Nationalist Movements

Edited by

Anthony D. Smith

Lecturer in Sociology, University of Reading

M

First published 1976 by
THE MACMILLAN PRESS LTD
London and Basingstoke
Associated companies in New York Dublin
Melbourne Johannesburg and Madras

SBN 333 18185 9 (hard cover)
333 18186 7 (paper cover)

Photoset, printed and bound
in Great Britain by
REDWOOD BURN LIMITED
Trowbridge & Esher

Contents

Acknowledgements

I should like to express my profound gratitude to Paul Wilkinson, who originally suggested the idea of an interdisciplinary volume on nationalist movements, and who approached me to edit it. His enthusiasm, untiring advice and help in matters of both conception and execution, and his kindness in agreeing to read the proofs, have greatly lightened the editorial burdens and helped to realise his original idea. In a very real sense, this has been a collective undertaking, although responsibility for the views expressed in each chapter rests with the editor and contributors.

I am also much indebted to Macmillan for their willingness to promote so novel and unusual a venture, and especially to Shaie Selzer for his constant interest and encouragement, without which this project could not have materialised.

Anthony D. Smith

Preface: Issues and Approaches in the Study of Nationalism

Nationalism is so central a feature of the processes of modern social change that no volume can attempt to broach more than a few of the many topics upon which it impinges – questions such as race and racism, the influence of colonial education systems, the relationship with economic development and 'modernisation', historical scholarship, demographic movements, scientific outlooks and bureaucratic variations, to mention just a few of the factors and problems which have influenced the rise and development of different nationalist movements. Clearly, limitations of space prevent more than a passing allusion to these and other questions. In the introductory chapter, I have selected only those issues and factors which have constituted recurrent themes in the literature on emergent nationalisms. Some of these I consider necessary conditions of their emergence, others important but alternative conditions. Generally speaking, the nationalist enterprise has been viewed here as a political consequence of the broader historicist movement which emerged first in late eighteenth-century Europe, and then in other areas, in response to certain kinds of geo-political frameworks, ethnic bases and social bearers, whose rise to prominence or revival at these times formed the matrix for historicism and nationalism. On the other hand, due allowance must be made for particular historical circumstances; there is a considerable difference in 'climate' and aims of nationalisms which arose in, say, early nineteenth-century Europe and mid-twentieth-century Africa or the Middle East. The changing circumstances of each movement promote and emphasize different types of framework, bases or bearers, and varying combinations of these three components. There are also circumstances of a more 'accidental' kind, such as the fortunes of war, the diplomacy of Great Powers and the incidence of famine and plague, which influence in particular the outcome of any bid for independence.

The chapters that follow therefore take up, each in their own way, some of the issues raised in preliminary fashion here, and add new themes often arising out of the cases considered. There is a similar range of approaches, from the philosophical to the historical and sociological. Nationalism touches on so many aspects of thought and life that no one approach can hope to tackle more than a few of its many aspects and dimensions. Hence these chapters also attempt to highlight the way in which quite different approaches can collectively illuminate various aspects of the formation of nationalist movements in several continents. No doubt there are further questions and problems raised by the very variety of these approaches, as well as by the specific contributions. But this is only to be expected of an interdisciplinary approach, one of the first of its kind in the field, to a subject of immense consequence in the modern world, but one which has been only partially explored, and in a descriptive and case-study fashion rather than through systematic analysis and comparison.

The arrangement of the chapters follows the division between geo-political frameworks, ethnic bases and social bearers which I have employed, with a concluding chapter by Calvert on the problems faced by nationalists on attaining independence. Similarly, Argyle's chapter covers questions about the dimensions of nationalist movements and the size of their constituency, but also broaches the question of the range of social classes involved in a 'successful' movement. In between, Minogue (Chapter 3) discusses the interplay of philosophical and political traditions of the polis and of absolutism, and their influence on modern European politics; Smith (Chapter 4) examines some of the ethnic bases of early European nationalisms, and especially the role of neo-classicism in French and German nationalism; Warburton (Chapter 5) compares the importance of linguistic divisions in the historical evolution of Canadian and Swiss nationalism and their relation to modernisation; while Kiernan's analysis (Chapter 6) of the social bearers of nationalism ranges across Europe and Asia, and leads on to the question of relations between nationalism and socialism.

Hopefully, the issues and approaches thrown up by this interdisciplinary venture will stimulate further research and discussion by historians, political scientists, sociologists and others, into a subject broad and important enough to invite and benefit by the sort of exchange of views and assumptions of which this volume affords an example.

Anthony D. Smith

1

Introduction: The Formation of Nationalist Movements

A. D. Smith

In this introductory essay I want to set out some of the main issues in the study of nationalist movements, with special reference to the conditions of their development into an effective social and political force. Nationalism has become so central a feature of contemporary social change that we are apt to forget its novelty and the originality of its message, and to read back into distant eras for those ideals and values which were first clearly enunciated in the French Revolution. For it is really only in the latter half of the eighteenth century that we can distinguish specifically 'nationalist' motifs and philosophies from the general ethnic and religious sentiments prevalent in pre-modern epochs. And it is only since the eighteenth century that the peculiar political, cultural and social conditions in which nationalism flourishes have become widely diffused, first in Europe and later in other parts of the world.

I. THE DIMENSIONS OF 'DEVELOPED' NATIONALISMS

Before turning to the analysis of the factors involved in the formation of nationalisms, something must be said about three preliminary problems: the definition of nationalism, the role and variety of nationalist movements, and especially the dimensions of fully developed nationalisms.

I shall define nationalism as an ideological movement for the attainment and maintenance of autonomy, cohesion and individuality for a social group deemed by some of its members to constitute an actual or potential nation.[1] In other words, nationalism is both an ideology and a movement, usually a minority one, which aspires to 'nationhood' for

For Notes and References to Chapter 1, see pp. 150–7.

the chosen group; and 'nationhood' in turn comprises three basic ideals, autonomy and self-government for the group, often but not always in a sovereign state, solidarity and fraternity of the group in a recognised territory or 'home', and third, a distinctive, and preferably unique, culture and history peculiar to the group in question. In more concrete terms, citizen self-government, a territorial home and a distinctive ethnic history, are the three fundamental goals of nationalist movements in every continent; and the nation they aspire to create through their movement is founded upon these three pillars, even where it seeks to import other elements such as language, will or religion. The nation, according to this view, fuses together three distinct elements: an ethnic principle, which emerged originally from kinship organisation, a territorial component, which derived historically from dynastic and colonial units, and finally a norm of political community found in the city-states of ancient Greece and medieval Italy. The nation is an abstract myth which nevertheless has deep roots in different levels of historical reality; and by fusing citizenship with ethnicity and territory, it has been able to satisfy many needs and inspire immense loyalties.[2]

So much for the problem of definition. The considerable variety of nationalist movements is closely bound up with their over-all role in history. Roughly speaking, and taking for the moment the standpoint of the nationalists themselves, that role was to provide a 'short-cut' to nationhood for communities unable to reach that goal without human intervention; while the different kinds of nationalist movement were specifically adapted to the various 'routes' along which diverse types of community had to travel in order to attain their 'national goals'. But, less teleologically, we may say that, wherever it has arisen, the nationalist movement has helped to turn a population into a nation, even if not quite so effectively as is sometimes supposed; and that it has taken a variety of forms as a result of very different initial conditions among various populations. Furthermore, not every population has become a national community through the operation of a distinct nationalist movement, but the vast majority have, and the nationalist movement has often had a revolutionary impact, implying a radical break with the past.

Here I can only briefly mention some of the more important types of nationalism, and merely allude to cases of nation-formation which had little recourse to a nationalist movement.

A.   GRADUALIST ROUTES

The populations in this category achieved their nationhood without a major rupture involving a developed nationalism. They fall into a number of sub-groups.

1. *State patriotisms*

Well-developed and ancient states often try to mould their populations into a unified, patriotic unit. Prussia, Burgundy, royal Ethiopia and Afghanistan, Bourbon France and Tudor England resorted to this policy, which is more concerned with loyalty to the state than the cohesion and individuality, let alone the autonomy, of the nation. Generally speaking, it has proved a failure, as in Prussia or Burgundy, or provoked a more thoroughgoing nationalist movement as in France and now in Ethiopia.[3] England presents a difficulty. It can be argued that the Puritan revolution was religious and social, rather than nationalist, in content, despite the theory of the Norman Yoke and Milton; and that subsequently, England has experienced no fully developed nationalist movement. If so, it is the only really successful case of a 'growth' route to nationhood (albeit much-punctuated growth), for the depth of English sentiment about country and mores can hardly be doubted, and there have been many 'surges' and revivals of national sentiment.[4]

2. *'Colonisation'*

In states formed by colonisation (and/or conquest) like Australia, Brazil and Canada, the nation has been slow to form. In Australia, Whitlam's fervent national sentiment implies less a radical break with the past than an intensification of existing trends towards individuality, cohesion and autonomy. In Canada, the situation is more complex, as Warburton's chapter points out, since Canadian national sentiment is confronted by a clear ethnic nationalism in Quebec, and by the claims of the Indians. Nevertheless, what sense of Canadian nationality there is has been the result of a gradual, if crisis-ridden, growth, rather than a decisive rupture, as has been the case in other countries. Likewise, the 1956–64 'developmental nationalism' of Brazil marked a surge of national sentiment rather than a radically new departure.[5]

3. *'Provincialism'*

Finally there are nation-states, or more often states in process of becoming nations as in some ex-French sub-Saharan states or Ecuador or Honduras, which never experienced a revolutionary nationalism, but quietly seceded, or were given independence by their imperial masters, and are gradually fusing into nations.

B.   NATIONALIST ROUTES

By far the greater number of today's nations and nation-states achieved this status largely through the often revolutionary and violent efforts of nationalist movements. They divide into two main types.

1.   *Ethnic nationalisms*

Here the nationalism arises in communities with a distinctive, often unique, culture and history, and operates solely on behalf of that ethnic group. There are several variants:

(a)   *'Renewal'*. Where the ethnic group possesses formal sovereignty, the nationalist movement comes as a renewal and rejuvenation of social and political life. Its adherents even regard the rulers as aliens, though they share their culture (or a version of it) as the 'Frankish' aristocracy shared the culture of their 'Gallic' French countrymen.[6] Or the rulers are regarded as collaborators with encroaching aliens, as happened in the 1890s in a Persia threatened by British and Russian economic intrusion. 'Renewal' nationalisms aim essentially to maintain the autonomy and restore the cohesion of a divided and declining *ethnie*.[7]

(b)   *Secession*. This is the commonest route to nationhood. The ethnic group is incorporated, allegedly against its will, in a wider unit, usually an empire (but also a modern nation-state, such as Bangladesh in Pakistan), and seeks to sever the bond through an act of secession. Thereupon it sets up a new state of its own (or, as in Poland and Hungary, restores an old one). So Italians and Czechs split away from the Habsburg Empire, and Arabs, Armenians and Serbs from the Ottoman, while Poles and Ukrainians sought to break away from Tsarist Russia in 1917. Today, 'secession' movements are very active in Brittany, Wales, the Basque country, among Nagas and Mizos, in Quebec, Kurdistan and Eritrea, and even the Swiss Jura wants a measure of autonomy.[8]

There are, in turn, a number of variant forms of ethnic 'secession' movements, which are really extensions of the basic urge to set up one's own state coextensive with the ethnic group. An interesting, but rare, type is the *diaspora* movement, in which a scattered ethnic group desires to return to its alleged historic homeland. The nationalism is accordingly an emigration movement, a movement of redemption through return from exile; and was so regarded by groups like the Greeks, Armenians, Jews and the Black emigration movements from America to Africa.[9]

More common is the *irredentist* movement. Usually it follows on from a successful secession nationalism. The new state does not include all the members of the *ethnie*, who live on adjacent lands under alien rule; they must therefore be 'redeemed' and the lands on which they live annexed. This was a familiar theme in Balkan nationalism, among Greeks, Serbs and Bulgarians, and in Germany and Somalia today. An extension of irredentist nationalisms seeks to unite culturally similar independent states into a single super-state. The *pan* nationalisms of

Africa, the Slavs, Turkic peoples and Arabs, though unsuccessful to date, take the historical–cultural aspect of ethnicity to its logical extreme.[10]

2. *Territorial nationalisms*

The nationalist movement which arises among heterogeneous populations is based upon the territorial unit in which they are forcibly united and administered, usually by a colonial power. The boundaries of the territory, and the administration of the colony, form therefore the chief referents and focuses of identification of the nation to be. On taking over the colonial territory, the nationalists' main attention is devoted to integrating a culturally heterogeneous or 'indistinct' population, a coalition of tribes or mixture of races, who possess neither myth of common origins nor shared history, except for the latest, often relatively brief, period of colonial subjection. In Tanzania, or Zambia, Nyerere and Kaunda must first ensure the cohesion of their states by welding together a series of culturally distinct *ethnie*; while in Argentina or Colombia, the successors of Bolivar and San Martín had to invent a literature and discover a history to invest creole independence with cultural depth and identity, and give meaning to the territorial cohesion of these former Spanish provinces.[11]

A variation of this territorial route to nationhood is furnished by those polyethnic colonies with one or more dominant or strategic *ethnie*, states like Burma, Indonesia, Malaysia, Kenya and Nigeria. Here we meet nationalist movements which define their aims and policies in terms of the wider territorial unit, yet are clearly spearheaded by members of one or other of the strategic *ethnie*, for example the Kikuyu in Kenya, the Javanese in Indonesia or the Baganda in Uganda. (Later their dominance may be challenged by other groups, as occurred in Uganda and to some extent in Kenya.) There is also the interesting case of Switzerland. Its late eighteenth-century nationalism is, from one angle, a clear case of a 'renewal' movement; but, because of the preponderance of Alemmanic Swiss in the Helvetic and other societies, and because, as Warburton underlines, Swiss nationalism is political and territorial rather than strictly ethnic, this movement falls into the *mixed* category, that is ethnic-led territorialisms.[12]

This discussion demonstrates the centrality of nationalism, in the sense of a radical ideological movement, in the process of attaining nationhood. Relatively few nations and nation-states have achieved this goal without the intervention of such movements. Hence the importance of nationalism as inaugurator, controller and interpreter of much contemporary social change, since the latter is in turn so heavily influenced by the framework of the nation-state. Nationalist movements, however, vary in intensity, duration, extent, force and clarity; those which were highly developed in these respects tended also to accelerate the process of turning a population into a nation, while those that failed to develop these qualities exerted little influence on the course of events, or even contributed to the break-up of the community.

We must therefore devote some space to the components and dimensions of developed and 'strong' cases of nationalism, before we can turn to a consideration of the factors which contribute to that strength.

To begin with, we must distinguish between the political *success* of a given nationalist movement, and its sociological *development* or strength. Politically, nationalisms are judged by a single criterion: did they gain sovereignty for their community? According to this test, Corsican or Tibetan nationalism has been no less (or more) successful than Armenian or Kurdish. The fact that Corsican and Tibetan nationalism was a short-lived revolt, fairly easily put down, while Armenian and Kurdish nationalisms involved dedicated, highly organised, articulate, widely diffused and long-lived movements, is politically irrelevant. The fact that the latter movements were as strong as, if not more developed than, the nationalisms of Sri Lanka or Sierra Leone, whose efforts met with political success, is also irrelevant on the sovereignty criterion.[13]

What application of the 'success' criterion of sovereignty yields is a threefold grading of nationalisms: at the top, those movements like the Rumanian or Indian which achieved sovereign statehood for their populations; next, those which like the Ukrainian or Biafran failed to do so, but achieved a measure of internal autonomy; and finally, those like the Breton or Basque which have to date failed to achieve even this.[14]

The other, sociological criterion for measuring the force and impact of a given nationalism is more complex. A classification (or better, continuum) of nationalisms according to the degree of their 'development' depends upon a number of criteria, whose presence or absence together will determine whether a movement should be labelled 'embryonic' or 'developed'. Here we are interested in such dimensions as: duration of the movement, complexity of its organisation, diffusion of its ideals and activities among the affected population, size of its membership, dedication and loyalty of its hard-core members, clarity and articulation of its ideas and concepts, and the priority of those ideas and goals over every other consideration.

In practice, these variables can be subsumed under four headings: a political dimension involving organisation and institutionalisation; a social one, concerned with mobilising the population; a cultural one aiming to create new communal values and new men; and finally a symbolic and mythopoeic component, in which nationalism becomes a 'religion surrogate'. I shall briefly elaborate these dimensions.

1.   A *'proto-state'*

By definition, every movement involves some conscious organisation. It must become a flexible instrument for fulfilling its aims. Embryonic movements, like the Coptic Assembly in the early twentieth century, never get beyond the ephemeral stage of mass protest or popular meeting.[15] But a nationalist movement, to stand any chance of gaining sovereignty for its group, must move well beyond this rudimentary stage and begin the process of evolving organisations, cadres and institutions able to act as a 'proto-state' the moment independence is achieved. It must, as it were, prefigure the polity it wishes to erect, by creating a counter 'state within a state' as part of the fabric of the 'movement', and train its followers in the political and administrative tasks they must perform when power is assumed. It was this sort of 'dress-rehearsal' institutionalisation which distinguished Algerian, Yugoslav and Israeli nationalisms as they fought for independence.[16]

2. *Mobilisation*

Nationalism holds that power emanates only from a 'people' who form a seamless whole, an indivisible brotherhood which abolishes all existing ties, whether of family, neighbourhood or occupation. The only genuine identity is a national one, and every man, be he peasant or worker, merchant or intellectual, can only rediscover self and freedom through that new collective identity. By sloughing off lethargy, passivity, ignorance, routine, tradition and the burdens of rural backwardness, and by joining the nationalist movement, subjects can become free citizens, and social divisions will be swept away through the unity created by a common struggle and purpose.[17]

Measured by this ideal of fraternity and unity, most nationalisms have been conspicuous failures. Whatever their populist rhetoric, the leadership has rarely involved the urban workers in their struggles; as for the peasants, only Maoism and 'national communism' have made a serious attempt to win their allegiance. Usually, nationalists confine their proselytising zeal to more educated strata in the main cities – officers, civil servants, merchants and intelligentsia. As Argyle demonstrates in the case of nineteenth-century nationalisms in Eastern Europe, the nationalist 'network' was fairly limited both in size and social range, even in the later phases of the movement. Nationalism is hardly ever a 'mass movement', though it may win the acquiescence of a majority of literate citizens, and quite often it fails to alter the position and life-style of even the 'lower middle classes' – clerks, domestics, secretaries and small shopkeepers – though it may benefit non-aristocratic status groups above them. Viewed strictly as social movements, the Italian Risorgimento and Greek independence struggle were revolutions *manquées*; in the Italian case, nationalism failed even to overcome the deep-rooted regionalism of the peninsula.[18]

3. *A 'culture-community'*

In view of their cultural origins, it comes as no surprise that nationalisms set great store by common values and tastes, customs and standards. All nationalisms view their movements as a cultural experiment, a kind of embryo 'culture-community', for forging common aspirations and life-styles. Some movements even go so far as to set up special associations to inculcate the appropriate moral and cultural qualities, some of them total and permanent like the early kibbutzim in Israel, others more segmental and recurrent like the Czech sokols, the Scandinavian culture houses, or the Swiss learned and agricultural societies. Their aim is fundamentally similar: to create the 'new man', healthy, vigorous and free.[19]

The cultural dimension of nationalist movements has two aspects: a populist and Rousseauan nostalgia for the simplicity and sturdiness of agricultural life, which embodies in pristine form the essence and inner virtue of the community, uncontaminated by urban luxury and corruption; and an academic, scholarly component, which is not only useful in undergirding the historic claims of the movement before the bar of world opinion and sceptical authorities, but can also provide the whole nationalist enterprise with a legitimacy based on scholarly research. It is history, and history alone, which can furnish the bases of ethnic identity and the psychic reassurance of communal security that goes with it. Hence the proliferation of historical, philological, ethnological, socio-demographic, art-historical, musicological, and other forms of historicist enquiries, and the appeal of nationalism for those engaged in such investigations.[20]

4. *A 'religion surrogate'*

Every movement requires a clear-cut, well-articulated system of beliefs and practices, and a set of myths and symbols. In nationalism, the 'mythopoeic' function is especially vital, since the doctrines embraced by nationalists are notoriously vague and even self-contradictory. Such themes, motifs or 'myths' endow nationalism with its power and attraction – myths of 'auto-emancipation', solidarity, ethnic 'authenticity' and 'self-determination'. Substituting the nation for the role of God and his saints, the flag for the cross or crescent, anthems for hymns, and national heroes for ancient prophets, nationalism evolves a whole pantheon of forces and ideas, whose diversity and colour are periodically celebrated in stirring ceremonies and solemn cults, like those of Brutus and the Supreme Being during the French Revolution. Similar quasi-religious symbolism may surround founders or leaders of the movement, or one of its 'prophets'; such charisma attached to Nkrumah and Nasser, or to Voltaire during the Revolution. Martyrs, too, add to the impact of the nationalist myths, a Rhigas in Greece or Marat in France; and where martyrs, prophets and ceremonies are lacking, the chances of a potent nationalism developing and taking root are correspondingly slim.[21]

A developed, strong nationalist movement will therefore manifest in high degree these four components: institutions and organisations, a fairly broad diffusion in the cities, a dedicated hard core steeped in the new values and tastes, and a set of clearly articulated myths and rites, which distinguish nationalism from other ideologies, as well as from religious doctrines and practices. For nationalism, despite its marked mythopoeic component, is not to be confused with religion. It is a movement of men, on behalf of men, and its referents are purely terrestrial. It has no place for a deity, nor for any salvation which is not of human origin and agency.

With this delineation of the nationalist movement and its varieties in mind, we can now turn to the task of isolating the main conditions in the formation and development of such movements.

II.   FRAMEWORKS OF NATIONALISM

The conditions that foster the formation of powerful nationalist movements may be divided into three categories: geo-political frameworks, ethnic bases and social bearers. Broadly speaking, the possession or presence in a given population of most, but not all, of the factors subsumed under these categories, facilitates the rise of a strongly developed nationalist movement; and conversely, the absence or deficiency of most of these factors is likely to weaken the movement and retard its development beyond a fleeting, or embryonic, stage. At the polar extremes, where none or all of the factors are present, nationalism either cannot arise, or is largely superfluous; in the latter case we find considerable national sentiment in a population, but few signs of a nationalist movement.

Which are the factors relevant to the development of nationalisms? Taking the categories in turn, the most important and recurrent are:

(a)   *Frameworks:* (i) an easily identifiable territory and location, (ii) a single political authority and bureaucracy, able to level and homogenise the population,

(b) *Bases:* (iii) a myth and cult of common origins and history, (iv) other cultural differences like language or colour, (v) partial secularisation of urban élites' traditions,

(c) *Bearers:* (vi) the growth and exclusion of an urban intelligentsia, (vii) an alliance between intelligentsia and one or more classes or status groups, usually urban, (viii) commercial penetration and mercantile assent.

Of these factors, some tend to be more vital than others. The most crucial involve bureaucratic authority, the myth of common history and the rise of an intelligentsia; a historical outlook and bureaucratic professionalisation do appear to be prerequisites for an effective nationalism. The other factors are more interchangeable: a 'territorial' nationalism has strong frameworks, but weak ethnic bases and social support, whereas the converse applies to 'ethnic' nationalisms. The factors also vary considerably in degree. The impact of bureaucracy, secularism and commerce are never uniform, especially relative to a given area or population, and it is not possible to correlate the 'development' of a given nationalism with a specific impact of any of these factors, since these factors may act as 'functional equivalents' in relation to the growth of a movement.

Therefore, all that we can say about the relations between these factors in the formation of nationalisms is that they constitute an overlapping 'family' of recurrent contributory conditions (allied to the three necessary ones); and that different combinations of these factors may accelerate the growth of nationalist movements. A nationalism can also be viewed as an instrument for supplying the 'missing' factors; it is the movement itself which aims to create appropriate frameworks (for example a state, natural frontiers) or bases (for example common customs or institutions, more secular education) where these are lacking, and to extend its social constituency where support is not immediately visible. Hence the optimal situation for the development of a strong nationalism requires that some, but not many, of the factors be to hand; and that the key characteristic of their relations be one of 'imbalance' as between frameworks, bases and bearers. It is just such an unevenness between factors that spurs nationalist activity and appeal, particularly when it is coupled with certain geo-political conditions, to which I now turn.

A.　TERRITORY

If, as we saw, social cohesion is an essential goal of nationalisms, then territorially integrated and compact populations are more likely to be susceptible to suggestions about their common 'nationality' than scattered and divided ones. Several writers have pointed to the profound influence of location and geography on Switzerland and Kurdistan; conversely, scattered tribes like the Masai or Udmurts, which are relatively small, lack a compact territory and a location between powerful neighbours, and appear to support this hypothesis in a negative manner.

In fact, the question of geo-political frameworks conceals at least three separate issues: size, scale and location.

1.　*Size*

Large numbers are often claimed to be a prerequisite for a population to develop an effective nationalism. Historically, the first European nations were large. Sociologically, too, small units are not politically viable, and any impersonal unit must be large scale.

It is true that very small units cannot survive politically and economically under modern, that is nation-state, conditions. But this presupposes the existing, nationalist, situation will continue to obtain, and it also confuses the conditions of nationhood with those of the formation of nationalisms. The Corsicans numbered only 200,000 at the start of their revolt against Genoa in 1734; and in the early twentieth century when the Yakuts raised their banner against Tsarist Russia, they numbered only about 240,000. Besides, as Argyle shows in Chapter 2, information on the size of movements or communities is often lacking, and even intense nationalisms tend to be tiny minorities of the presumptive population.[22]

Besides, though nations are larger than face-to-face groups, it does not follow that they must be 'large scale', a criterion of great elasticity in practice. It is true that very small ethnic groups or 'tribes' in Africa and Siberia have not succeeded in developing strong nationalisms, and would, like Anguilla or the Isle of Man, be unable to maintain a meaningful independence (though they might attain a measure of autonomy). But the range of size manifested by existing nations is so great, that arguments about a lower limit, below which nations are 'unviable' and nationalisms unlikely to develop, are difficult to sustain.[23]

2. Scale

A more serious geo-social candidate for nationalist prerequisite is the notion of 'scale'. The latter term, too, contains a number of facets. There is, first, the idea of scale as geographical extent, the argument here being that nationalism requires for its development (and nations for their sustenance) a fairly large territory and 'living-space'. As far as the development of a strong nationalism is concerned, the argument is extremely dubious, especially as it rarely specifies the lower limit of territorial area required; island nationalisms in Corsica, Cyprus and Iceland have shown considerable power, even virulence, while very large territories like Brazil and Australia have proved relatively free of nationalism. Communications, or lack of them, over a given territory are a vital factor; and it is really the density of different ethnic populations, in confined and economically developing areas, that counts. Rapidly expanding population in ethnically mixed and confined areas does foster a nationalism, once it has emerged. In that sense, the 'scale-cum-population' argument is relevant to the development of strong nationalisms, but only under conditions of ethnic antagonism and new social processes.[24]

The other main sense of 'scale', as social range, is taken up by Argyle, who again underlines the absence of any correlation between the strength and success of a nationalism and the range of social classes represented in it. Apart from members of the intelligentsia, no social group's presence in the movement is an absolute prerequisite for its growth and success. On the other hand, it can be argued that the intelligentsia's efforts are likely to be rewarded more swiftly, and to possess greater resonance, if it can succeed in gaining recruits from one or other of the main urban 'middle-class' status groups. This is a position I shall develop later.

3. *Location*

One other geo-political factor is sometimes cited as influential in the growth of a nationalist movement, namely the location of the chosen population and its relations with neighbouring groups. Switzerland, Bohemia and Kurdistan are the classic instances of nationalisms exacerbated by geo-political location, being situated at key points along trade and military routes. In each case as well, the actual shape and terrain of the area helped to foster a sense of common ethnicity, and later a fully fledged nationalist movement. Early Romantic sentiment among writers and artists for the Alps or fjords shows the cultural influence of such 'geographic' nationalisms, which found a recent echo in the Jura and Tyrol.[25]

Such cases are pronounced instances of the impact of geo-political frameworks on the growth of nationalisms. As constants, such factors as the shape of 'natural' frontiers or location between neighbours affect the subsequent delineation and attraction of the movement rather than its origins; and this is only to be expected of an ideology which emphasises social cohesion in a recognised territorial 'home'. That emphasis also helps to explain the peculiar bitterness of frontier conflicts like those in Transylvania, Macedonia or the Middle East; or the defiant insurrection in nineteenth-century Poland, wedged in between a strong, populous Russia and Prussia.[26]

Even alleged counter-cases turn out, in fact, to lend support to this influence of location and territory. Nationalism was often initiated by exiles and expatriates who only then began to understand the position of their homeland, or felt that it was indeed their home, like the Irish exiles in America, the Armenians in India and the Serbs in Vienna and Paris. Similarly, the Jewish case, often treated as proof that territory and location are irrelevant for the growth of nationalism, involved not only religious longing for Palestine, but also the birth of Zionism among Western- and Central-European emancipated exiles. At the same time, the effective support for Zionism came from the rapidly expanding Jewish population of the Russian Pale, which constituted an enforced territory for Russian Jewry, in which they formed dense, compact communities, resembling an autonomous 'state within a state' hemmed in by Tsarist restriction. Without that geo-political framework, it is doubtful if Jewish nationalism would have achieved a powerful following.[27]

B. THE STATE

Of all the factors involved in the formation of nationalist movements, the state and its bureaucratic structure is perhaps the single most decisive agent and framework. It is against a given state structure and political style that nationalists battle in the first instance, and their demands for autonomy are often related to allegations of neglect or discrimination (or both) on the part of successive administrations.

There are three aspects of this bureaucratic matrix I want to touch on: the historical origins of early European nationalisms within an absolutist framework, the ideological component of the *polis* tradition, and a wider sociological aspect of urban bureaucratic practices, especially in the colonies.

1. *Absolutism*

Historically, the first European nationalisms in France, Germany and Poland operated within the context of monarchical absolutisms; even English national sentiment in the eighteenth century took the rejection of princely tyranny as its starting-point. This does not mean that all democratic-nationalist revolts like those of Geneva in the 1760s and 1782, of Corsica from 1734 and especially in the 1760s, in America, in the United Provinces of 1784–7 and the Austrian Netherlands in 1787–90, were conceived in opposition to princely tyranny or resulted from the reforms of absolute monarchs. At the same time, oligarchic aristocracies, whether in Holland or Switzerland, came under increasing pressure both from the rising bourgeoisie and intelligentsias, and from the example and ideas of enlightened despotism in neighbouring territories.[28] For all the attempts of the princes to fashion and rule clearly demarcated and sealed-off realms, their activities and policies were part and parcel of a delicately balanced European concert of power, such that reforms in any one territory were bound to have marked repercussions in others. The fact is, as Minogue argues in Chapter 3, European nations (and nationalisms) have been formed in the framework of the monarchical state; but the uneasy alliance of ruler and 'middle classes' against aristocratic privilege soon collapsed under the new social pressures and revolutionary ideas after 1780. In this context, the reaction of many intellectual and professional groups against even an enlightened despotism, because of its bureaucratic regimentation and arbitrary remoteness from the interests and needs of educated subjects, constitutes a recurrent leitmotiv in early European nationalisms. Equally important, however, and less remarked upon, is the use which nationalists were to make of the concept of sovereignty derived from the absolutist tradition of kingship: as Cobban points out, the sovereignty of the nation is but a step from the sovereignty of the state, embodied in the prince.[29]

2.   *The 'civic republic'*

That step is nevertheless of immense ideological significance, representing as it does the attempt to reincorporate the *polis* tradition into European political thinking and practice. Herein lies the political dimension of the first of those 'historicist' cults which swept Europe in the later eighteenth century, a neo-classicism which owed more to Sparta and above all to Republican Rome than to Athens. Part of a broader yearning for simplicity, heroism and purity, the neo-classic cult which banished rococo styles in England, Germany and Scandinavia achieved its greatest impact in France after 1770, where it inspired images of republican stoicism and virtue even before the Revolution attempted to put them into practice, or Napoleon could propagate them on his missions of conquest. Neo-classicism, among other things, provided a new political framework, and a congenial philosophical arena, for emergent nationalisms, namely the civic republic of the various patriot parties. Politically, this concept involved the transfer of power to the urban bourgeois and intelligentsia, men who shared similar tastes and ideas, and thereby constituted an 'educated public' and the core of the sovereign nation. Ideologically, the neo-classic tradition of the *polis* preached that freedom lay ultimately in stoic self-sacrifice on behalf of the community, an idea that was soon to be adapted to the more 'organic' ethnic community ideals preached later in France and in Germany and Eastern Europe. Socially, the appeal to the ancient *polis* reasserted the role and vitality of educated, self-governing urban communities, and the leadership of networks of urban trading interests within the emergent nation. In every respect the revival of the *polis* ideal reinforced the dominance of the capital or a few key cities over the hinterland, and of educated urban groups within them.[30]

3.   *Bureaucracy*

Romantic reaction against the levelling effects of bureaucratic absolutism was by no means confined to early nineteenth-century Europe. As the range and effectiveness of centralised bureaucracies has grown, in the overseas colonies as well as the Eastern empires, ethnic reaction, especially on the part of educated élites, has intensified. In Africa, especially, bureaucratic administration provided the basic framework for nationalisms, as well as the immediate catalyst of discontent, by its tendency to exclude a swollen army of graduates from all but the lowest echelons of the civil service. This was also true in India, Burma and Malaysia. This phenomenon of bureaucratic exclusion has both structural and cultural elements, which I have discussed elsewhere;

and several writers have drawn attention to the psychological indignities suffered by highly educated non-Europeans at the hands of colonial governments.[31] In Eastern Europe, a similar pattern of imperial discrimination and exclusion assumed a more overtly ethnic (and religious) tone; imperial governments might play *ethnie* off against each other, as the Porte did with all non-Greek (or rather non-Phanariot) *ethnie*. More than any other factor, rationalist bureaucracy has proved the decisive instrument in welding, as well as dividing, populations and inciting revolts.[32]

III. ETHNIC BASES OF NATIONALISM

At the core of the study of nationalist movements lies the vexed question of ethnicity. A highly influential stream of thought, originating with the German Romantics, holds that a nation forms a community of culture, especially language, and that possession of a common and distinctive culture entitles a population to constitute itself into a nation and claim a separate state. Conversely, populations which lack common and distinctive cultural traits cannot be regarded as genuine nations (or nationalities); and hence their 'nationalism' must be largely spurious. However, the advent, especially in tropical Africa, of territorial nationalisms bearing important family resemblances to the better-known European types has forced a revision of the earlier Europocentric view; and thereby contributed to a more profound understanding of the role of 'ethnic bases' in the rise of nationalism.

If, as we saw, centralised bureaucratic reform (at home or in neighbouring territories) is an essential framework and catalyst of nationalist revolt, then equally the possession of at least some 'ethnic bases' is a prerequisite for the development and sustenance of a strong nationalism. Though Weber was right to emphasise that it is political action over several generations which binds together ethnic communities, that action requires for its success sufficient common interests in a population, coupled with a modicum of communal sentiment deriving ultimately from either close kinship ties or common values, customs and codes, or both. In other words, for a nationalist movement to gain adherents, it must be able to point to some common cultural 'materials', some roots or 'bases', which the chosen population can recognise; and, further, for a nationalist claim to originate, it must arise on the basis of ideas and sentiments about a specific category which affords a platform for constructing the nation. Even territorial nationalisms, therefore, require some 'ethnic materials' to give shape and depth to their claims, in their own eyes as much as in others'.[33]

If some kind of ethnic base is a prerequisite for an effective and developed nationalism, two questions arise. First, which ethnic bases are most conducive to nationalisms, and which are simply important but contributory factors? Second, under what conditions do these bases, which have often been fairly constant over centuries, begin to furnish materials for an emergent nationalism and the new identity it wishes to create? These questions may be conveniently treated under three headings: the myth of common history, language and cultural equivalents, and secularisation.

A. HISTORY AND HISTORICISM

The discovery and uses of a common history constituted one of the fundamental goals of the nationalist ideal of individuality. Even among populations which lacked a common history, nationalisms have sought out any common myths of origin and common memories, often oral ones, not just to mark themselves off from alien rulers, but to meet the more fundamental cultural need for a component of 'authenticity' for the new collective identities they are forging. In sub-Saharan Africa, where colonial boundaries sometimes divided ethnic groups like the Bakongo, Fang and Ewe, ethnic historicism was pursued at three levels. There were ethnic historical renaissances, often inspired by foreign missionaries and researchers; the influence of Protestant missionaries from Bremen – such as Reverend Jacob Spieth and the great linguist, Dr Diedrich Westermann – on Daniel Chapman and Reverend Kwakume, the Baetas and Armattoe, helped to foster an Ewe cultural revival from the 1910s onwards, and was an important factor in the genesis of Ewe nationalism.[34] Similarly, growing anti-European sentiment in Nigeria found early cultural roots in the Yoruba revival of the 1890s, which led to the discarding of European names and dress, as well as research into Yoruba history and arts.[35] The second level of ethnic historicism was a good deal more tenuous. It involved the discovery of historical roots on a territory-wide basis, such as the adoption by the Gold Coast independence movement of the name and memory of the empire of Ghana. This in turn extended the range and uses of African history, and cannot be separated from the third and highest level of African historicism, the elevation of the 'African race' or even the Black people as a whole, through a deeper study of its contribution to world culture and history. From Blyden and Horton to Senghor and Nkrumah, this sense of African roots and a pan-African set of traditions diametrically opposed to Western materialism has reinforced the separate African nationalisms at the state level, and helped to counteract an exclusive pursuit of local ethnic histories with their consequent autonomist pressures.[36]

Outside Africa, ethnic nationalisms are more numerous and often intense. In many cases, possession of a common history, which is both eventful and well-documented, has inspired heroic resistance, in successive Polish revolts, in various Irish conflicts, among Arabs and Israelis, in Greece and the Balkans, Hungary and Rumania, among the Tatars and Mongols, in Java and Burma, Mexico and Peru; but even the lack of records and memories has not prevented the development of fairly intense nationalisms. In Slovakia and the Ukraine nationalists had to forge a new historical consciousness, with the aid of folk-tales and poems, because of the relative paucity of materials documenting the distinctiveness of these *ethnies*.[37] Similar problems have faced Welsh nationalists (let alone those of Cornwall), whereas Basque and Breton separatist nationalisms can take a long and fairly well-known history for granted.[38]

This lack of correlation between the strength of historical memories (and records) of distinctive ethnicity, and the intensity of nationalisms illustrates that it is 'historicism', rather than ethnic history itself, which is the essential 'base' for nationalist movements. Of course 'historicism', the cult of particular histories and a belief in historical explanation and reconstruction, requires some antecedent history to work on. But it is not the amount of such history, or even its dramatic value, that is important; what nationalists require from their historical researches is the definition of a particular ethnic atmosphere, unique to that community, and the provision of moral qualities (and heroic embodiments) peculiar to the group. The discovery of this atmosphere and set of values confirms and undergirds the growing sense of 'alienity' felt by members of urban groups exposed to secular doubt and to rapid, but uneven, mobility.

The essence of a sense of ethnicity lies in a myth of common origins and historical traditions, often in conjunction with an association with particular territories or migration routes. In pre-modern eras, such myths and traditions were embodied in religious conceptions and rituals; and from time to time they provided bases for messianic ethnic revolts against alien repression.[39] From the later eighteenth century, there has been a revival of ethnicity in new forms; even territorial nationalisms have returned to myths of common origins, history and migration/territory memories. Such a return, however, is deliberate and conscious, part of an over-all conception of society and life, one which applies organic and historical notions to the explanation of all phenomena. The Celtic cult of Ossian and Arthur, the Teutonic one of Arminius and the Nibelungen, the Indian glorification of Kali and the Vedas and the Pharaonic cult in Egypt, all exemplify this historicist outlook whose clear ethnic overtones prepared the way for nationalist claims.[40]

B. LANGUAGE AND CULTURE

While historicist search for ethnic roots is a vital element in the

development of strong nationalisms, other ethnic bases are generally interchangeable. What is essential is not any specific base such as
language, customs, religion or institutions, but an ability to communicate and a modicum of shared values among the majority of educated
members of a given population. In addition, any cultural traits which
serve to differentiate a population from its neighbours will tend to
strengthen its nationalism, once it has emerged; while secondary cultural traits which subdivide the population may provide the basis for a
subsequent 'secession' nationalism, as has occurred in Flanders, Biafra
and Bangladesh.

Language is often singled out, following Herder and Fichte, as the essential criterion of nationhood and basis for nationalism. Only through
a vernacular and its literature can one grasp the 'personality' of a
nation; and only through the communication of messages in an agreed
code can a sense of nationality develop. With regard to nationalist
movements, language differences have been the chief source of ethnic
tensions since the eighteenth century, and every secession movement is
fundamentally a linguistic movement. It is therefore hardly surprising
if language reform and philological research figure so largely in
nationalist programmes, or that nationalism is so often accompanied
by literary renascences. As men cease to define themselves through traditional religious categories, they require alternative focuses of solidarity and compensating modes of identity; and language, it is claimed,
can provide both.[41]

Both historians and sociologists interested in the cognitive dimension of social life have tended to embrace this linguistic account, though
without its Romantic accretions; and they point to the way in which
language does appear to define new identities in polyethnic states like
Belgium, Canada or Yugoslavia. There are, however, a number of ob-
jections to this inflation of the linguistic factor. To begin with, there are
several powerful nationalisms which do not invoke language, and
indeed avoid it, as far as possible; India and Burma are obvious cases.
The Indian case is particularly interesting since here we have an ethnic
nationalism (Hindu Indian) comprising several sub-*ethnie*, the first
defined by religion, the second by language and territory.[42] Second,
there are several nationalisms whose emergence did not in any way
depend upon the possession or properties of a common language: Irish,
American, Argentinian (nineteenth-century), Swiss, Serb, Pakistani,
even Algerian nationalisms, let alone those of tropical Africa – none of
these depended upon language as their main focus of solidarity or identity. Third, and following on from this, nationalisms have with perfect
equanimity treated different cultural bases like customs, language, institutions and so on, as substitutes for each other, particularly when it
came to defining boundaries for their new states. In particular, religion
and common institutions have often performed the role of creating

solidarity in nationalist theory, in place of language; Rousseau and Montesquieu as well as Burke and Bolingbroke thought in terms of institutions and mores rather than language (and so did Jefferson), while Tilak, Aurobindo and Gandhi, as well as Iqbal and Jinnah, utilised the religious community to define their nations. The point is that language by itself is incapable of sustaining a collective identity; to do so, it requires the 'support' of the historic core of ethnicity, a cult of common origins and common development.[43]

Under modern conditions, language undoubtedly provides a vital mode of communication and a repertoire of symbols and values, since an ancient tongue carries with it innumerable historic associations and allusions. But there are other modes of communication and cultural expression open to nationalisms, beyond the administrative requirement of a *lingua franca*. Art and music, though in principle universally accessible, also afford possibilities for 'national self-expression', for creating images and tonal ideas which capture the atmosphere, moral quality and aesthetic uniqueness of particular historic communities, often with greater force and clarity than the more discursive modes of literature; paintings by David, Fuseli, West and Delacroix, operas of Verdi, Wagner and Mussourgsky, and the music of Chopin, Dvorak, Elgar and Bartok – not to mention the ballads and folk-songs, the dances and music dramas in places like West Africa or Indonesia – remind us of the way in which non-linguistic modes of expression can evoke strong national passions among wide audiences to this day.[44]

C. SECULARISATION

An essential cultural condition for the rise of historicism and an ethnic revival is a measure of secularisation among élites in the cities. This does not mean that nationalism, as a political offshoot of historicism, cannot accommodate itself to religious interests nor assume traditional forms. In Burma, for example, it was political monks (*pongyis*) who led the national revolt against British occupation after the First World War;[45] and in Greece, Armenia and Rumania, priests played an important part in the national awakening and revolt. In the Middle East, nationalism is even more closely intertwined with religion: the highly political tone of Islam, and the close identification of Arabs with the *umma* and the Arabic Koran, appear to confirm the hypothesis that nationalism is really a political extension of traditional religions.[46]

This argument nevertheless underestimates the complexity of relationships between a religious base and nationalism. Most nationalist leaders are either irreligious or at least non-traditional; and, more significant, nationalism, as we saw, is an ideology, a strictly secular doctrine of autonomy and individuality. Burmese monks and European priests embraced nationalism, either as an offshoot of heterodoxy, as in

Rumania, or at any rate without the blessing of the ecclesiastical authorities.[47] Traditionalist priests and rabbis generally condemn nationalism, along with other ideologies, as godless and arrogant perversion; and even in the Middle East, pan-Islamic crusades have to be distinguished from secular pan-Arabism, which embraces Christians as well as Muslims, and is increasingly permeated with Marxist concepts.

For historical reasons, however, the Middle East is exceptional. Islam's early involvement with politics, its refusal to separate the political from the social or personal spheres, and its peculiar concept of the *umma*, or community of believers, has led to subtle and powerful, if uneasy, blending of religion and nationalism. In Turkey, it required a veritable revolution to break this tie, and even then the rural population remains permeated by Islamic customs and beliefs. Among the Arabs, who identify far more closely with Muhammad and Islam, and particularly the Arabic Koran, there is much greater reluctance on the part of nationalists to undermine Islam. Arabs face greater dilemmas than most peoples in exchanging a religious base for their solidarity for a linguistic or an institutional base. Their territorial expanse and ragged boundaries, the separateness of their evolution, in kingdoms and states as far apart as Morocco and Iraq, as well as the differences of their colonial and post-colonial histories, all militate against the political unity and psychological fraternity to which their common cultural heritage makes them aspire. Moreover, it is the most secularised, even non-Muslim, Arabs who are as vehemently nationalist as, in another sense, are the neo-traditionalist Muslim Brethren. Neo-traditionalism simply underlines Islam's political dimension and its ethnocentric attitude to other cultures. Secular Arabism, by contrast, seeks to bypass Islam, but cannot afford to do so without destroying the main bond of Arabs and reinforcing the centrifugal tendencies among them. A truly secular, political nationalism in the Middle East would inevitably end by creating separate state identities, by turning believers into citizens, and fostering a sense of belonging to Syria, Iraq, Egypt, Algeria, rather than to a single Arab nation.[48] The only parallels in this respect are afforded by Burma, Serbs and Croats, and Israel, though in all these cases their territorial compactness and location counteracts centrifugal tendencies consequent upon secularisation.

Where nationalism has penetrated in force, it has come on a wave of secularisation of the urban educated, exactly because that education tends to be secular and rationalist in content, westernising rather than traditionalist. Scientific methods and temper, rational modes of discourse, reliance on observation and induction, as well as specific rationalist attacks on tradition and religion in the West itself, have affected members of these élites, particularly when they travelled abroad. More important, colonial and imperial bureaucracies increasingly required appropriately trained personnel, and demonstrated their effectiveness in coping with problems which religious tradition had assumed to be beyond the powers of man. Training and effectiveness alike depended upon rational organisation, as well as a view of society which placed self-reliant and perfectible man at the centre of all activity. Bureaucracy also helped to implant a purely utilitarian ethos based on welfare ideals, and a more rigorously economic attitude to men and institutions. The result, in the West and outside, has been increased questioning of traditional explanations of the ethnic community; its destiny and history are no longer seen as part of some supernatural salvation drama, but simply as a theatre for social action which men by their own volition can mould to their ideals. The concept of the community is accordingly secularised and democratised; and the rediscovery of historic ethnicity is self-consciously theoretical.[49]

It is in this context of partial secularisation (affecting only some members of the élites) and religious doubt, that the ethnic 'bases' which I have discussed become alternatives for defining new nontraditional types of community, in terms of historicist attitudes and outlooks. The cult of history, the desire for exact period reconstruction, the belief in organic communal growth through time, the yearning for primordial origins, all these facets of 'historicism', whose political outgrowth is nationalism, are inconceivable without some degree of secularisation of attitudes and thought among sections of the intelligentsia.

IV. SOCIAL BEARERS OF NATIONALISM

Every movement has its originators and what Weber termed its peculiar 'bearers'—a stratum or strata for whom a given set of ideas has a particular attraction and who, in adopting them, mould them to their own material and 'ideal' interests.[50] The distinction between originators and bearers is not so clear-cut in the case of nationalism, since its doctrine is vaguer and more plastic than other ideologies. Nevertheless, nationalisms in every continent manifest certain leitmotivs, and these owe most to that stratum which originates and most zealously promotes nationalist ideas—the intelligentsia.

A. THE EXCLUSION OF THE INTELLIGENTSIA

If by 'intelligentsia' we mean 'professional strata' and not just intellectuals, men, that is, who apply and disseminate ideas, not only create and analyse them, then nationalism appears to exert a peculiar attraction for these occupations. Of course, every ideology requires, by definition, some westernised and secular intellectuals to elaborate and systematise it; and, as we shall see, other strata are needed if nationalism is to develop into a fully-fledged movement. Nevertheless, professionals have provided the backbone of most nationalisms, as well as much of the leadership; and, in some cases, they constitute the main bearers of the movement, since it provides a practical programme for fulfilling their needs, material and mental, and answers closely to their vision of the world and their place in it. Hence the rise and exclusion of an intelligentsia must be regarded as a necessary, though not sufficient, condition of the development of nationalism.

The link between nationalism and the intelligentsia stretches back to the fifteenth century, when the word 'natio' began to be used in something like its modern sense in the universities of Prague and Leipzig, and in the Church Councils, as at Constance, to signify divisions of the educated or clergy according to territory and culture.[51] In seventeenth-century England and eighteenth-century France it was mainly these professional classes – doctors, architects, artists, journalists, teachers, and especially, lawyers – who evolved the puritanical ideas behind nationalist doctrines.[52] In Germany, poets and professors were among the foremost apostles of an ardent, romantic nationalism, partly because it afforded a wider, worthier theatre for an educated public claiming a voice in civic affairs than the *Kleinstaaterei* of the petty despotisms with which they had to come to terms.[53] Rousseau's cult of nature and Winckelmann's of Greece were early expressions of this desire to escape the boredom and oppressiveness of a cramped small-town social life and the whims of officials and princelings. Imagination, channelled into poetry and history, soon extended this dual cult of nature and antiquity into a passion for everything unique and authentic.

The early Middle Ages offered a particularly fertile ground for imaginative escape from the drab provincialism of society and the mechanical routine of bureaucracy, and inspired the medievalist romanticism of Klopstock and Novalis, as well as the organicist conceptions in Herder's cultural populism and Fichte's nationalism.[54] The Italian intelligentsia were even less united than their German counterpart, partly because the Metternichian settlement had, if anything, accentuated the regionalism of the peninsula, partly because Napoleon's incursions had divided the politically educated into 'internationalist' revolutionaries like Buonarroti, radicals like Mazzini and the Carbonari, and 'moderates' who wanted the restricted suffrage of the 1814 French constitution – journalists and writers like Silvio Pellico, Cesare Balbo and the economist Carlo Cattaneo, bent on industrial and social progress.[55] What they shared with their German contemporaries, and with intelligentsias in other areas, was the frustration bred by cramped horizons and impaired mobility, both political and social.

Another major source of discontent among the intelligentsias was the increasing obscurantism and exclusiveness of religious authorities in their areas and communities. Suspended intellectually midway between their own traditions and the secular, scientific thought pioneered in England and France, excluded by arbitrary, if reformist, courts and bureaucracies, the qualified but untraditional professional found himself unable to return to his ethnic traditions or embrace a dogmatic faith. Kiernan remarks here on the 'unattached' and 'unanchored' quality of lower-middle-class individuals or clusters, who opt for incorporation into the nation with an emotion corresponding to their lack of social roots. But it is not only teachers, artisans and small traders who experience this need; more upper-middle-class individuals, who have been frustrated and disturbed by secularism and provincialism, also become fervent adherents of nationalism. Even the gentry were affected, as in Poland and Hungary; and in 1812, we find Baron Stein writing:

> 'I have but one fatherland, and that is Germany . . . to it, and not to any part of it, I am wholeheartedly devoted. I am completely indifferent, in this historic moment, to the fate of dynasties, my desire is that Germany shall grow large and strong, so that it may recover its independence and nationality, and maintain them against both France and Russia.'[56]

Similarly, Mirabeau and Lafayette supported the 'moderate', but fervent, nationalism of the American colonies;[57] and the early phases of Arab, Jewish and Indian nationalisms had upper-middle-class leaders or supporters like Abduh, Rida and Kawakibi, Herzl and Nordau, or Naoroji and Nehru, particularly where they turned to journalism and the law.[58]

Nationalism offers this new intelligentsia a practical way of translating into institutional reality their imaginary vision of freedom, their utopia of fraternity, based upon affiliation which reaches back into a mysterious and pure era of virtue and innocence, uncontaminated by market forces, urban luxuries and petty officialdom. It also offers a chance for finding a niche for their education and talents, a project where their knowledge is needed for social guidance and construction. Specific utopias and programmes may differ, but only the 'nation' and its state can confer on them the power and status to implement their ideals and fulfil their needs.[59]

B.   BEARERS OF NATIONALISM

Though professional clusters can achieve a considerable degree of expertise and organisation, they need the support of other strata if they are to convince the powers-that-be of their capacity and intention. Hence the tendency for other groups to take up the nationalist programme, altering it to suit their specific interests and conceptions. The very 'classlessness' of nationalist ideology facilitates its acceptance by different strata with conflicting aims. The result is several competing nationalisms within one movement; and often the competition assumes organisational form.

With such a plastic ideology, nationalism's bearers become highly variegated. Usually, however, one stratum (apart from the professionals) appropriates the movement from the first, stamping it with its own goals. Thus, the nationalisms of Poland and Hungary led by the declining gentry and middle nobility differ considerably from those of the French bourgeoisie or the klephtic leaders and priests of the Pelopponese. Outside Europe, too, as Kiernan's discussion reveals, there is much social variety. Students have been prominent in China, Burma, the Pan-African Manchester Congress of 1945 and the First Arab Students' Congress in Brussels in 1938.[60] Officers have assumed the leadership in Turkey and later in Egypt and Iraq, as well as in Latin America.[61] Their nationalism takes a strongly puritanical and *étatiste* form, quite different from the more enthusiastic, ideological student congresses. Yet another popular form is the 'national communism' found in Yugoslavia, Vietnam and Mao's China, which seeks the support of a peasantry threatened by alien rule.[62] Religious personnel often play a considerable part in nationalist movements, particularly in Asia where ethnic groups are identified (and identify themselves) by their religion, as in Pakistan or Burma. In the latter, however, the more traditional interests of the *pongyis* (political monks) clashed with those of the students and officers after the Saya San revolt was crushed; and in other countries like Indonesia, an initial religious stimulus gave way to more socialist-minded strata.[63]

The malleability of nationalism, its capacity for 'social distortion' by the interests of particular strata, can be illustrated briefly in both France and Greece. In the Dreyfus Affair, when nationalism re-emerged in France after the loss of Alsace-Lorraine, there were at least two conflicting versions of nationalism, the one Barrès's traditionalist 'integral nationalism' with its mystic and monarchical underpinnings, embraced by the army and the church, the other republican and democratic, harking back to the Jacobins and favoured by Jaurès's socialists and the liberal sections of the intelligentsia.[64] In Greece, the social situation was more complex at the time of the War of Independence, and the nationalist movement accordingly resembled an ideological patchwork. On the one hand, some priests and merchants dreamt of the Megale Idea, a restoration of Byzantine wealth and glory. On the other, more westernised merchants shared the Hellenic visions and enlightened, republican sentiments of Adamantios Koraes and the exiled professionals. Sailors and peasants were mainly concerned with freedom from taxes and restrictions levied by the Sultan, or the pashas and the primates on land; while the klephtic leaders were latterday warriors against the infidel, to whom they might go over and become guards (*armatoli*), fiercely independent outlaws who understood nothing of Hellenism, men like Nikotsaras who is reputed to have replied to a Greek scholar who acclaimed his prowess by likening it to Achilles': 'What nonsense is this, and who is Achilles? Did the musket of Achilles kill many?'[65]

C. COMMERCE AND MERCHANTS

Quite apart from nationalism's abstraction, its growth *pari passu* with the development of first commerce, then capitalism and finally industry, has subjected its social composition to still further variation and ideological colorations, which Kiernan explores in Chapter 6. In some cases, particularly in Eastern Europe, class conflicts generated by capitalism have been so bitter that they have often weakened the social penetration of nationalism beyond the élites. This is certainly true of nationalism's later development. At the same time, the initial stages of many movements were dominated by commercial (though not strictly 'capitalist') interests. Serbian pig-dealers, Greek merchants like John Riggos and Norwegian traders followed in the nationalist footsteps of the French bourgeoisie.[66] Outside Europe, commercial interests tended to be less developed, but merchants continued to play vital roles in the early phases of nationalist movements, for example in the Indonesian Sarekat Islam,[67] or the pan-Turkist jadid movement among the Tatars around 1900.[68] Even more crucial was the role of Armenian merchants in India and elsewhere,[69] or of the cash-crop farmers and traders in the Ivory Coast.[70]

The African case is particularly instructive of the *indirect* influence of commerce on the rise of nationalism. Generally speaking, African business and managerial organisations were small, and the number of entrepreneurs and merchants tiny in comparison with their intrusive European counterparts. At the same time, businessmen were very well-represented in most of the legislatures in which power was formally vested upon independence, and many of the intelligentsia who became leaders of the nationalist movements were sons of urbanised merchants who engaged in trade in the commodities which the Europeans were developing with the help of African labour. In certain cases like Ghana, Sierra Leone and the Ivory Coast, the links between merchants or cash-crop farmers and the nationalist movement were intimate. In other cases, it was a more general process of commercialisation of labour and services, mediated especially through secular education, which fostered the growth of nationalism. The nation-state provides obvious security and markets for traders and businessmen in a world of such states; hence it is hardly surprising to find this close link between nationalism and commerce, particularly as trading interests tend to promote secularism in order to provide vocational training as well as general education for their children. This is especially marked in those areas, the vast majority in fact, where the commercial class is fairly small and either overshadowed by competition from merchants of other ethnic groups, or hemmed in by political and economic restrictions, and where of course a suitable political framework for their activities was lacking.[71] The French bourgeoisie were perhaps restricted, yet they did possess a state framework; the Greek and Armenian merchants were both restricted and without an appropriate framework.[72]

V.   HEROES AND CITIZENS

If men's visions are as compelling as their interests, then nationalism's relative success lies in its ability to harmonise a pictorial abstraction which fires the imagination with practical, concrete programmes to serve the interests of several strata. Fatherlands and *ethnie* can be on the one hand decked out with vivid images and striking symbols, and on the other adapted to the most specific situations. At the same time, its pictorial abstraction means that nationalism, of all ideologies, is one of the most remote from immediate social and economic concerns, and so can embrace many groups with conflicting goals within its fold.

But this very heterogeneity of social composition poses grave problems after independence is attained. This is the issue to which Calvert addresses himself (in Chapter 7), when he considers the sources of continued integration or opposition for nationalisms after independence. Here we move from consideration of the factors – frameworks, bases and bearers – involved in the growth of nationalist movements, to the additional conditions of its political 'success' in retaining sovereignty and in state-building. Here, the main factors are the existing social and ethnic composition of the new state, its geo-political situation, and the quality of its leadership. A mono-ethnic, and socially homogeneous, state possesses overwhelming advantages in this respect. But few states have been free of minorities, and the imperatives of social cohesion and individuality have generally entailed a policy of nationalisation of personnel, sometimes involving expulsion. As Calvert argues, the costs and adversity that nationalist policies of integration entail are more easily borne if the nation can be personified in the figure of a charismatic hero–leader, who can wield the aggressive power of the new state, without the checks and balances found in older nation-states. For attaining independence, however, leadership and even ethnic homogeneity appear to be less important than the geo-political context. What determined the successful attainment of independence by Greece, Albania, Israel, Belgium and Bangladesh was as much the alignment of Great

Power interests in the area, and their role as sponsors, as their social homogeneity (often defective) or leadership and organisation, effective though these were.[73] Movements like the Biafran or Kurdistani, which have, to date, failed to gain independence, lacked neither unity nor leadership compared to the cases of Greece or Bangladesh; but they failed to find Great Power sponsors willing to protect their cause.[74]

Mention of the geo-political context's continuing influence brings us to a more fundamental consideration about the long-term 'success' of a nationalist movement. This is the need for the new state and regime to be accepted by the 'community of nations' as a familiar and 'normal' part of the international scene. To fulfil this requirement, to meet the test of world approval and respectability (which in practice means at first securing the recognition of powerful member-states of the world community), nationalist movements have to 'normalise' themselves and their populations. 'Normalisation', which of course negates nationalism's cult of ethnic uniqueness, is the price of continued independence; and normalisation, in the long run, is measured by nationalism's ability to transform a movement of heroes into one of citizens.

This process of 'normalisation', this transformation of nationalism, is full of dangers. The movement has drawn its rationale and inspiration from the world of heroes, saviours and prophets, from the esoteric and magical nuances and chords that kindle the ethnic imagination. The world of citizenship, by contrast, is uniform and unremarkable. It levels men through the device of formal equality of rights and duties before an impersonal state. Beneath the flamboyant fantasies of national liberation and mystic ties, normalisation reveals in the legal status of the citizen the hard bureaucratic structure of the nation-state. But, in the process of transformation, disillusion bred by over-centralisation and lack of local participation may easily slow down the social and political mobilisation necessary to attain economic autarchy, integration and other goals of the new regime. Even more profoundly, planning and standardisation threaten the very legitimacy of the nationalist enterprise by eroding the cultural individuality to which nationalists aspire. If the nationalists are simply improving on the bureaucratic work of 'alien' rulers – colonial or imperial – wherein lies the rationale of their act of secession and their sense of alienity?

These questions have found no lasting solutions. Instead, the method of the French Revolution has been copied: mass levees, societies and clubs, fêtes and ceremonies, flags and anthems, have rehearsed the rites of citizenship in every continent, proclaiming their true freedom and equality, under bureaucratic law.[75] Together with the censuses and plebiscites, the constitutions and legal codes, oaths, presidents, assemblies, congresses, proportional representation and similar devices for securing world recognition, these rites and symbols simultaneously perpetuate and standardise ethnic differences. They create a sense of solidarity, a corporate will (or the semblance thereof), and thereby delimit the nation and define the outsider. Moreover, central administration which regulates the symbols and rites, as it does everything else in the new state, intervenes unevenly in the affairs of every section of the people. Discrimination or neglect on its part, coupled with a passion for downward government, has stimulated new movements for autonomy and secession in areas where economic change appears to threaten ancient cultures and institutions. Scotland, Brittany and Wales are some of the better-known examples of a type of 'reactive nationalism' which resists incorporation with, they allege, second-class status.[76]

Yet even secession movements cannot carry their need for cultural separateness too far. The condition of attaining their political goals remains recognition by the world, or at least by the Great Powers; and that means some degree of conformity to international norms. It is a well-known dilemma of guerrilla movements on the brink of diplomatic recognition; but it also applies to every nation-state, which must steer a middle course between cultural uniqueness and international comparability, between the vitality of distinctive ties and the security of cross-national standardisation.

The rival claims of uniqueness and universalism which nationalism embodies are further highlighted by its relations with socialism and Marxism. From this standpoint, two tendencies unfold within the original Enlightenment versions of nationalist doctrine, one of which constitutes a Romantic exaltation of the people, while the other views nationhood in more pragmatic and instrumental terms as a prelude to, and instrument for attaining, a mature revolutionary consciousness and *praxis*. The first of these tendencies gives rise to various types of 'populist' nationalism ranging from Mazzini's Young Europe to the recent appeal of Nasserism in the Arab world.[77] In Africa, too, 'populism' may be regarded as a phase of the independence struggle and an attempt to broaden its social base. Yet, despite the use of a radically democratic vocabulary and the exploitation by élites of local popular grievances, the disjunction between the interests of the élites in the towns and the rural tribesmen often turns national consciousness in Africa into what Fanon called an 'empty shell'.[78] In other colonies like India, the 'populist' appeals of Tilak and Gandhi reflected a neo-traditionalist rejection of Western, including rationalist and Marxist, values, while emphasising community and solidarity.[79]

The other tendency which traces its descent from Jacobin centralisation and revolutionary expansionism has been inherited by Marxist socialist parties, especially in developing countries. While in Europe the emphasis of orthodox Marxists (especially those indebted to Engelsian determinism) upon the class consciousness of a revolutionary proletariat allowed only compromises and alliances with strong nationalist sentiments whether in Germany or in Poland, in Asia and Africa (and Cuba) much more subtle blends of nationalism and communism have appeared, notably in China, Yugoslavia, Algeria and Vietnam. Here, social democracy of the British variety has had no appeal against the identification of the peasantry as the revolutionary class on the Maoist model. The 'nation' accordingly became in theory an instrument of revolutionary action and a model for other revolutionary movements. At the same time, the consolidation of national communist regimes has bred a subtle re-emergence of national sentiment, indeed an overt nationalism based on Leninist notions of self-determination, in each of these countries, reinforced of course by their having to fight wars of liberation against invaders.[80] In many ways, such 'communist nationalisms' have been pace-setters in ex-colonial territories, outstripping the more emotional, fragmented populisms, except in sub-Saharan Africa, where the élites have so far contained incipient class conflict.[81] They have also provided inspiration for the loose international networks of terrorist guerrilla resistance movements who attempt to combine notions of world revolution with their particular nationalist wars of liberation.[82]

It is, however, important not to overemphasise the impact of Marxian or more generally revolutionary guerrilla groups, who often constitute a tiny minority of the resistance movement, despite their ability to bring unresolved conflicts to world attention. Moreover, the attitude of more orthodox groups within resistance movements, and of the central administrative and party leaderships in national communist regimes, to their revolutionary cousins, is often ambivalent, if not hostile. For most, the revolutionary horizon is bounded by ethnic and territorial limits set by an overriding sense of national identity; and acceptance by the 'world community', recognition of the justice of their claims, is in the final analysis of greater importance than the export of their revolution, let alone the sinking of their identity in a true class revolution. In other words, the need for international recognition regulates both the degree to which national distinctiveness may be emphasised, and the extent to which world revolutionary ideals may be pursued outside one's own borders.

CONCLUSION

The final test of every nationalism is its capacity to confer dignity and security on individuals by means of a novel theory of the relations between culture and politics. But modern political conditions create a continual tension in trying to fulfil both needs. The quest for dignity entails an emphasis upon the uniqueness of a citizen's identity which threatens to upset the international balance and the criteria of 'normalcy' and general human advance. This, in turn, jeopardises the quest for individual security, of which a precondition today is a measure of world stability, and hence social progress. To settle for complete security on the other hand, through revolutionary advance within a global framework, risks a loss of inner meaning in the collective life of the regimented citizen. Both normalcy and material progress require continual renewal of purpose and enthusiasm, which nationalism, with its characteristic quest for purity and identity, can inspire. Among the developing countries, citizenship is barely established. The need there is for a greater measure of security through material and social progress; hence the appeal of Marxian socialism in conjunction with nationalism. In the industrialised nations, however, the malaise is rather a loss of purpose, identity and, ultimately, dignity, in the face of increasing bureaucratisation. For here, it is the state which has come to dominate the nation; and, paradoxically, the very quest for that sovereignty which would afford security and well-being in one's own homeland has ended up eroding the autonomy and individuality in whose name sovereignty was sought. Originating as a passionate reaction against state power and authority, against the dulling uniformity of bureaucratic encroachments, nationalism has in fact succeeded in strengthening that power and increasing those encroachments. Yet for all its shackled respectability in the West today, the evidence suggests that nationalism has not yet lost its inspiration and appeal for the unprivileged and aspirant across the globe.

2

Size and Scale as Factors in the Development of Nationalist Movements

W. J. Argyle

Whatever else nationalism may be, I take it to be a process by which a social or cultural category may become a corporate group. By construing nationalism in this way, I am not of course defining it, for the same general process occurs in modern times at many different levels, so that, for example, the category 'homosexual' becomes the Gay Liberation Front or the category 'student' becomes the National Union of Students or the category 'doctor' becomes the British Medical Association. The level of the 'nation' is then only the most inclusive at which the process has so far effectively occurred.[1]

Nor am I proposing a new 'theory' of nationalism. Instead, I am simply using and linking two concepts which have not, so far as I know, been applied in this particular way to the study of European nationalism (with which I am here principally concerned), but have been elaborated in several other contexts by a number of anthropologists. The concept 'category' was, for example, used some time ago by Professor Evans-Pritchard[2] in something like one of its dictionary (*S.O.E.D.*) definitions of a 'class, or division, in a scheme of classification', in order to distinguish relationships between kin from those between unilineal descent groups. Following his example, many other anthropologists have written of 'kinship categories', but some have also extended the notion to describe as 'social categories' certain collectivities of people who share a particular set of characteristics, but who lack any organisation for the management of their common affairs. It is this lack that principally distinguishes them from 'corporate groups' which do have internal organisation.

So, for Bohannan, an 'estate' in medieval Europe, such as the serfs, is a 'category of people who are not organised' whereas a caste in India is 'a corporate group . . . made corporate by the fact that it has organisation'.[3] A more conspicuous example is M. G. Smith's increas-

For Notes and References to Chapter 2, see pp. 157–60.

ingly elaborate typology of 'corporations' in which two key types are the 'corporate category' and the 'corporate group'. For him, corporate groups are 'presumptively perpetual aggregates with unique identities, determinate boundaries and memberships, and having the autonomy, organization and procedures necessary to regulate their exclusive common affairs'.[4] Corporate categories are similar in 'having presumptive perpetuity, determinate boundaries, identity and memberships', but differ 'by their lack of the organization, procedures and capacity necessary to regulate the common affairs of their collective membership'.[5] The distinction is more systematically (and more profusely) made than Bohannan's, but corresponds to his in its main feature, the presence or lack of organisation. My own usage conforms more or less to this distinction, though I have not followed such a precise definition of 'category' nor the attachment of 'corporate' to it, since this seems to me[6] an idiosyncratic departure from previous convention which had established that a category was precisely *not* corporate.

The clearest anthropological precedent for my assumption that a category can be converted into a group is Cohen's remark, in his recent important study of what he calls 'retribalisation' amongst Hausa migrants, that 'an ethnic category often becomes an ethnic group'.[7] This remark can indeed be taken as a bare summary of the topic of his work, but he does not use it as a specific framework for his analysis in the way I have tried to do with mine.

Besides such anthropological precedents for my general approach, there are some much earlier ones established by historians dealing with the specific topic of nationalism. There is, for example, the distinction made by Meinecke (in a work first published in 1908 and frequently reprinted) between *Kulturnationen* and *Staatsnationen*, a distinction which further implies, in Cobban's summary of it, 'an effort on the part of these cultural nations to become state-nations'.[8] Essentially the same distinction and the same process was stated by one of the pioneer American students of nationalism, Carleton Hayes:

A nationality, by acquiring political unity and sovereign independence, becomes a 'nation', or . . . establishes a 'national state' . . . . A state is essentially political; a nationality is primarily cultural.[9]

Both this quotation and the one from Cobban state the process almost as if it were impersonal, self-generating and self-sustaining: the 'nationality' itself 'becomes' or 'establishes' the 'nation-state'. Of course what actually happens is that a succession of human agents first define a particular national category and then proceed, more or less deliberately with varying degrees of success, to try and convert that category into the corporate group of the nation. These agents, by which I mean those who are particularly active in a movement, are usually called nationalists and, since the process cannot occur without them, they must obviously be included in it.

This initial statement of the process, of its specific terms and agents, may seem fairly obvious. But it is a necessary preliminary to my discussion of the significance of size and scale in the formation of nationalist movements (which is the topic assigned to me). For their significance must vary at different phases of the process which may, after all, take a century or more to complete, though it can be much more rapid, as in some of the most recent cases. An indefinite number of such phases could be distinguished. I recognise four, which are: proposing the category, elaborating the category, making subsidiary corporations, mustering the people.

Before I consider these phases, I should emphasise that they are more analytical than historical; that is, they do not form an invariable sequence in real time: there, indeed, the episodes that compose them sometimes overlapped. They are, however, inductively derived from historical data, some of which I reproduce as 'apt illustrations' of the phases. Having thus derived the phases and arranged them in an order that is mainly logical, but also roughly chronological, I examine as far as possible for each phase, first, the 'size' of the categories or corporations, then their 'scale'; next, the 'size' of the promoting nationalist agencies; finally, the 'scale' of these agencies. By 'size' I generally intend 'number of persons', though it is never in fact possible to state precisely what the number is so that I have to make rough judgements of relative size. 'Scale' I usually interpret as 'social range' and try to determine briefly which social classes were comprehended in the various national categories and which were most prominent in the agencies.

I follow this procedure in relation to examples, drawn mainly from monographs in English, of the nationalist process amongst peoples in Central and South-east Europe, particularly some of those in the Habsburg Empire during the period from about the mid-eighteenth to the late nineteenth centuries. These examples seem to me to represent the process in some of its most intense and prolonged forms, and they therefore serve to bring out features which are not so evident elsewhere, though I believe they are always present in some measure wherever the process occurs.

I. PROPOSING THE CATEGORY

It is sometimes claimed (especially by nationalists) that national categories are 'natural' divisions of mankind, marked by definite cultural characteristics which are readily apparent to any ordinary observer. The categories are therefore self-evident and do not need 'proposing' by anybody. This claim is, of course, unacceptable. People only become members of national categories when they have been taught what these are and have accepted that they belong to them. The point is clearly illustrated by the statement of a former peasant in Galicia, published as late as 1941, that he had not realised he was a Pole, until he started reading books and newspapers which he thought were also the most likely source of his fellow villagers' sense of national identity.[10]

This example of acceptance suggests how the category develops exogenously, once it has been proposed, from some original point which may be quite remote in space and time from the populations which it eventually comes to comprehend. This point may indeed lie in such an obscure setting as that of the meeting in 1737 of the Transylvanian Diet, where the Uniate Bishop Innocentius Klein-Micu may be said to have first publicly proposed the Rumanian national category by presenting to the Diet (of which he himself was a member by right of his Bishopric) 'a memorial "in his own name, and in that of the whole nation of Wallach[11] name in Transylvania"'.[12]

The background to this memorial was that the Bishop was trying to get recognition for the Rumanians as a fourth 'nation', alongside the three 'nations' of the Magyars, the Szekels and the Saxons who were already represented in the Diet and in the lesser assemblies of local government. Indeed, the term 'nation' (*natio*) at this time often applied only to a category which had such representation and could be defined even more narrowly to refer exclusively to that class from which the representatives were actually drawn, so the Magyar 'nation' was in this sense not the whole Magyar people, but only the Magyar nobility. The Transylvanian Diet, like all others in the Habsburg Empire, was subordinate to the Imperial authority, but played a significant role in securing and maintaining the hereditary privileges attaching to the 'nations' and particularly to the 'political classes' within the 'nations'. In my terms, therefore, the three national categories were already partially incorporated through their representation in the Diet, and the Bishop was trying to obtain a similar degree of incorporation for the category of which he regarded himself as a member.

He did not succeed, for his memorial met with a very hostile reception in the Diet, including cries of 'There is no Wallach nation, there is only a Wallach plebs'[13] – in my terms, again, there was no Rumanian corporate group, only a Rumanian category. Some members of the Diet would have denied there was even a category, for they refused to allow that the Rumanians were a 'gens', let alone a plebs. Yet this episode and the Bishop's other, ecclesiastical and educational, activities on behalf of his Rumanian flock can be seen as an early,[14] perhaps the earliest, attempt to propose not only a Rumanian national category, but also its partial incorporation. His example was soon taken up by other Rumanians and, after the whole process had been accomplished, the ultimate result was the achievement of the Rumanian national state.

Although Klein-Micu's case is especially striking, it is by no means unique. An even more obscure figure, the monk Paissi (1722–98), may be said to have first proposed the Bulgarian national category from the isolation of his monastery cell in Mount Athos, where he completed in 1762 his *Slavo-Bulgarian History*, a work which circulated in manuscript until printed in 1844 and which has been described as 'the Gospel of the Bulgarian revival'.[15] In the preface to this work, he exhorted Bulgarians to know their own history, language and characteristics and not to be ashamed of them in comparison with other peoples'.[16] Similar exhortations were subsequently addressed by, amongst others, Obradovic (1742–1811) to the Serbs; Dobrovski (1753–1829) to the Czechs; Bessenyei (1747–1811) to the Magyars.[17]

These examples may justify some observations about, first of all, the factor of size in relation to the categories proposed. My initial observation is that the only one of these early 'nationalists' who is said to have referred to the size of his 'nationality' was Klein-Micu. He seems to have used the figures from a census of taxable families in Transylvania made in 1733 to show that the 'Wallach nation' far outnumbered the other three nations combined and that it therefore deserved to be 'recognised', as the other three already were.[18] This kind of argument was, of course, much favoured by later generations of nationalists all over Europe and elsewhere. But Klein-Micu's use of it at that time seems to have been as unusual as some of his other claims and arguments. My impression is that he could use it mainly because of the rather peculiar political structure of Transylvania, with its various 'nations' which for some reason were enumerated in the census. Elsewhere in the Habsburg Empire, the official censuses apparently did not record language (the usual test of nationality) until after 1790,[19] and in Hungary the Magyar nobility (obstreperous as always) prevented any official census from being taken at all between 1781 and the middle of the nineteenth century. As for the Ottoman Empire, if any official censuses were taken there, it seems most unlikely that Bulgarian or Serbian nationalists would have had access to them.

In any case, my second observation is that the first step in proposing any national category must be to state, or at least imply, its defining characteristics. Only when they have been formulated is it possible to begin trying to count those who conform to them. It is likely, therefore, that the nationalists of this phase were preoccupied with the first step and did not concern themselves much with numbers.

My inference about numerical size is, then, that it was not and usually could not be a crucial factor in proposing the categories. This inference does not, however, preclude the possibility that a category might comprehend a large number of people; it does preclude the possibility of stating what that number was. Given this impossibility, any judgement about the *relative* size of a proposed category must depend partly on the suggested scale of the category.

This scale is sometimes almost certainly an expanded one, as when Paissi equates the 'Bulgarians' he is apostrophising with the 'simple, harmless peasants and shepherds', and excludes from that national category the traders and other 'prudent' (= 'cunning'?) people whom he puts in another category as 'Greeks'.[20] This dichotomy reflects the contemporary social division in that part of Europe between the ordinary rural population which was predominantly Slav-speaking and the largely urban commercial and administrative class which is being called 'Greek'. Yet in addressing all these rural people as his 'Bulgarian kin', Paissi must have been newly stretching an old category, for it is most unlikely that their mental horizons would have comprehended the 'Bulgarian fatherland' that he was inviting them to know and understand. They are virtually certain to have been like those Galician peasants before they read the Polish books and newspapers or like those other twentieth-century peasants in Upper Silesia who, when asked what they were, tended to reply, 'I am a man from here.'[21] Similarly, not all those classified as 'Greeks' would necessarily have accepted the term as applying to themselves.

To that extent, then, Paissi's categories were transcending many of the divisions and boundaries which actually obtained in the society around him. Indeed, it is difficult to know just where the Bulgarian category might end, since there were no clear distinctions on linguistic or cultural grounds between 'Bulgarians' and, for example, 'Serbs', as may be seen from the later controversies over that very issue. It follows that one cannot safely say more than that the categories proposed were generally 'wider' and therefore their membership 'larger' than those previously employed are likely to have been. I cannot see that such a conclusion allows of any connection between the size or scale of particular categories and the ultimate success or failure of the nationalist agencies proposing them.

I can, however, be rather more definite, though still not precise, about the size and scale of the agencies themselves. Of size, I can declare immediately that it was ordinarily very small: perhaps as small, in some cases, as one person. Bishop Klein-Micu was not leading a party in the Diet (though he certainly had supporters outside it in his own Church); he apparently stood alone there and, as his opponents said, he spoke up for 'things which no one has ever demanded from our ancestors'.[22] Since Paissi was not a Bishop, he was perhaps an even more singular figure; certainly, Kohn twice characterises him as 'lonely' in his advocacy of Bulgarian identity[23] and Macartney gives a similar impression.[24] Other sources frequently single out an individual as the initial proponent of a particular national category.

It is of course true that none of these individuals, not even Paissi, was completely insulated from all contact with other minds. They did not create their categories *ex nihilo* and they did not propose them without effect. But nor were they at the head of large movements; at the most, they collaborated with one or two associates and usually propounded their views through the then rather confined medium of the written word.

Since they were so few, it is not surprising that they represented a rather limited range of the contemporary social orders. Of those men already mentioned, four (Klein-Micu, Paissi, Obradovic and Dobrovski) were clergy or ex-clergy and there were others from that order. I attribute the prominence of the clergy to the interaction of three factors: the circumstance that the church was often the only significant organisation other than the state itself; the virtual monopoly that the churches had over education; the urge to proselytise, especially amongst the peasantry which could be reached only through the 'national' vernaculars.

The clergy did not, however, always have the field to themselves. In Hungary their nationalist role was overshadowed by that of some members of the Magyar noble order, which was itself partially corporate, who had some education, and who favoured Magyar, instead of German, as the official language. Amongst the Greeks of the Hellenic diaspora, merchants or the children of merchants, such as Adamantios Korais (1748–1833), played an unusually important part in the Greek nationalist movement. Such cases reflect the differing social composition of particular nationalities and suggest that the proposal of categories was not the prerogative of the same class everywhere. On the other hand, they also confirm what the numbers already imply: that in no case did an early nationalist movement include equally prominent representatives of all the social orders within that category. These conclusions and all the previous ones about the size of the agency and the size and scale of the category have to be modified, but not fundamentally changed, as the process moves into the next phase.

II. ELABORATING THE CATEGORY

In this phase, as my label for it suggests, the definitions of the categories became increasingly elaborate. Apart from such well-known manifestations as the proliferation of literary and linguistic works in or about the vernaculars, all of which gave extra substance to the categories, there were other elaborations that had the apparent, but not real, effect of adding to the categories the dimensions of number, space and time.

Amongst those who gave an increasing emphasis to the numerical size of national populations were some of the more prominent Slav nationalists who 'often played on the chords of statistics'.[25] One way in which they played on them was by composing what can be called 'super-national' categories, of which the most extensive was that of 'Slav' or 'pan-Slav', for which estimates of about eighty million people were made[26] and widely used to assert the potentially overwhelming superiority of Slavs over other nationalities, especially over Germans and Magyars. Another, less extensive, but popular one among the South Slavs for several decades was the category 'Illyria' which comprehended varying combinations of Croats, Slovenes, Serbs, Bulgarians and other Southern Slavs. An early example of the statistical use, or rather misuse, of this super-national category was that of the spokesman at the (Hungarian) Serb 'National Congress' of 1790 who claimed 'to represent four million [sic] "Illyrians" of Hungary against only two million [sic] Magyars'.[27] Many other variations on such themes were played later by other Slavs, and they tended to evoke contrapuntal responses either from Magyars, such as Kossuth's remark in the Diet just before the 1848 revolutions about Croatia being 'so small that it is not enough for a breakfast',[28] or from Germans, such as the rejoicing of the Viennese newspaper, *Volksfreund*, in 1848 over 'a small, defeated party like the Czechs, against whom there will always be forty million Germans'.[29]

In this sort of atmosphere, the meaning of the figures, which were usually arrived at by tortuous manipulations of censuses with dubious validity, was largely symbolic. In other words, it was becoming important to claim a size for the category and to make that size as impressive as possible, but there was in reality no way of calculating an 'objective' figure, since the boundaries, social and spatial, of the categories were still not established.

Some nationalists did indeed attempt in this phase to deal with the problem of spatial boundaries by constructing maps showing the extent of the territory claimed for the category. One conspicuous example is the map of 'Illyria' drawn by the Croat, Ljudevit Gaj (1809–72). Jaszi, who mentions this map and who himself lived under the Habsburg Empire, adds the following interesting general comment:

> How seemingly useless a play it is for the nationalist to draw maps of territories whose inhabitants scarcely know anything of each other. And still there is a kind of political magic in such jokes . . . . Men not inclined to abstract reasoning visualise at once things unthinkable.[30]

In other words, the maps were symbols of the category's territory, not as it existed, but as nationalists wanted it. They also gave an answer to those who, like Kossuth, claimed to be 'unable to find Croatia on the map'.[31] Furthermore, they provided the basis for claims in the real world, such as that of the Czech newspaper in 1848: 'The Danube is a

Slavic river',[32] to take only one, not especially bizarre,[33] example of what became an increasingly common trend.

Such claims were reinforced by asserting primacy of occupation in the territories delineated on the maps. This assertion meant projecting the existence of the national category as far back in time as possible. So modern Greeks said their ancestors were the Ancient Greeks; Transylvanian Rumanians argued that they were descended from the inhabitants of Roman Dacia; the Magyars indignantly rejected this argument and boasted that their own 'thousand-year state' gave them priority there and in the rest of Hungary; the Czechs claimed immemorial antiquity for Bohemia. Sometimes the claims were carried to the point of fabricating historical evidence, as when V. Hanka successfully imposed on his Czech contemporaries a forged collection of manuscript poems depicting 'a glorious Czech civilisation allegedly existing in the Dark Ages'.[34] Yet other claims went quite beyond the range of any evidence, real or forged, like that of the scholar (Magyar of course) who showed Adam to have been a Magyar, or that of Karadzic (see below) who included Jesus and the Apostles amongst the Serbs.[35] Ludicrous as they seem, such fantasies, like those about numbers and space, were part of the gradual conversion of the category into the corporate group. For the projection of the categories back through time gave them that 'presumed perpetuity' which is one of the commonly used criteria for corporateness. Similarly, the attribution of numbers to the categories implied a move towards a more definite membership which is another criterion. The claims to national territories defined by maps amounted to assertions of rights over 'estates', which some anthropologists, following Radcliffe-Brown, have seen as characteristic of corporations.

I should perhaps emphasise that many of these elaborations already had marked political implications because they entailed, in Macartney's words, 'the gradual transformation of the [Habsburg] Monarchy from something which could be ruled as a non-national State to something the multi-national nature of which had to be admitted'.[36] The emerging corporations were therefore essentially political, even if their ultimate metamorphosis into independent nation-states was scarcely yet imagined.

These political implications were also evident in the fluctuating definition of the categories which was occasioned by the elaborations to which they were subjected. For the competing assertions about size, space and time enjoined the more ardent nationalists to declare publicly their personal commitments to particular definitions. For example, in 1846, the Czech publicist, Karel Havlicek (1821–56) published a series of articles in which he described his own progresssive disillusionment with the (pan-) 'Slav idea' during his travels in Russia and Poland, from where he 'returned to Prague as a Czech, a simple determined Czech, even with some secret sour feeling against the name

Slav'.[37] Two years later a more famous declaration of Czech identity[38] was made by Frantisek Palacky (1798–1876) in refusing the invitation he received to attend the Frankfurt Assembly, an invitation made because of the then common pan-German assumption that Bohemia was a German territory and perhaps also because Palacky's own work on Bohemian history had been initially written and published in German.

But even this narrower, 'Czech' identity was too wide for some, who otherwise shared many of the nationalist assumptions. For example, the nobleman, J. M. Thun, a member of a family conspicuous for its support of the Czech cause, declared (in German),[39] 'I am neither a Czech nor a German, but only a Bohemian.'[40] Comparable sentiments were expressed by many Czech-speakers in Moravia who held themselves to be not Czechs but Moravians.[41] Some Slovaks, such as Ljudevit Stur, also began to resist identification with the Czechs, who roundly castigated them for their resistance.[42] Elsewhere in the Habsburg Empire, similar disagreements about the scope of the category 'Illyrian' (later 'Jugoslav') stimulated a sharper sense of more restricted national identities amongst Croats, Slovenes and Serbs. I may therefore repeat, in summary form, the 'segmentary principle' that is apparent from many studies of nationalism: a national category usually emerges only in opposition to other categories.

The eventual outcome of such opposition was, on the whole, a reduction in the appeal of the wider categories and a correspondingly higher degree of commitment to the narrower ones. In that sense, elaboration of the categories may be said to have diminished their scale in relation to each other, but to have expanded the scale within each one by encouraging more individuals to associate themselves with it. This expansion of the 'internal' scale can also be noticed at the collective, rather than the individual, level in the growing popularity of the notion of the 'folk' or 'people' which made up each national category and enabled, in theory at least, the calculation of its numbers, the definition of its territory and the reconstruction of its past. So Palacky 'made the whole Czech people the bearer of the Czech idea',[43] and the Magyar, Count Szechenyi (1791–1860), wrote that 'Hungary will be neither happy nor of exalted position until the people are admitted to the ranks of the nation'.[44]

Such statements should not, however, be taken as evidence of a willingness to admit the 'people' to anything like full participation in the existing or future political life of the nation. In general, it seems that the nationalists of this phase were willing to emancipate the peasants (who formed the overwhelming majority of the 'people') but not to enfranchise them. My interpretation of the expansion of internal scale to include the 'people' is therefore that it was conceived almost entirely in cultural and social, rather than political, terms. It follows that nationalism was still a long way from becoming a mass political movement for the total incorporation of the nation. This conclusion may be readily supported by an examination of the size and scale of the nationalist agencies during this phase.

Some increase in the size of the agencies would be expected from the proliferation of written works which were still the main medium for the communication of nationalist ideas and sentiments. The sources do usually give an impression of a growth in the relative size of the agency, even though it may not have been large in absolute numbers. A sufficiently striking illustration is that of the so-called 'Transylvanian Triad' who carried on the cause which Klein-Micu had begun solo. These three men, Petru Maior, George Sinkay (1756–1816) and one of the Bishop's own nephews, Samuel Klein-Micu (1745–1816), were products of the educational system he had instituted in his Transylvanian diocese. Between them, they produced a number of linguistic, literary and historical works, all tending to elaborate and glorify the Rumanian nationality.[45] For that reason, they provoked considerable official hostility, so it is not surprising that, to judge from the sources, they remained a Triad, though doubtless their books found some eager readers.

Although the numbers of the major figures in other nationalist agencies of this phase cannot be so neatly stated, there is evidence that they, too, were often small. Certainly Palacky once claimed, when reviewing the progress of the Czech national movement, that if the ceiling of the room where he and his associates used to dine in the early days had collapsed on them, it would have been the end of the movement.[46] Perhaps he was overstating the point, but at least he was a leading participant in the movement and the modern sources, with their recurrent, short lists of the same names, offer little reason for challenging Palacky's estimate.

The evidence on other nationalities tends in the same direction, emphasising the importance of a few individuals in each case. Sometimes, indeed, a crucial role at particular moments is attributed to single persons, as Macartney, for example, does to Count Szechenyi amongst the Magyars and to Ljudevit Gaj amongst the Croats.[47] Obviously, though, such men could not have had the influence they did have without gaining support – which has at least to be mentioned, when dealing with the size of the agency (and also with its scale, as I shall show below). Szechenyi, though never the leader of a party, had his followers in the Hungarian Diet and in the country at large. He reached an especially wide audience, though some of his books were written in Magyar at a time when it was still not common to use the vernacular for such works. One of them sold over 2000 copies in five months, which was considered a very large sale at the time.[48]

It is not, of course, very helpful to consider all those who agreed, wholly or partially, with Szechenyi's views or who read his books as part of the nationalist agency – they were rather its constituency – but they do show again the difficulties in discussing the factor of size. Perhaps the only generalisation which should be made is that the agencies were still small, but growing. Amongst Czechs and Magyars, the active agents who devoted a large part of their efforts to the nationalist causes might perhaps now be numbered in tens, rather than singly. They were proportionately fewer amongst the other smaller or less 'advanced' nationalities, such as Croats, Slovenes, Slovaks and Rumanians.

Since the increase in numbers was small in absolute terms, it is not surprising that the scale of the agency often remained much the same as in the first phase. The Transylvanian Triad were all clerics, as were at least two of the Slovak nationalists, Josef Hurban and Michael Hodza. Amongst the Magyars, the upper and middle nobility continued to be well represented in the persons of Count Szechenyi and his like-minded compeers, who also had, to a degree, counterparts amongst the Croats, such as Count Draskovic, and amongst the Czechs, such as Counts Leo Thun and Anton Kolowrat.

On the other hand, as this phase developed, the movements started to attract more persons whose origins or stations lay lower down the social scale. One very conspicuous case is that of Louis Kossuth (1802–94) who 'was a member of that dangerous class which possesses birth and brains, but no means'.[49] That is, he belonged to the increasingly large section of the Magyar nobility which was impoverished and even landless. Such men had to find other sources of income than the land, and neither the church nor the army could absorb all of them. They were averse to commerce (which was in any case poorly developed), and so they tended, if they had the ability, to congregate in the professions (especially law), in the expanding central and local bureaucracies, in higher education and (a small but growing number that included Kossuth himself) in writing and journalism. It seems inappropriate to label them a 'middle class', since so many were nobly born and those that were not often became 'quasi-noble', through achieving the status of *honoratior* which was conferred by the Imperial administration on those of its subjects who gained certain academic qualifications.[50] 'Intellegentsia', with its modern connotations, is not much better and I prefer 'literati' as perhaps the least misleading term.

Such literati (and *honoratiores*) were also evident in other nationalities amongst which, however, they were quite often recruited from below rather than from above. The great Czech scholar and nationalist, Josef Jungman (1773–1847), was the son of a village cobbler, the Croat publicist Ljudevit Gaj, of a village apothecary, and the Serb folklorist and lexicographer, Vuk Karadzic (of whom more below), of a peasant. Since the clergy, to whom I have already referred, were not born to that status, it is possible that some of them were also of humble origins, as they certainly were later on.

In general, then, it seems that some agents were now coming from the upper and lower levels of society into a not new, but newly expanding, order of literati which, in turn, was contributing a greater proportion of recruits to the nationalist movements. The movements also continued to attract persons from the same orders which were prominent in them during the first phase. This summary refers, however, only to the agents more or less continuously engaged in the movements and does not take into account those sympathisers who gave occasional support or encouragement to the agents themselves. It would be too large a task to search the sources for details of such sympathisers amongst the various nationalities, but I can do it partially for one case from which it is possible to draw some tentative general conclusions which I think serve to give a more comprehensive, but also more elusive, idea of the scale of the movements both in this phase and in the later ones.

The case is that of Vuk Stefanovic Karadzic (1787–1864) who played a significant part in the Serb nationalist movement through his contributions to the developing administrative services of the new Serb state, as well as through his better-known linguistic and literary works. He has recently been the subject of a most useful biography[51] from which it is possible to reconstruct a partial 'network'[52] of some of those who were linked to him, in one capacity or another, in those activities which I would describe as serving to elaborate the Serb national category. The network shows, first of all, the remarkably wide geographical spread of Karadzic's contacts, stretching from Moscow in the East to London in the West, and from Germany in the North to Italy in the South. It also shows an equivalently wide range of social types who participated in Karadzic's literary efforts, from a sometime Russian Minister of Foreign Affairs, through Goethe and Ranke, to a blind singer of Serbian oral poetry.

These features themselves testify further to the degree of social mobility that could be achieved through the devoted pursuit of a nationalist cause. That a man from an obscure peasant community, and hampered by physical and educational disabilities, could acquire such a network is itself impressive evidence of how the interest in 'folk' literature could open doors that would otherwise have certainly been closed to him. Of course this interest was not always explicitly, or even at all, 'nationalist'. It is unlikely that Goethe was much interested in fostering the emergent Serb nation (though he may well have had some sympathy for it); he was more concerned with encouraging the development of literature. I doubt, too, if those few Serb merchants who were amongst the numerous people successfully pestered by Karadzic for money expected to have their names enshrined in a national roll of honour; they apparently thought it sufficient if they got a mention in the prefaces to his books. As for the peasants who sang their songs to him, some, by his own account, were interested in the drink, others in the money, he gave them; perhaps one or two were also proud that he should record the products of the tradition they represented.

But whatever the standing and whatever the motives of those who entered Karadzic's network by engaging in transactions with him, they all contributed through him to the same nationalist movement of which he himself was only one outstanding member. It is also noticeable that some of these contributors were not Serbs, but of several other nationalities: Slovene, Czech, Russian, German and English. Examination of such networks (other revealing ones would certainly include those of Szechenyi and Palacky) therefore permits the generalisation that the scale of a national movement can be extended if one wishes, well beyond the social limits of those actively engaged in it and also far outside the limits of the national category to which it pertains. From this point of view, the size of any movement then becomes considerably larger, but just how large it remains impossible to say.

These revisions of the notions of size and scale depend, of course, on the presence of such informal clusters of persons centred, for the purposes of analysis, on one or more key figures. The boundaries of such clusters are not self-evident but can be determined only according to criteria selected by the analyst of them. The clusters are, however, perhaps more characteristic of the earlier than of the later phases of the process of nationalism. As the process continues, it begins to generate formally constituted groups which are bounded by criteria decided by those who create them and which therefore might be supposed to specify more closely the limits of the national category and of the movement by instituting more exclusive criteria for membership in them. The appearance of such groups can therefore be treated as the next phase of the movement from which it appears that size and scale remain elusive concepts.

III.   MAKING SUBSIDIARY CORPORATIONS

The corporate groups which emerged in this phase were subsidiary in the two dictionary senses of being 'subordinate' to the whole category which included them and of 'aiding' the conversion of that category into a fully comprehensive corporation. That is, members (and sometimes employees) of the groups constituted only a proportion (usually small) of a whole category and were predominantly supporters if not agents of the national movement. Hence, it is of little use trying to maintain a distinction between the size and scale of the groups and those of the agencies: to a large extent they were one and the same thing. Consequently, after mentioning some of the main types of these corporations, I shall simply present what information there is on the size and scale of some of them.

One type of these subsidiary corporations was that of the learned or antiquarian association for which one nationality often gave the example to another: the Royal Bohemian Society of Sciences (1794), the Magyar Academy of Sciences (1825), the Jugoslav Academy of Science and Art (1867), the Magyar National Museum (1807), the Bohemian Museum (1818), the Society of Friends of the Bohemian Museum (1822), and so on for other nationalities. Of those listed, the Magyar Academy was intended by its founders to be 'a workshop of universal national culture',[53] and the Bohemian Museum was converted by Palacky 'into a vehicle of the Czech national movement'.[54] Similar motives inspired the foundation or subsequent direction of all the others.

Another type of corporation which proliferated amongst the different Slav peoples was that of the national literary and publishing organisation called, in the vernaculars, *Matica*. The first one was founded by Hungarian Serbs in 1826, and by 1869 there were eight more.[55] Besides such cultural associations there were social clubs, with strong nationalist leanings, which began to appear amongst the Magyars (who called them 'national casinos') from 1827[56] and amongst the Czechs from at least 1845, when they were allowed to open a 'Citizens' Club' in Prague.[57] More mundane interests were catered for amongst Magyars, Czechs and, subsequently, other nationalities by various national economic, agricultural, industrial and commercial organisations.

Since these different types of association generally had 'determinate memberships', I can cite some apparently more precise indications of their size than I could for the unstructured categories. When the first 'national casino' opened in Pest in 1827, it had 127 'subscribers'; by 1831 it had 370 'shareholders' and 520 later in the same decade.[58] Following this original foundation, the clubs spread quickly to other parts of Hungary and there were 28 of them by 1833. There was a comparably rapid growth in the membership of the Czech *Matica*, which grew from 35 members in 1831 to 190 in the following year and to 2329 in 1847.[59]

Of these two national movements, it can therefore be said that there were eventually hundreds who sympathised sufficiently with the movements to make the effort and pay the money to join organisations devoted to them. I must add immediately, however, that not all those who did join were equally enthusiastic for the nationalist causes; many were primarily interested in the social amenities and opportunities provided by the organisations.[60] So even these apparently definite figures present insoluble difficulties of interpretation in determining the size of the corporations as nationalist organisations. Another problem with no obvious solution is to decide if employees of the organisations, as distinct from members, ought to be included in any calculation of their size. The lack of comparable figures in my sources for the subsidiary corporations of other nationalities was therefore not a great disappointment to me. I simply infer that they, too, were able to recruit scores and perhaps hundreds of members, some of whom had a strong sense of national identity and others of whom did not. It is therefore probable, but not demonstrable, that these subsidiary corporations did in general add to the size of the nationalist movements.

It might be expected that the additional numbers would go with a further expansion in scale, but what in fact seems to have happened in most cases is that the corporations simply attracted more of the same social types who were already prominent in the second phase. This development is especially evident for the Magyars. The first national casino, founded by Count Szechenyi and some of his associates, consisted mostly of magnates, and the annual net income of the eventual 520 shareholders was given by Szechenyi himself as more than twelve million florins.[61]

Although membership was supposed to be open to all, attempts by Szechenyi to lower the subscription and to admit Jews as members were rejected by a large majority of other members. Later, Szechenyi himself persuaded Kossuth to withdraw his application to join and did not welcome the proposal to make him a corresponding member of the Academy.[62] These measures were justified by Szechenyi on the grounds of Kossuth's unpopularity in governing circles, but they offended him and, since he was an influential figure amongst the literary, had the effect of further restricting the membership. There may, however, have been imitative alternatives for those excluded from the original clubs, since Barany mentions 'Casinos of Law Students' and 'Clubs of Poor Fellows'.[63] The total effect of Szechenyi's example may thus have been to draw into these subsidiary corporations a wider range of social types than might at first appear.

In Bohemia, there was again a tendency for the scale to be similar to that of the second phase. The nobility there took the initiative in founding the Society of Sciences and the Museum, but the former was soon dominated by literati of whom Dobrovski was the most eminent, and the latter by Palacky and others.[64] The Czech parallel to the Magyar casinos, the Citizens' Club, differed from them in its social composition, in line with the general difference in the social structure of the two nationalities. For the Club membership was drawn from the 'burghers' of Prague, that is from those holding property or having comparable qualifications.[65] This requirement kept out the majority of the population and in that sense it was about as socially exclusive as the Magyar casinos were.

Consequently, although all these groups were significant for the

nationalist process, because they displayed that organisation for the
regulation of common affairs which is the ultimate criterion of corporateness, I cannot see that they greatly expanded the scale of the
movements. On the other hand, they probably drew more people into
the movements, though it is impossible to say even approximately what
the numbers were. To detect both an expansion of scale and an ac-
companying substantial increase in numbers, one must look to the next
phase.

IV. MUSTERING THE PEOPLE

I have chosen a slightly old-fashioned verb to characterise this phase
because 'muster' means both 'to show or display' and 'to collect or
assemble' (*S.O.E.D.*), which I find most appropriate for activities that
often assembled relatively large numbers of people in displays of their
attachment to a national cause. These assemblies were generally of a
public or semi-public nature, in contrast to the usually more private activities of the subsidiary corporations.

Interesting examples of such assemblies were the balls organised as
displays of nationalist sentiment. What Pech describes as 'the first
Czech ball' was held in Prague in 1840.[66] Deliberately designed to
muster Czech-speakers, it was also meant to display the suitability of
Czech as a vehicle for polite social intercourse, which had previously
been dominated by German. Pech claims that it was successful enough
to give 'the cause of Czech nationalism . . . a mighty thrust forward'.[67]
Another such ball was held in the same year in Agram, where the Croa-
tian women present wore on their dresses stars, of which the points bore
the names of the 'Illyrian' peoples and of which the centres bore the
legend 'God help us to union'.[68]

Another kind of public assembly, with a permanent institutional setting, was the theatre of which the conversive implications had earlier
been recognised by Schiller in Germany: 'Should we achieve a national
theatre, we would become also a nation.'[69] This sentiment was shared
by Magyars who had been proposing a national theatre since at least
1790 and who finally opened it in 1837. The Czechs followed suit in
1868 and when the building later burnt down they built another, again
from public subscriptions which were acknowledged in the suitably
corporative inscription over the stage: 'The People to Itself'.[70] Other
nationalities, such as the Croats, also eventually opened their own
national theatres.

Another sort of occasion which assembled even larger numbers of
people were the funerals of leading nationalists. That of Josef Jungman,
the great Czech scholar and patriot, was 'attended by thousands [and]
represented the first great Czech national manifestation'.[71] Similar

demonstrations occurred amongst other nationalities, and as the nineteenth century wore on tended to get larger, culminating in the funeral
of Kossuth in 1894, which some half a million people are said to have
attended.[72]

The Imperial authorities were suspicious of all such musterings of
the people, but at least they allowed them. Other, more explicitly political gatherings were not permitted. It was therefore only during the
1848 revolutions, when the authorities were temporarily unable to prevent them, that such gatherings occurred. They were then so numerous
among the various nationalities, and of so many kinds, that I can only
note some of their usual titles. There were National Congresses and
National Committees which formulated political programmes and
tried to implement them. Parallel to these rudimentary national
governments, there were military musterings of National Guards and
Academic Legions. In addition, there were various loosely organised
'clubs' representing special interests or political viewpoints which often
held their own public meetings and demonstrations.

Some of these musterings were not very big: the indoor meetings sig-
nalling the Czech uprising took place in a hall which held about 800
people. Others brought out probably more people than had ever before
assembled in any particular national cause. The open-air meeting of
Transylvanian Rumanians on the 'Field of Liberty' outside Blaj on 15
May 1848 may have attracted 40,000 people.[73]

In general, the numbers involved imply an expansion of scale of
which details are sometimes given. The more purely social gatherings
attracted predominantly 'the bureaucrats, officers, merchants, artisans, professors and artists'[74] who came to the Czech ball and, no
doubt, to the National Theatre. The bigger public assemblies, such as
the funeral processions through the streets, were open to whoever cared
to join them. With the outbreak of the revolutions, there were many
opportunities for more intensive participation by social types who
were not in evidence during earlier phases. Conspicuous additions in
Prague were the students and some industrial workers. The students
were themselves of mixed social origins, some noble or bourgeois, but
mostly from poor families,[75] including presumably those of artisans
and peasants, as were many Viennese students.[76] The industrial workers who participated in the Prague demonstrations were mainly skilled
or semi-skilled men.[77] Neither the students nor the workers were
necessarily all inspired by nationalist motives; many were simply pro-
testing against their social and economic condition. But in Prague, as
elsewhere in the Empire, the revolution assumed more 'nationalist'
forms as it progressed.

The general effect of all this mustering was therefore to show that
participation in 'national' affairs had certainly widened compared
with other phases. Yet it was still nothing like representative of

national categories as wholes. For the assemblies were largely confined to the main cities; most of the smaller towns saw few of them and the rural population had little or no part in them, even during the months of revolution, except in so far as portions of it were recruited into the rebel and the Imperial armies. It seems indeed that most peasants continued to be either ignorant of the 'national' causes or indifferent to them.[78] This ignorance or indifference prevailed despite the fact that sections of the peasantry, unlike most other classes, derived some immediate and lasting benefits from the revolutions which hastened the abolition of several of their legal disabilities. With the possible exception of some Bohemian peasants,[79] they did not asociate these improvements with membership of national categories which still had little, if any, meaning for them. Even in the cities, the majority of the adult, male population (for nationalism and revolution were predominantly male activities) cannot have participated in the assemblies and demonstrations, with the possible exception of one or two of the biggest.

Perhaps, therefore, the title of this phase ought to be mustering *some* of the people, especially if one takes into account the size and scale of the agencies which organised or precipitated the musters. For it is quite clear that the initiative was again usually taken by small groups or cliques. In the case of the more formal assemblies, such as the theatres or balls, it came from some of the nobility like Szechenyi (again) or from the more established of the literati, such as Frantisek Rieger (who later became Palacky's son-in-law). The literati were also prominent in the early assemblies of 1848. Once the revolutions were well under way, however, the initiative tended to pass into other hands, especially those of students and workers, except in Hungary where it remained with the gentry and literati, led by Kossuth. But even these hands were not numerous. When the barricades finally went up in Prague, they were manned by 1200 to 1500 men. The students amongst them were less than a quarter of the total student body; the majority had prudently gone on vacation.[80] There is also the puzzling fact that the most complete surviving casualty list shows that about three-quarters of the dead were workers and none were students, although there had been even fewer workers than students on the barricades. On the other hand, it is possible that the workers would never have been there at all if it were not for the few students who provided them with what leadership they had. Indeed, the workers had previously been so small a part of the 'nation' that the only links of communication which the police and later the burghers had with them were through doctors who saw some of them as patients.[81] Their marginal situation was not much changed by the events of 1848, so that their participation in them was not in itself a major expansion of the nationalist movement.

I do not think, therefore, that the importance of this phase lay simply in the changes of size and scale that accompanied it. Of equal importance were two other aspects, one of which was summarised by a Russian speaker at the close of a Pan-Slav congress at Moscow in 1867: 'The Slav question has been transferred now from books and private studies to the street, to public squares, to churches and to theatres.'[82] Being a Russian, he was at least twenty years late with this observation as far as the Western Slavs were concerned and he failed to mention that others, besides Slavs, had made the transfer, but he had correctly appreciated its significance. The other important aspect of this phase, and particularly of the 1848 revolutions, was the demonstration that the creation of national political communities was a real possibility even for 'small' nationalities with 'weak' national movements.

The continuing significance of these two aspects was demonstrated by the failure of the Imperial authorities to eliminate their effects during the years of 'absolutism' after 1848. This failure led in turn, during the latter part of the nineteenth century, to the gradual concession by the authorities of much that had first been demanded in 1848. It is true that the principal beneficiaries of these concessions were Magyars, Czechs and Poles, and they were also the nationalities which eventually achieved the ultimate 'success' of forming nation-states in which they were dominant. By comparison, the movements of, say, Croats, Slovaks and Slovenes seem less successful.

It is, however, important to remember that the achievement of national independence depended on the destruction in 1918 of the Empire, which was not brought about by the nationalist movements and which they scarcely anticipated until near the end. It is therefore misleading to infer that 'success' or 'failure' depended, in any absolute sense, on the size and scale of particular nationalities and of their nationalist movements. The only reasonable inference is that, *in relation to those particular circumstances*, some nationalities and movements were 'large' enough for success and others were not. In other conceivable circumstances, it would have been entirely possible for a nation-state to have been achieved by a nationality like the Slovaks with a presumptive population of less than two million in 1918 of which Seton-Watson estimated (I know not how) that 750 to 1000 were 'conscious and active Slovak nationalists'.[83] For, in precisely other circumstances, the states of Albania and Estonia did come into existence, each with a population of about one million. I may reinforce the point of these examples by adding that there are now at least sixteen 'independent sovereign states' with populations of less than one million and some of them have fewer than half a million.[84]

I suggest, then, that if the process of converting a national category develops as far as the fourth phase, or somewhere near it, then there is what Weber called an 'objective possibility' that it will culminate in the formation of a nation-state. This 'objective possibility' should in itself prohibit any general statements that some categories are 'too small' ever to become nation-states. However, such statements are still commonly made, and the prohibition on them therefore needs to be strengthened by pointing out that they imply at least two preconditions for making them which, in practice, cannot be met. First, they imply some absolute criteria of political and economic 'viability' which potential contenders for nationhood must meet. But, as Abbott has recently argued,[85] it is very doubtful if there are such absolute criteria. Second, such statements imply that the sizes of national categories can be known with some accuracy before they have been converted into states. This implication I have contested in the body of this chapter by insisting that membership of a national category is, particularly in the early phases, optional and situational and is therefore inherently incapable of enumeration, except in gross, provisional terms.

Similar considerations apply to any attempts at relating the actual or potential success of a national movement to the size of the movement itself. For, as I have shown, it is impossible to assign any absolute size to a movement. The size must vary from phase to phase and, unless its membership is contained only and entirely within subsidiary corporations (I know of no such case), there is no way by which size could be determined for any phase, except, again, in the grossest terms. Even if a more precise statement of a movement's size could be made, it would only be meaningful in relation to the size of the category comprehending it, since a movement of, say, 500 persons would have differing significance in categories of half a million and of five million. But I have already stated that the size of the category cannot be specified in this way, and therefore the proportional size of the movement is also unspecifiable.

The most that can be done is to make relative and necessarily impressionistic assessments of size. I have recorded my own impression that the movements in the Habsburg Empire and in the European parts of the Ottoman Empire were very small in the first phase and became bigger, but never very big, in the later phases. Such an imprecise assessment may seem hardly worth the effort made to arrive at it. I suggest, however, that it is more reasonable than the elaborate attempts to quantify the inherently unquantifiable which are to be found in some parts of Deutsch's work[86] and in the works of his imitators.

It is a fairly safe inference from this assessment that the active agents in the movements formed minorities, often very small ones, amongst the presumptive memberships of the categories they claimed to represent. This inference does not necessarily conflict with those theories, again deriving mainly from Deutsch, which explain the nationalist process in terms of the 'mobilisation' of increasingly large sectors of the population. However, I believe that it is more in line with the argument of Olson that unless the number of individuals in a group is quite small, or unless there is coercion or some other special device to make individuals act in their common interest, *rational, self-interested individuals will not act to achieve their common or group interests*.[87]

If Olson's argument is correct, then it follows that nationalist movements must generally be small minorities, unless and until they can either offer what Olson calls 'selective incentives' for joining them or can coerce people into supporting them. During the phases I have examined, movements could usually offer only limited incentives and had little, if any, capacity for coercion. Hence they remained minorities, though in later phases, when they had already begun to acquire control of the resources of the state, they could offer more benefits to individual supporters and could even penalise some of those who withheld support. It was, I suggest, only in those final phases that the movements became at all large and even then I doubt if they formed majorities within the national categories.

The other assessments I have made on the scale of categories and movements are not novel, but are perhaps especially striking in a situation like that of the Habsburg Empire where there had

evolved herarchies of national cultures, not . . . in the sense that any people lacked its unprivileged masses, but that some national cultures stopped short at the peasant–village priest level, while others continued upward through some or all of the higher grades of bourgeoisie, professional classes and lower or higher aristocracy.[88]

The fact that categories could be defined and movements be developed for all these 'national cultures', no matter what social level they reached, is clear evidence that there was no correlation between the presence or absence of any particular class and the occurrence of nationalism. At the same time, the examples show that nationalism did generally involve an expansion of scale through the inclusion in single categories of those who previously belonged to different categories. They also show some expansion of scale within the movements, as these developed through the various phases, though this expansion was often not sufficient to secure widespread participation by the peasantry which formed the majority of the population.

In general, then, my assessments of the nationalist process are opposed to those of others who have set lower limits for the size of nations, or have held that nationalism requires large movements, or have claimed that nationalism is always an expression of particular class interests. I also disagree with those who try to show that in these or other respects nationalism differs significantly from the processes that are variously labelled as tribalism, regionalism, communalism or separatism. But I do not want to end on this contentious note; I would rather emphasise that wide areas of agreement become possible if nationalism can be interpreted through the use of concepts developed mainly in the study of societies remote in space and time from those with which this contribution has been concerned.

3

Nationalism and the Patriotism of City-States

K. R. Minogue

It is a curious paradox of European history that, for all the monarchies and empires under which Europeans have lived, the characteristic political units of the area are the city-state in ancient times and the nation-state in modern times. The more one explores the paradox, the stranger it becomes. The Romans thought of the political unit they inhabited as a *civitas* long after they had succeeded in dominating the whole Mediterranean area; and when, late in the day, St Augustine transposed some of their political ideas into theological terms, he called his work *De Civitate Dei*, not *De Regno Dei*. Nor is this addiction to political fictions confined to classical times. The nation-state of modern Europe is almost entirely a fiction. Its two most celebrated exemplars are the United Kingdom and France, but a glance at the realities will immediately show how completely unreal it is to describe these states as nations. The United Kingdom contains four obvious nationalities – the English, Scots, Welsh and Irish – without in any way exhausting the plurality of her populations. Inherited from the past are such groups as the inhabitants of the Guernsey, Jersey, Shetland and other islands; Cornwall is a county with claims to nationhood, and history records regions (such as Northumbria) which, given the impulse of economic circumstance and intellectual cultivation, could easily be promoted as independent nationalities. Nor is this to consider the French Huguenots, Poles, West Indians and inhabitants of the Indian sub-continent who have settled in significant numbers within her borders. France was, till quite recent times, construed as a union between the Germanic Franks and the Latin Gauls; but it has also absorbed Basques, Italians and the Germanic peoples of Alsace-Lorraine. The memory of a split between the *langue d'oc* and the *langue d'oïl* occasionally generates the project of resuscitating a new realm of Occitanians. Nor should we forget the Celtic Bretons. If, then, these are the

For Notes and References to Chapter 3, see pp. 160–2.

models of a nation-state, how can we possibly take the idea seriously. The truth of the matter has been clearly recognised by Pilsudski: 'It is the state that makes the nation, not the nation that makes the state.'[1]

City and nation, then, are the permanent aspiration of European peoples. But if this is true, what are we to make of the monarchies and empires they have generated? For it is obvious that many of these nation-states have been monarchies, and all of them have been empires, at least in the sense that they are forms of rule incorporating a plurality of peoples. Part of the answer is that necessity has often thwarted choice. Athens grew so large that it became an empire, and it was in turn subjugated by Alexander of Macedon. The Roman city acquired the hegemony of the Mediterranean, if not in a fit of absence of mind, at least without ever quite setting out to do so. Again, European nation-states were constructed by kings, and always contained subjects who were unhappy with the monarchical usages under which they lived. The institution of monarchy was, to a large extent, a European inheritance stemming from the barbarian nomads who broke up the Roman Empire, and many Europeans came to feel (along with King Farouk) that the only place for royalty was adorning a pack of playing cards. We shall return to this question, but for the moment it is enough to observe that all modern states have *tended* to be republics, that is to say states composed of citizens legally equal to each other in rights; though (as Rousseau pointed out) there is no essential incompatibility between a republic and a monarchical office-holder.

The statement of this preference has often taken precedence over the recognition of political reality. Thus it has often been found strange that Aristotle should have argued for the political ideal of a small-scale city-state just at the moment when history was about to disclose the much grander construction of Alexander the Great. Aristotle's point is a philosophical argument about the appropriate size of anything: 'Ten people would not make a city and a hundred thousand would exceed its natural proportions.'[2] Neither a pygmy nor a giant can, in other words, be classed as a man. His figures include Athens, which was huge by Greek standards, and exclude Persia, which was not properly a state at all, but rather a despotism, a family writ huge, a victim of political elephantiasis caused by the slavish disposition of its inhabitants. The tolerable limits derive from functional criteria. What limits the smallness of a city is the principle of self-sufficiency or *autarkia*, for no family or village can be counted a state. What limits its largeness is a principle of intimacy: 'What constitutes a polis is an association of households and clans in a good life. . . . This consummation, however, will not take place unless the members inhabit one and the self-same place and practise intermarriage.'[3] Thus did the Greeks canonise, as it were, what had been given them by historical accident, and thus create the aching nostalgia of European peoples for a community in which they would be fully human and fully themselves.

What this doctrine rejects is just as important as what it affirms. The Greeks looked East and saw large oriental empires which were not at all to their taste. They identified these realms partly in terms of monarchy, and thus helped to associate freedom with republics. The Romans fell into line with this view because of their own memory of kings, so that even as Rome moved towards a monarchical structure of government under Augustus, it did so crab-wise, under republican forms. Monarchy and empire were inevitably associated ideas, for the principle of unity in a monarchy rested in the king himself, and this allowed a greater heterogeneity of subjects than was possible in republics, which must necessarily find their principle of unity in some sort of homogeneity of the citizens themselves. Besides, it came to be observed both that kings sought to expand, and that expanding republics tended to become monarchical. Hence the idea of monarchy and that of empire were to be closely linked as antipathetic to the idea of the political community with which they associated their highest achievements; and they passed this view on to their modern successors. Thus Hobbes comments upon the propensity of classical literature to encourage subversion of the modern European monarchies:

> And by reading of these Greek, and Latin authors, men from their childhood have gotten a habit, under a false show of liberty, of favouring tumults, and of licentious controlling the actions of their sovereigns, and again of controlling those controllers; with the effusion of so much blood, as I think I may truly say, there was never anything so dearly bought, as these western parts have bought the learning of the Greek and Latin tongues.[4]

Rousseau, who was one of the many striking voices to articulate Europe's allegiance to city and nation rather than to monarchy and empire, teased his contemporaries and successors by outlining a form of community, which, as he admitted, would inevitably have to be of the sort of diminutive size that all the social tendencies of modern Europe had made impossible of realisation.

For two centuries, whilst civilisation developed apace in many directions, the political ideal of many Europeans living under monarchy was a declining city-state, set on the Adriatic and far from the creative centres of modern civilisation.

The reasons for this widespread political preference are, of course, complicated, but one central question revolved around the disjunction between Christianity and early modern states. From at least Machiavelli onwards, some men yearned for a state in which religion and politics were completely integrated. Rousseau expressed this feeling in the *Social Contract*, and it was also before his mind when he turned to practical matters. In relation to Poland, he wrote: 'If we assemble, it is in the temples of a cult which is in no sense national, and which does nothing to remind us of the fatherland.'[5] Nor is this pervasive discontent with the plurality of the European inheritance confined to philosophers, or indeed even to Europe itself. After the independence of the Belgian Congo, for example, President Mobutu moved towards a systematic removal of all Christian usages on the ground that they were 'a form of mental alienation repugnant to the public'. What he sought was to make himself the central figure of a cult which would unite political and religious allegiances.[6]

To understand nationalism in this context, the widest available to us, we need to consider several closely related points. One of these is the difference of *scale* in ancient and modern political units. The smallness of cities makes them essentially different from nation-states, even if political accident should (as in the case of Rome as she expanded) have left the tidy taxonomist with a significant measure of overlapping. The second consideration arises from what I shall argue is a conflict between the traditions we have identified in terms of monarchy and empire on the one hand, and state and nation on the other.

But this distinction, as we have so far discussed it, would suggest that nationalism is merely the modern version of the patriotism of the ancient world, and such a view is in very important respects fatal to an understanding of their true relationship. One aspect of this very complicated question may be grasped if we note that Machiavelli was both a patriot and a nationalist. His *patria* was Florence whilst his nation was called *Italia*, a picture of whom had been painted in the Florentine office in which he worked. His call in chapter 26 of the *Prince* for Italian unification represented a kind of national ideal, but the patriotic attributes characteristic of all Italians of his period made this an unreal aspiration.[7] That patriotism and nationalism may work against one another is argued by Arnold Toynbee in discussing the risings of Milan and Venice in 1848: 'The Venetian and Milanese exploits of 1848 were foredoomed to failure because the spiritual driving force behind them was not modern nationalism but an idolization of their own dead selves as medieval city states.'[8] The difference between nationalism and patriotism is to be found, then, both in the unit to which allegiance is given, and also in the very manner of that allegiance. Nation and *patria* are indeed linked ideas in the history of European political experience, but the link is complex. In discussing it, we need first to look at the character of the city-republics which have so long both inspired and tormented modern Europeans.

I

The key to the fascination exercised by the *patria* lies in the idea of freedom, though it is freedom in the sense of communal self-determination, rather than in any idea of liberty of the subject.[9] Both the Greeks and the Romans thought that the office of monarchy restricted communal self-determination unbearably. The subject of a monarch can often seem barely distinguishable from a slave. In medieval Europe, these classical ideas were not pervasive, and in early modern times the idea of freedom might be used in quite different ways. That loving monarch James I, for example, was kind enough to explain to his subjects what their obligations were, and this service he performed in a pamphlet called *The Trew Law of Free Monarchies*. The word 'free' here is in the body of the pamphlet yoked with 'absolute', and it means that the king is free, whilst the subject is obliged. Although James sees politics as a matter of reciprocal duties between monarch and subjects, he also sees himself as the natural Father of his people, and there is no question of equality between father and children. It came to seem obvious that a monarch was altogether too superior a creature to inhabit a republic; so much so, indeed, that in the first wake of the impact of classical ideas, sundry monarchs came to describe themselves as the servants of their peoples. It seemed that an absolute sovereign power was tolerable to modern Europeans only so long as this power was not incarnated in a particular person. The very existence of such a person qualified some essential equality of citizens. Similarly, the institution of representation came to seem an inadequate exercise of citizenship for those who were represented. A strong strand of European thought has identified the idea of freedom with institutions barely distinguishable from the individual decision of each citizen. Perhaps the most extreme case of this situation is that of the Italian communes of the early Middle Ages in which it 'was quite usual for communes to bind themselves to the terms of diplomatic contracts by agreeing that the entire adult male population should take an oath to obey the treaty'.[10] This extremity of individual participation in communal decisions is both impractical and inconvenient, but it may be said with confidence that the majority of the most popular mechanisms invented in modern politics (the general will, the notion of a vanguard of a particular class, and so on) are designed to go beyond mere representation in producing a fictional simulacrum of exactly this situation.

The general theme that nothing must be remote from the citizenly centre of the life of the *patria* can be seen most clearly in the case of religion. What has ever been peculiarly attractive about the *patria* has been its unity of religion and politics. The ancient city was the centre of a cult. Life was lived within a context of divinities whose favour or disfavour was believed to determine events, and a variety of usages, and of officials to conduct these usages, was intimately involved in the life of the city itself. It was true that, as Fustel de Coulanges puts it: 'Two cities were two religious associations which had not the same gods.

When they were at war it was not the men alone who fought – the gods also took part in the struggle.'[11] And he quotes Euripides: 'The gods who fight for us are more powerful than those of our enemies.' There is no doubt an element of exaggeration in this view, but only because Fustel de Coulanges generalised both Greek and Roman experience over a long period of time. Institutions such as the lot, and the Olympic Games, were both, in origin, devices for discovering the will of the gods. In the history both of the Greek cities and of Rome this religious aspect undergoes considerable change; but the literature generated presented its European admirers with the picture of a civilisation that was ideal because the citizen and the believer were one and the same.

The politico-religious unity of classical cities is evident even during the Peloponnesian wars, a time when a certain theological *insouciance* had begun to spread amongst the more sophisticated Athenians. Alcibiades was solemnly cursed after the desecration of the Hermae, and had to be equally solemnly uncursed when he returned to Athens in 407 BC. Both the ordinary ceremonies of life and the extraordinary events of crises were carried on within a framework of established ceremonies whose significance a modern reader is likely to underrate. 'No political action of any importance, no assembly of the people, no meeting of a board of officials or a court could take place without an introductory sacrifice and prayer. If the sacrifice proved unfavourable the meeting or whatever it was had to be postponed.'[12] These acts were performed not by professional priests who tended the central shrines, but by political officials, one of whom was a vestigial survivor of the early Greek kings in their priestly role, and was called the *archon basileus*. The *rex sacrorum* was a corresponding official at Rome. So far as the political cohesion of the city was concerned, this permeation of the sacred and profane allowed for the extensive reliance upon oaths in both private and public business.

What has attracted modern writers was a situation which prevented the sort of fundamental bifurcation of allegiances to which the Christian member of a medieval realm or modern state might be thought to be subject. The significance of this, however, is spiritual and philosophical rather than practical. The feud between the Guelfs and Ghibellines that ravaged the Italian city-states in the thirteenth century, for example, was but one of the many causes of civic strife and disunity. Its full significance appears only when the matter is raised to a more abstract level, as it was in Machiavelli's famous disjunction between caring for one's immortal soul, and caring for one's *patria*.[13] This idea reappears in the socialist view that Christianity's individualist emphasis on the salvation of the immortal soul has the effect of disrupting the solidarity of proletarian movements. In nationalist movements, religion may or may not become important according to circumstances, but if religion is already strong, it may be turned by nationalists into a fundamental constituent of national identity (as in Irish nationalism for example), and this device may diminish the possible conflict between religion and politics.

It is significant that the close association between politics and religion in the ancient world was no less strong after the cities had succumbed to monarchical government; yet it is not this latter kind of unity which has struck a responsive chord in European thought. The hellenistic monarchies which succeeded to the empire of Alexander adapted oriental notions of the divinity of the monarch, notions of a kind which were also to become influential in the later stages of the Roman Empire. Ideas of this kind have a resemblance (though it is but superficial) to the divine-right-of-kings doctrine as it was developed in Europe after the fifteenth century. No doubt one reason why these practices were unattractive to classically educated Europeans was that the revival of an admiration for classical politics took place largely amongst a set of writers who were fundamentally hostile to monarchical prerogatives. It is also, no doubt, important that deification of rulers was usually a sentiment confined in the ancient world to the less educated sections of the population. The more educated regarded these beliefs largely as formal rituals; and hence the regimes of semi-divine monarchies were extraordinarily tolerant and hospitable to whatever cults (for example those of sun-worship and Manichaeanism) were circulating at various times.[14] The temperament of modern Europeans, is, for the most part, sufficiently Christian to be impatient of merely formal religious observances. Worship of rulers is not the sort of cult that can usually incite enthusiasm in educated men; and the exponents of modern nationalism were nothing if not educated.

Most of what we have so far discussed of European city-states suggests the picture of an ideal community, at one with itself in a manner which the complexity of modern life has rendered impossible of achievement. The reason is that we have largely been concerned with idealisations. The reality was not only much more varied (for we are concerned with a multitude of scattered communities over a period exceeding a thousand years) but also a good deal less appetising. The very unity of cities in all its hothouse intensity (rather similar to that of families) meant that conflict took on a ferocity which, if not without parallel in modern Europe, was all the more destructive because of the small scale of the communities involved. The alternation of oligarch and democrat in Greece brought death and exile in its wake, just as did the struggles between the partisans of Marius, Sulla, Pompey, Caesar, and their like. The Italian communes were so full of civil strife that eventually most of them succumbed to tyrannical masters. The physical consequences of internal strife are to be seen in the towers built in Italian cities for purposes of self-defence: a kind of urban version of the castle in the countryside. A long list of distinguished exiles – Aristides,

Ovid, Dante – testifies to the hazards endured by citizens as a result of the intense factional strife of city politics. Thucydides has some grim passages (which no doubt impressed themselves on his translator Hobbes) about this kind of internal strife:

> During the seven days that Eurymedon stayed there with his sixty ships, the Corcyraeans continued to massacre those of their own citizens whom they considered to be their enemies. Their victims were accused of conspiring to overthrow the democracy, but in fact men were often killed on grounds of personal hatred or else by their debtors because of the money that they owed. There was death in every shape and form. And, as usually happens in such situations, people went to every extreme and beyond it. There were fathers who killed their sons; men were dragged from the temples or butchered on the very altars; some were actually walled up in the temple of Dionysus and died there.[15]

The problem was in part constituted by the fact that the world of city-states, especially that of the Greeks and the Italians, was made up of networks of friends and enemies, both within cities and between them, and hence any cause of dissension could immediately seep along channels of passion to involve large areas of the political world.

This hothouse element of human passions in a city meant that it was extraordinarily difficult to attain any degree of detachment from city life. The study of Aristotle has often accustomed us to think of Greek politics in terms of the *agora* and the *hestia*, of a public and a private realm; and it is easy to associate this distinction with that respect for individual rights expressed in the notion that an Englishman's home is his castle. Should we not regard the Greeks as people like ourselves when we read in the Funeral Oration:

> And just as our political life is free and open, so is our day-to-day life in our relations with each other. We do not get into a state with our next-door neighbour if he enjoys himself in his own way, nor do we give him the kind of black looks which, though they do no real harm, still do hurt people's feelings. We are free and tolerant in our private lives; but in public affairs we keep to the law.[16]

But such a view needs to be seen in terms of other passages in the same speech; such as: 'We do not say that a man who takes no interest in politics is a man who minds his own business; we say that he has no business here at all.' It is also to ignore much other evidence, such as the way the Corinthians characterised the Athenians to the Spartans at the beginning of the war: 'As for their bodies, they regard them as expendable for their city's sake, as though they were not their own; but each man cultivates his intelligence, again with a view to doing something notable for his city.'[17] In short, the Corinthians aver, the Athenians 'are by nature incapable of either living a quiet life themselves or allowing anyone else to do so'. Compare the duties of the Roman Censor:

> The Romans did not think it proper that anyone should be left free to follow his personal preferences and appetites, whether in marriage, the begetting of children, the regulation of his daily life, or the enter- tainment of his friends, without a large measure of surveillance and control. They believed that a man's true character was more clearly revealed in his private life than in his public or political career, and they therefore chose two officials, one from the so-called patricians and the other a plebeian, whose duty it was to watch, regulate, and punish any tendency to indulge in licentious or voluptuous habits and to depart from the traditional and established way of living.[18]

The Athenians were a large group of people pre-eminent amongst the Greeks for their openness to foreign influences and their capacity for cultivating individual expression. How much more restricted was life in smaller communities – and above all in Sparta – may well be ima- gined.[19] At Locri, the state forbade men to drink pure wine, whilst at Rhodes and Byzantium the law forbade men to shave the beard. Fustel de Coulanges exaggerates, though not by much, when he says: 'The citizen was subordinate in everything and without reserve, to the city; he belonged to it body and soul.'[20] The Italian communes were no less comprehensive, regulating prices, what should be planted in the soil, how sewerage should be disposed of, the number of pearl buttons or the length of scarlet robes on women, and so on.[21] And beyond the regu- lation of law, one would expect that the power of public opinion in small communities would be restrictive in a way that few citizens of a modern state would find easily tolerable.

Since our main concern is with the relation between ancient cities and nationalism, it remains to consider the relation between culture and politics in these cities. With the qualified exception of the Romans, each group of cities lived within an area of common culture. The Greek cities shared many institutions, and above all a language and a pan- theon of Olympic gods, with their neighbours. It has often been found puzzling that the Greek states were unable to unite in the face of the Macedonian threat; and Aristotle's view of the ideal size of the city has been taken as a symptom of Greek short-sightedness, generally by European commentators who have before them the modern tendency for national groupings to generate states. Yet the problem rests upon a number of fundamental misconceptions of the life of city-states. As Fustel de Coulanges remarks on the profound gulf which always separated two cities:

However near they might be to each other, they always formed two completely separate societies. Between them there was much more than the distance which separates two cities today, much more than the frontier which separates two states; their gods were not the same, or their ceremonies, or their prayers. The worship of one city was forbidden to men of a neighbouring city.[22]

For this reason, union between two cities was extraordinarily difficult; the best that might be hoped for was the federal union of cities such as had been suggested by the sages Bias (that the Ionians should emigrate to Sardinia) and Thales (that they should set up a federation based on a common centre of government at Teos).[23] But then Thales at least was said to be of Phoenician descent, and besides regarded civic pieties with philosophic detachment. Certainly the Athenian empire was always seen in terms of hegemony rather than in terms of a common growth of institutions, and given the particularist passion of each of the cities, it is difficult to see how fusion could have occurred.

These considerations can be seen vividly at work in the military relations between Greek cities. Defeat meant destruction, total defeat meant annihilation, with death for the citizens and slavery for the women and children. Such was the fate of Plateia at the hands of the Spartans, and that it was not the fate of the rebellious Mitylenians was the result merely of a change of mood at Athens from one day's debate to the next.[24] This situation looks rather fearsome to Europeans, who, in spite of the ferocity of modern wars, can look back to centuries in which the conduct of war was entrusted to a somewhat cosmopolitan class susceptible to intermittent fits of chivalric respect for the rules of the war, and a craftsmanlike respect for one's opponent's skill and bravery. Yet it is important to realise that the ferocity of ancient cities has often been admired as giving to life a seriousness entirely lacking in the limited wars of modern times. Machiavelli's lesson from his reading of Livy is that 'The condition for many virtuous men is many states.'[25] The replacement by a single empire of many small warring cities resulted in a considerable diminution of *virtu*. This association between large-scale monarchies and corruption was to be one of the dominant notes of modern political thought.

Being so small, city-states did not usually involve such close attachment to a native soil as modern states. The Ionian Greeks are perhaps peculiar in this respect, but it appears that, faced with the threat of Persian domination, the Phocaeans 'Launched their galleys, put aboard their women and children and moveable property including the statues and other sacred objects from their temples – everything, in fact, except painting, and images made of bronze or marble – and sailed to Chios.'[26] There were, of course, spirits of the place; and the heroes whose cult often played a more important part in civic feeling than the worship of the Olympians had local graves. Once a city had dug itself as deeply into the soil as Periclean Athens, or Rome, or any of the larger cities, then such reminiscences of a nomadic past would be much less conceivable. Yet it remains important to remember that, by contrast with modern nations with their romantic attachment to the native soil, city-states were associations of citizens, and to be cut off from the city was to be cut off from the life of the association rather than to be cut off from one's native soil. Indeed, it is notable that exiled parties from Italian communes would establish themselves in friendly neighbourhoods with the full corporate organisation of the city itself; almost as if one could create out of faction a shadow of the city itself.

These then are the materials out of which an ideal of patriotism was constructed for modern Europe. What made it attractive was that 'two opposed principles, that of rule and that of equality, were the two creative forces which, on the basis of civic freedom, determined the political form of the Polis'.[27] Modern Europeans lived with a feudal inheritance of inequality, and came to see this as the source of whatever alienation they felt for the communities in which they lived. Hence it is that Fustel de Coulange's comment, 'It is a singular error, therefore, among all human errors, to believe that in the ancient cities men enjoyed liberty', may well be close to the truth of the matter, but his has not been the established opinion. Hobbes, as we have seen, recognised the danger, insisting that freedom meant the self-determination of the community. He tried to ward off the republican tendencies of the classicists by insisting that, 'Whether a commonwealth be monarchial, or popular, the freedome is still the same.'[28] It has not proved a very popular opinion. There has always been a strong disposition to agree with Cato that 'a king is an animal that lives on human flesh'.[29]

II

What we have so far been discussing is a form of patriotic community constituted by an association of equal citizens. The reality of many city-states may well have been very different, but the literature of city-states has always sustained this idea. Our next task must be to consider what it was in modern European states that would make the revived patriotism of the classical republics so devastatingly attractive. Ideals are, of course, always constructed out of past and present experience, but it is unusual for men to find an ideal in a historical period more than a thousand years old. What features of modern states might help us explain this?

It is obvious that the modern state was essentially feudal so far as the beginning of virtually all its important features is concerned, and it is by no means irrelevant to note that feudalism is a form of social life that derived from the countryside, and in that respect contrasts with the urban life from which classical patriotism was derived.[30] Several features immediately command our attention. The first and most obvious is that these realms were all monarchical, and that the particular principle of monarchy found here (derived from the arrangements of vassalage) brought in its train an unequal and hierarchical society. Below the king were dukes, and below the dukes were various grades of landholding nobility, and these people continued into modern times as in some degree a warrior class whose business it was to look to the military vitality of the realm.

In medieval times, kings had exercised a pre-eminence which had been qualified by feudal law and the rights of vassals, but in the early modern period new circumstances had made the king much more powerful. The religious features of his coronation had been converted into a belief in his divine appointment. By the theory of sovereignty, his growing power to legislate for his realm had been explained and legitimated, thus making him much more than the fount of justice he had been in the Middle Ages. And his affairs were now conducted in the middle of a court, something so elaborate and complicated as to be almost a factory of monarchical decisions. The modern evolution of kingship appears as replete with just the features that might tempt an opposition based on classical precedent to come into being.

The significance of early modern monarchy is that it owed less to its subjects than any other form of government ever experienced by Europeans. Provinces changed hands according to the accidents of war and marriage, with little concern for any preference the inhabitants might have. Sometimes this use of districts as if they were merely pawns in some grand game of territorial chess might provoke difficulties, as the Habsburgs found in the Netherlands, but for the most part populations were remarkably long-suffering. They were often too busy thinking about religion to be much worried about masters; but it must also have been the case that a change of masters made relatively little practical difference to life. *Plus ça change, plus c'est la même chose.* The most unpleasant feature of all rulers was their avidity for money to fight their wars with, and this varied little as between one ruler and another. The conclusion that came in time to be drawn from this situation was that wars were caused by dynastic competition, a conclusion that was to lead on rapidly to the view that if kings were abolished, war would soon disappear.[31]

A second and related feature of this early modern world was the relatively cosmopolitan character of the nobility. Religious divisions were often serious, but in the end (which means by the eighteenth century) they too gave way to a world in which aristocrats spoke a common language, literally French, metaphorically a set of understandings about good behaviour. It was a cosmopolitan world which even fought its wars according to chivalric and well-recognised rules. Reason, it seemed, spoke French and could make herself understood anywhere between Lisbon and Moscow. This was, of course, the world from which nationalism arose by direct opposition. Within the area that used to be called 'Christendom' and was now coming to be called 'Europe', a common culture seemed for a time to mean more than a dividing politics.

Further, this was in essentials a Christian world, even if by the eighteenth century the Christianity was worn in many places with a lighter touch than had been the case in earlier centuries. A common substratum of Christian beliefs was one of the essential elements of the cosmopolitan world; the eighteenth century had an internationality similàr in some respects to the medieval period. Christianity is, in this context, more important than might seem the case to those impressed by the sceptical aspects of the century, for it seems indispensable in explaining the element of personal loyalty on which this sort of politics rested. Englishmen needed a heady draft of constitutional and theological ideas before they could nerve themselves to cut off the head of Charles I. They meditated in the most meticulous fashion about the character of their loyalties even in 1688; and a significant number of them came to the conclusion that they had an overriding loyalty to the House of Stuart. It is said that a few Jacobites survived as eccentrics into the third decade of the twentieth century. It is clear that to have a king as master could operate for millions of Europeans as a form of chivalric identity no less powerful than the patriotic attachment to a city in the ancient world.

Let us consider at random two examples of this kind of chivalric loyalty. One is the case of Blaise de Monluc, a Gascon soldier who served Francis I and Henry II, the latter of whom he described as 'the King my good master'. In 1554 he was the Governor of Siena which was being besieged in the Habsburg interest by the Marquis of Marignano. On Christmas Eve, the Marquis 'by one of his trumpets sent me half a stag, six capons, six partridges, six *borachios* of excellent wine and six loaves of bread, wherewith the next day to keep the feast'. Some Greek wine was also sent because Monluc had spoken of little else when he was sick, and Monluc comments:

'Such little civilities as these are very gentle and commendable, even betwixt the greatest enemies; if there be nothing particular betwixt them, as there was not betwixt us two. He served his master and I served mine. He attacked me for his honour, and I defended myself for mine. He had a mind to acquire reputation, and so had I. Tis for Turks and Saracens to deny an indifferent courtesy even to an enemy; but then it must not be such a one, or of such importance as to break or damage your design.'[32]

This is a contrast with the Peloponnesian War; and its usages are exactly what are criticised in Machiavelli's conception of war.

The second case is a reminiscence of Alexis de Tocqueville in a letter to Lady Theresa Lewis, who had sent him a book on Clarendon:

> One sentiment especially, dead in the hearts of our generations, lives in your pages, the idolatry of royalty which made obedience noble, and the greatest sacrifices, not merely to a principle, but to the person of the sovereign, easy. Throughout the world this sentiment is going; in France, it is gone. Even its traces have disappeared. You give to it its real power and importance. I recognised it with a pleasing remembrance, for it is associated with my earliest infancy. At this day, I remember, as if it were still before me, an evening in my father's château, when some family rejoicing had brought together a large number of our near relations. The servants were gone, and we sat round the fire. My mother, whose voice was sweet and touching, began to sing a well-known royalist song, of which the sorrows of Louis XVI and his death were the subject. When she ended we were all in tears; not for our own misfortunes, not even for the loss of so many of our own blood, who had perished on the field of civil war and on the scaffold, but for the fate of a single man, who had died fifteen years before, and who few of us who wept for him had ever seen. But this man had been our king.[33]

Here then is a focus of a political community which we may suitably call *legitimism* because its focus is a monarch believed to have a right to be obeyed. It obviously derives from the practices of the barbarian tribes who invaded the Roman Empire, but it has equally clearly been modified and developed by a variety of influences, ranging from medieval practices of representation to the equally medieval creation of an ethic of honour and a chivalric way of life. It is to be found, for example, in the fate of the blind king of Bohemia, whose motto was *Ich Dien* and whose body was found amongst the dead at the battle of Crecy in 1347. It was always the basis of medieval fighting, and it is no less evident in the appeal made by Queen Elizabeth to her troops at Tilbury. It has been powerful in modern times, in the opposition both to the Roundheads in England and to the Revolutionaries in France, but its effects on modern politics have been obscured by anachronistic interpretation of earlier conflicts in nationalist terms. But its effects have also been obscured by a much more significant confusion between medieval notions of consent and classical notions of liberty.

Consider, for example, the view that

our Government may truly be called an Empire of Laws, and not of

Men; for every Man has the same right to what he can acquire by his
Labour and Industry, as the King hath to his Crown, and the mean-
est Subject hath his Remedy against him in his Courts at *Westminster*:
No Man can be imprisoned, unless he has transgressed a Law of his
own making, nor be try'd but by his own Neighbours; for that we
enjoy a Liberty scarce known to the ancient *Greeks* and *Romans*.[34]

As the reference to an Empire of Laws reveals, this is a Harringtonian
argument, published in 1697 (probably by Walter Trenchard) attack-
ing the idea of a standing army. Trenchard is concerned with 'that
precious Jewel Liberty' and is one voice in that chorus of self-
congratulation about the liberties of England, which he attributes to
the benefits of Neptune, which was to become a powerful theme in
eighteenth-century political thought. Other countries, he reveals, have
become 'subject to the lawless Fancy and Ambition of the Prince, and
the Rapine and Insolence of his Officers'. England, however, has a
balanced constitution and rests, he argues, upon the support of its
people; hence it does not need a Standing Army which, however small,
could not be trusted not to threaten the liberties of the people. As John
Pocock has argued,[35] Whigs of this period tended to identify the
English country gentry with the citizens of the ancient city-republics.
What we find here, then, is a manner of thought tending to transpose
legitimism into the language of patriotism. In many respects, this was
an admirable Whig tendency, but one of its features was to edge
modern monarchies closer to an abstract ideal which was dubiously
compatible with it.[36] Nor did this tendency go unnoticed.

Halifax in the seventeenth century, like a good Trimmer, could assimilate patriotism to monarchy without any fear of conflict: 'Our
Trimmer is far from idolatry in other things, in one thing only he
cometh near it; his country is in some degree his idol.' But Halifax,
being an aristocrat, was a good mixer. Dryden thought that appeals to
patriotism were less to be admired:

> Gull'd with a Patriots name, whose modern sense
> Is one that wo'd by Law supplant his Prince;
> The Peoples Brave, the Politicians Tool
> Never was Patriot yet, but was a Fool.[37]

And Dr Johnson, of course, regarded patriotism as the last refuge of a
scoundrel, though it was added that 'he did not mean a real and
generous love of our country, but that pretended patriotism which so
many, in all ages and countries, have made a cloak for self-interest'.[38]
The conflict of Whig and Tory in eighteenth-century England had
many complicated facets, but one of them may be seen in terms of the
encounter of patriotism and what I have called 'legitimism'. Some

people saw it in just these terms, and one of them, Bolingbroke, attempted to reconcile the two strands of feeling in the 'idea of a patriot king'.

Britain has, of course, often managed to make cohabitate in practice things which are blindingly contradictory in theory. The French, however, have a notorious habit of pushing things a bit too far. Observe then how the *Encyclopédie* treats the idea of patriotism:

> Le rheteur peu logicien, le géographe qui ne s'occupe de la position des lieux, et le lexicographe vulgaire, prennent la *patrie* pour le lieu de la naissance, quel qu'il soit; mais le philosophe sait que ce mot vient du latin *pater*, qui représente un père et des enfants et conséquemment qu'il exprime le sense que nous attachons à celui de *famille*, de *société*, *d'état libre*, dont nous sommes membres, et dont les lois assurent nos libertés et notre bonheur. Il n'est point de *patrie* sous le jou du despotisme. Dans le siècle passé, Colbert confondit aussi *royaume* et *patrie*.

The various jumps in this particular argument (by de Jaucourt) are worth noting. Family imagery bears the burden of the argument and (contrary at least to the Greeks) the family is linked with liberty. De Jaucourt has a maternal image of the *patrie* and at one point describes it as a divinity, and as something which is superior to any of the officers who from time to time administer its affairs. We have reached the point where a metaphorised abstraction has replaced the personal loyalties of legitimism.

The evolution of modern classicism has often been seen in terms of enthusiasm for two co-ordinate standards of judgement. One of these was the standard to be derived from classical models, the other the abstract standard of Reason itself. The Renaissance was a domination of the European mind by classical standards, but by the seventeenth century, classical models and rational standards were co-ordinate points of reference for men engaged in most of the more prominent civilised activities. From the early eighteenth century, the classics begin to fall into second place before the onrush of reason, and this is not less true of politics than of other spheres of thought. Concrete models came to be replaced by what Bolingbroke called 'Platonick politics'. It is an important sign of French revolutionary thought when the Abbé Sieyès throws over the traditional French admiration for English liberties in favour of a rational constitution which will be free of all admixture of contingency. The American colonists were great readers of the letters of Cato, and the French revolutionaries played out a charade in Roman dress. Yet by the nineteenth century, the classical models of the city-state were mere decoration; but they were only decoration because the ideals they declared had been thoroughly assimilated into European thought.

There is therefore a considerable pathos in Burke's famous passage about Marie Antoinette in his *Reflections on the Revolution in France*. Poor Tom Paine, who never failed to utter the superficial, remarked that Burke pitied the plumage but forgot the dying bird;[39] but there was more to Burke than mere sentimentality. It may indeed look like a piece of monarchical triviality to grieve for Marie Antoinette as a romantic figure affronted by the muddy-booted disrespect of the Parisians who had marched to Versailles. But when Burke announced his shock that a thousand swords had not sprung from their scabbards to protect her, he was recognising a violent shift in the underground terrain of European political feeling. The age of chivalry was dead; legitimism had become a relic. The stage was set for the dominance of a set of abstract creeds which can, as we shall see, barely be adequately differentiated one from another.

III

We are concerned with the history and character of three clusters of thought: Nationalism, Patriotism and Legitimism. The French Revolution was clearly a decisive event in the character of all three. We have space for nothing more than the sort of sketch of future developments which Victorian novelists provided in their final chapters.

The French Revolution was a direct assault upon feudal usages, and particularly upon that feudal type of political cohesion which we have called 'legitimism'. But like all deeply rooted political sentiments, legitimism was to take an unconscionable time a'dying. Indeed, observers in the latter half of the nineteenth century, observing the power of thrones and the tendency of Balkan nationalisms to add new monarchies to the world, might well have thought that monarchical institutions were riding on a crest of faith in progress into a happy future. By 1919, however, it was clear that legitimism was largely extinct. For it was a universal tenet of the new ideological theory that the rulers had to be members of the nation itself; they must not be foreigners. Monarchs, of course, were often more foreign than national, for their marriage-pool was largely cosmopolitan. Most English monarchs, for example, have been of foreign extraction. They have ranged from conquering Normans to a Hanoverian dynasty which had to change its German name as late as 1914. The principle of self-determination, whether interpreted in a republican or a nationalist manner, was equally hostile to kingship.

The reason legitimism took so long to disappear is that it combined two elements always to be found in vital political doctrines. One of these elements was a belief, inherited from earlier times, that certain families had a right to rule. The decline of legitimism is simply the slow erosion of this belief from generation to generation, and its replacement by democratic beliefs deriving a right to rule from some form of election. But vital beliefs of this kind are generally supported by something much less subject to historical erosion: namely, a more or less natural propensity. Legitimism rests upon a propensity amongst human beings to invest certain men with symbolic and representative status. Beliefs change slowly enough; propensities change even more slowly, if indeed, they change very much at all. Hence it is that we have had to employ ideas like 'charisma' or (in a different type of context) leadership-principle to describe passages in modern politics which are analytically similar though historically distinct from what I have called 'legitimism'. Indeed, the career of some political families, from the Bonapartes to the Kennedys, suggests that legitimism is not entirely extinct, even though the feudal beliefs on which it rested in earlier centuries cannot be revived.

The career of patriotism in the last two centuries has been remarkably similar. The beliefs associated with it, as we have described them, have moved elsewhere, and we are again left with a natural propensity which has been remarkably little intellectualised. Patriotism now describes a sentiment derived from attachment to one's native soil and scenery, to its mode of life and its inheritance of tastes. Foreign threat can make this into a powerful political feeling, but normally it has been quiescent. George Orwell's comments on patriotism seem to me to catch its character accurately: 'By "patriotism" I mean devotion to a particular place, a particular way of life, which one believes to be the best in the world but has no wish to force upon other people. Patriotism is of its nature defensive both militarily and culturally.'[40] This clearly means that patriotism is largely conservative in its operation, and in the twentieth century it has supported traditional governments like those of Britain and Germany in 1914, and revolutionary governments like that of the Soviet Union in 1941, with equal doses of enthusiasm. As an idea, patriotism used to subvert European states; now it sustains them in whatever form they happen to have.

We are left with the fate of nationalism itself, and it is here that the complexities threaten to become unmanageable. Just as classicism became increasingly rationalist in the period between the Renaissance and the Enlightenment (the very terms themselves supply the clue to the drift of development), so classical patriotism had turned, by the beginning of the nineteenth century, into a version of rationalist politics. Classical ideas which had been sustained by a kind of nostalgia turned into abstractions sustained by a kind of hope. For, as we have seen, classical patriotism affirmed the moral value of communities composed of citizens who were both self-determining and more or less equal. But what was the bond holding these citizens together as a community? Loosely speaking, it might be said that they had *chosen* to come together, for a city was not a natural unit, like a tribe, but an association of diverse elements. No doubt in most generations they were simply born to their communities, and in this sense constituted both a *patria* and a *natio*. But for a variety of complicated but familiar reasons, many nineteenth-century thinkers sought to discover bonds more natural and more determinate than either choice or mere accident of birth, and they were thus launched upon the quest for a variety of different ways of characterising the members of a community, such that it might be more scientifically or philosophically understood.

To characterise these citizens as members of a nation was to see them in historical terms as members of something that had developed its collective character over the experience of many generations. But this membership came now to be seen, not as a notionally chosen bond but as actually constitutive of the human character of the members. For outside of such historic communities (it was argued) what would the individual human organism be? Lacking speech, customs, moral values and all the other attributes now plausibly being attached to collective entities, it would be nothing at all, something unrecognisable as a human being, an 'it' rather than a 'he' or a 'she'. The individual, whom earlier modern political thought had liberated from feudal bonds, was now becoming attached (in the name of sociological realism) to his community by links even tighter than those of feudalism. Thus was the community made the basis of a new type of political thinking.

But it was a type with many varieties, for there were inheritors of this stock of thoughts who did not find the nation the most convincing description of the new moral community. One group of these thinkers was concerned with the race, whilst an even more influential group was concerned to build the community out of the supposedly productive (by contrast with parasitic) classes of existing states. The most influential version of this latter strand was, of course, the productive classes construed as the proletariat; but very similar ideas lay at the root of populism, which focused its thoughts around the rural population and called them 'the people'. But whatever the variations (and they were very extensive indeed) the general thrust of this tradition of thought was to construct a community purified by the amputation of some significant imperfection. Such imperfections might be parasitic classes, or foreign rulers, or inferior races, or urban manipulators, but each version derived all evils from the imperfection that concerned it.

What I am suggesting, therefore, is that to see nationalism as the outcome of the tradition of thought deriving from modern nostalgia for ancient city-states is like trying to mate an elephant with a mouse. The outcome of that tradition was, rather, the entire spectrum of ideologies which have been so dynamic a part of modern political thinking. Many attempts have been made to distinguish one ideology from another, and sometimes these attempts have moved beyond classification into the attempt to supply different lineages for each. But the fluidity of the material, in which Plato, Rousseau and Hegel turn up more or less indifferently as ancestors equally of all these ideologies, suggests that they can only be distinguished in terms of local circumstances rather than fundamental principle. Fully explored, each ideology tends to exhibit the full range of feeling, the practices and the devices found in most of the rest. Hence it is that each ideology may conceptually expand to absorb the rest. Thus Orwell argues that nationalism means the habit of assuming that human beings can be classified like insects, and that whole blocks of millions or tens of millions of people can confidently be labelled 'good' or 'bad': 'The abiding purpose of every nationalist is to secure more power and more prestige, *not* for himself, but for the nation or other unit in which he has chosen to sink his own individuality.'[41] This is an account of nationalism which explicitly includes communism, Zionism, anti-semitism, Trotskyism, and so on. It is a polemical piece, written at a time of high emotion, but it does illustrate the way in which not only political scientists, ever prone to the dangers of isomorphism, but acute observers of everyday political reality, are prone to assimilate any ideology to the fundamental pattern that each one exhibits.

Nationalism may be taken as a paradigm of modern ideological thought because it tends to be egalitarian and democratic. Like all ideologies, it seeks both to understand and to organise human beings in terms of a pure, integrated community, a community so pure as almost to make redundant the kind of political activity which has hitherto sustained amongst Europeans a sufficient unity in which to seek the good life, at least as that expression might be understood by a collection of freely willing individuals. Thus has the essentially urban ideal of public-spiritedness tended to replace that complex mixture of feudalism and Christianity in terms of which modern Europe has so long lived.

4

Neo-Classicist and Romantic Elements in the Emergence of Nationalist Conceptions

A. D. Smith

Western and Central Europe in the later eighteenth century witnessed the rise of two major cultural movements, a civic neo-classicism and a 'historicist' Romanticism. In this chapter I want to examine the interplay of these currents, and their contribution to the formation of the ideas inspiring the earliest nationalist movements, particularly in France and Germany. In doing so, I hope to show the common cultural and social bases of early European nationalism, at least up to 1800. For this purpose I shall confine attention to the ideology of nationalism rather than the separate, if related, phenomena of the diffusion of national sentiment and the growth of nation-states.

I

Certain assumptions underlie this examination of early European nationalism's cultural roots. The first is that the term 'nationalism' refers, not to a single unitary concept, but to a family of related propositions. Some of these are descriptive, others normative. The descriptive assumptions relate to the idea of the 'nation' and its role in history. They assume that the world is indeed divided into unique cultural communities and that world history is the story of their interplay. This in turn gives rise to the belief that such communities have a history and destiny which is of profound significance for their members, and that the only legitimate government is one which represents the community as a whole. The ethic of nationalism is accordingly founded on a premise of collective autonomy, in which the supreme good is felt to be the freedom of the communal will. In addition to the right of self-determination, nationalists generally subscribe to a belief in the duties of self-sacrifice for the community, of self-purification by the community and of political activism on its behalf. Finally, most, though not

For Notes and References to Chapter 4, see pp. 162–6.

all, nationalists aim for political sovereignty – which in practice means that each 'nation' must have its own state.[1]

Second, for present purposes I am assuming that the ideology of nationalism, as just outlined, is a relatively modern phenomenon. To be more precise, the nationalist conceptions and ethic appear no earlier than the latter half of the eighteenth century, perhaps first in Corsica, America and Poland, but most clearly in 1789 and the Revolutionary Wars. Certain elements of nationalism, and especially certain components of 'nation-states', may be traced back much earlier, even into antiquity; but no clear conception of nationhood or of self-determination appears before the Enlightenment, and only fleetingly during the Netherlands revolt or the Puritan Civil War in England. If this is true, then we should also avoid talking about the growth or development of nationalism in evolutionary terms. The period prior to the rise of nationalism is indeed one of social and cultural gestation, in which various currents of thought and emotion are adapted and synthesised; yet there are no clear-cut stages of growth through which the nationalist idea or ethic may be said to pass, but rather a fairly sudden upsurge of nationalist ideas among an élite, after the period of 'gestation'.[2]

Third, in examining the cultural roots of nationalist ideologies, I do not wish to imply that the cultural sphere provides the most important, let alone the sole, motivations for nationalism. In one sense, cultural factors are clearly dependent on more fundamental social and economic changes, which they mediate; and from another angle, it is the political frameworks and agencies which act as the catalyst of nationalist rebellions. Nevertheless, over and above the tautological sense in which the cultural sphere is vital for any ideological movement requiring coherent intellectual formulation, culture provides an essential key to the understanding of the *nationalist* variety of secular ideology. This is because, as I hope to show, nationalism represents a fusion of elements from movements whose attitude to politics is at best ambivalent, at worst negative, and which look to culture itself to provide the missing qualities in political life. Literature, the arts and social philosophy furnish, therefore, important clues to the sources of nationalist conceptions, although at first glance they appear marginal because apolitical.

II

The starting-point for an understanding of the cultural roots of early European nationalisms is the consolidation of territorial units by bureaucratic absolutist states. The various bureaucratic despotisms which sprang up in Western and Central Europe in the seventeenth and eighteenth centuries ranged from relatively large and efficient states like Prussia and France to tiny duchies and principalities like those of Wallerstein or the Reichsritter of Swabia. The character of these regimes varied with the personality of the rulers and their chief ministers, and with the degree of bureaucratic efficiency built up by the dynasty. Generally speaking, however, bureaucratic despotism, enlightened or reactionary, gradually proved its effectiveness as a form of political organisation, especially in regard to large territories and populations. It is hardly surprising, therefore, if such bureaucratic despotisms provided not merely a target for the competition of the rising intelligentsia for power and status but also a mould and an instrument for the incipient nationalist movements. Moreover, by demanding a rational training and utilitarian outlook, by instilling a belief in man's ability to solve his problems unaided, the bureaucratic machine and ethos encouraged the trend to secular education so conducive to nationalism.[3]

To this bureaucratic phenomenon, there corresponded certain theories and assumptions. In the first place, the bureaucratic type of state tended to be viewed as the product of outstanding personalities, men of heroic stature, princes, warriors and lawgivers, a tradition which can be traced back to the Renaissance. This meant that the bureaucracy was held to be dependent on the will of the absolutist monarch. On the other hand, this dependency was modified by the belief in *raison d'état*, the superiority of technically required action to moral standards, of purposive rationality to transcendent or permanent principles. The rational monarch was accordingly bound by the principles of administrative efficiency and expediency, as embodied in his bureaucratic instruments.[4]

A consequence of this partnership between heroic absolutism and bureaucratic *raison d'état* was their encroachment on traditional liberties, whether of regions or estates, in the name of legal frameworks and territorial standardisation. This in turn provoked a challenge to bureaucratic absolutism, in the name of that very concept of sovereignty which the monarchs had appropriated.[5]

In the cultural sphere, therefore, no less than in the political, bureaucratic and princely absolutism and its consequences contributed an essential motif to incipient nationalism: that of external and internal sovereignty. The foundations for the concept of external sovereignty stretch back, well beyond Bodin, to the fourteenth century; indeed, the maxim 'Rex est imperator in suo regno' remained the foundation of statecraft from Philip the Fair to 1789. Internally, too, we can trace the assertion by the lawyers of royal power over all other parts of the state, conceived of as an organism, to the thirteenth century; and as monarchical power increased and attracted the services of administrators and lawyers, often from the ranks of the Church, the rulers' demand for internal sovereignty, for the levelling of every intermediate or rival centre of allegiance, became more insistent and successful. When, therefore, the nationalists began to stake out their claims in the late eighteenth century, they found a ready-made legal and political tradition of imperial sovereignty waiting, as it were, to be transferred into the hands of the 'people'. An essential part of nationalism's appeal lies in its ability to harmonise other, often conflicting, cultural elements with this imperial and absolutist tradition of sovereignty.[6]

III

It was nevertheless in militant opposition to the claims of bureaucratic absolutism that the nationalist movements first arose. They made their demands in the name of a set of assumptions and precepts, which were couched in terms of two rival cultural movements, the neo-classical and the romantic. These later eighteenth-century movements were heirs, in turn, to broader cultural traditions, and in different ways gave meaning and direction to the social processes and ethnic bases which cut across the political frameworks I have described.

The first of these cultural movements, the 'neo-classical', arose in the 1750s and 1760s and reached its climax during the Revolution. It represents an intensification of certain elements in the wider rationalist tradition of the Enlightenment which, until 1750, was marked by a spirit of sceptical enquiry and secularism, at once benevolent and optimistic. But around the middle of the century, a new moral seriousness, even pessimism, made its appearance in the writings of the literary men, and in the arts. In 1759 d'Alembert noted the 'remarkable change in ideas', the 'intellectual revolution', that was currently taking place. Against the flippancy, hedonism and cynicism of the Rococo, the enlighteners and the neo-classicists in the arts set purity, simplicity, high-mindedness and stoicism. In the arts and philosophy, education and social criticism, a regenerative impulse appeared: in 1769, Gluck appealed for a 'noble simplicity' and harmonious clarity against the artifice and decorous sophistication of Italian opera, in architecture, Laugier as early as 1753 pleaded for a return to pure and simple forms, even deriving the temple form from the primitive hut; while even so representative a Rococo artist as Fragonard was influenced enough by the prevailing tide to turn away from depicting *fêtes galantes* to paint themes of self-sacrifice like Corresus and Callirhoe (1765). The same serious, moralising tone pervades the literature of the period, whether in the plays of Lessing and Diderot, or the poetry of Cowper and the novels of Richardson.[7]

Now, in turning away from the courtly hedonism and feminine ideal of the Rococo, neo-classical artists and writers sought and encouraged a manly simplicity and heroism which appealed to the rising strata of the intelligentsia and bourgeoisie who had been exposed to the growing secularisation of education. Among these strata, the first sceptical phase of the Enlightenment had eroded traditional Christian beliefs, and encouraged an aristocratic taste for cultural and social models drawn from a pre-Christian milieu, that of a classical antiquity. It was to this educated 'public', in search of enlightenment through literature and art, that the neo-classicists appealed.

We should, however, beware of relating the rise of neo-classicism too closely to the growth of the 'middle classes'. Even if it were possible to give a precise definition to so all-embracing a category, and one so subject to historical fluctuations, there is the fact that both aristocrats and the state frequently patronised the products of the neo-classical artists and writers; and the taste for the values and forms of Roman antiquity was widely diffused over the several strata, in both France and Germany.[8]

At the same time it is difficult to imagine the classical revival without the antecedent confluence of three social processes in early eighteenth-century Europe: namely the rise of a wealthy commercial bourgeoisie, the growth of cities (especially capitals) and the beginnings of secular thought following the Wars of Religion. The union of these three long-term processes encouraged the growth, in turn, of groups of professionals interested in science and social enquiry, and the formation of an 'educated public' bound together by newspapers, organisations and coffee-houses or salons in the fast-growing cities. Now one of the mainstays of neo-classical ideals is the very idea of an 'educated public': a body of men united by common tastes, ideals and sympathies, rather than by natural ties, and committed to the dissemination of knowledge and virtue. This was the ideal of the influential German publicist A. L. Schlözer (1735–1809) in the 1770s and 1780s. His paper, *Stats Anzeigen*, which had a circulation of 4000 copies, preached the necessity of a civic spirit to combat absolutism and revolution in the interests of a constitutional monarchy; there was no evil, he believed, which a free exchange of opinion by citizens could not eradicate.[9]

Neo-classicism presented a number of ideals and aspirations which gave meaning and direction to this idea of an 'educated public'. To begin with, it tended to equate that public with the 'patriot' community, lovers of liberty, extolled by early eighteenth-century English writers like Bolingbroke. In doing so, it gave substance to that equation by defining the community as one of common sentiments and purposes, a community of common will. Second, to agree to live under common laws and institutions, as 'citizens' enjoying equal rights and common duties, was to assert the primacy of the communal will. From this it followed that the noblest action of the individual was the submergence of his desires and will in the common will of his fellow citizens. Third, neo-classicism introduced a new note of political activism. Rather than simply imitate the 'noble simplicity and calm grandeur' of

Winckelmann's Greeks, the neo-classical ideal took as its models those ancient states in which martial valour and stern resolve defined the content of virtue. Self-sacrifice for the community, the pursuit of stoic virtue rather than pleasure, the superiority of a citizen's duty to affection or the claims of family – virtues which were thought to inform the life of Sparta and republican Rome – these were active qualities, the political virtues, which the neo-classicists admired. They were also acquired virtues, the result of years of internal struggle for mastery over the baser desires. Hence political activism implied striving for self-control, and this in turn bred a fourth ideal: education of character. To build character requires a harnessing of all the moral energies; hence the appeal to sentiment and the heart, the reaction against the primacy of intellectual education, can be explained by reference to the communal ideals of neo-classicism rather than in general psychological terms. When that seminal figure of neo-classicism, Diderot, extols the moral truths, the emotional simplicity and veracity of Greuze's didactic scenes or Chardin's still-life pieces, and contrasts them with the decorative artifice of their Rococo contemporaries, we must interpret his comment in terms of this wider 'republican' ideal of neo-classicism.[10]

Nowhere is this republican ideal of virtue more forcibly presented than in David's celebrated *Oath of the Horatii* (1785). Nowhere also can we gain a better idea of that controlled violence which lies at the core of neo-classicism. The revolutionary dynamism which demands the surrender of individual desire to communal dictates, expressed in the outstretched arms of the Horatii brothers; the unity of purpose symbolised by the swords of liberty against tyranny; the emphasis upon heroic struggle at the cost of their wives' affection; and the moral lesson of their pure act of self-sacrifice: all these facets of neo-classical ideals, which were to provide the components of the ethic of nationalism, are presented by David with stark simplicity and vivid tension. To his contemporaries it seemed a worthy vision of antiquity, of a Europe regenerated by classical ideals of martial simplicity, to set against the decadence of the absolutist state, its lack of social purpose and solidarity.[11]

IV

The neo-classical revolt against Rococo absolutism was essentially an urban protest of an educated public excluded from participation in political life. By contrast, romanticism extended that protest to include the corruption of urban life and rationalist education; it represented, therefore, a reaction against those social processes which fostered the rise of an intelligentsia, on the part of circles within that stratum. But the contrast between the vision of an unspoilt nature and urban luxury, which marked the point of departure of early Romanticism, helped to reinforce the ethical bias of neo-classicism, while at the same time extending its conceptual content.

Before about 1800 the conflict between neo-classical and Romantic aspirations was latent. In the so-called 'pre-Romantic' phase of the 1760s and 1770s, Rousseau and his followers provided, in their cult of Nature, a bridge between the two movements. The imitation of Nature was, after all, also the goal of the more rationalist neo-classicists. The effect of Rousseau's influence was to augment that cult of sentiment and fantasy to be found in such different mid-century products as *Clarissa* or Piranesi's *Antiquities* (1748). By the 1760s, the Rousseauan contrasts of urban luxury and untainted nature had entered into the Arcadian idylls of the Swiss poet and painter, Salomon Gessner; and by the 1770s Schiller and the *Sturm und Drang* had developed the essential Romantic dichotomy of classic universalism and creative individualism. For all that, the drama and passion expressed by the music and poetry of the period was as yet no more than an extension of neo-classicism's controlled violence to aspects outside the urban domain.[12]

Apart from the general discovery of nature as an elemental force, such as inspired Hans Bull's eulogies of the Norwegian fjords, or British water-colourists' pilgrimages to the Alps in the 1770s, two aspects of pre-Romanticism are particularly significant for the emergence of nationalism. The first is the emphasis upon historical origins, the second is the admiration for genius and the concept of the sublime. Quite often they were combined, as in Wood's *Essay on the Original Genius of Homer* (1769), or in the widespread admiration for Macpherson's forgeries of Ossian. Homer, the Bible and Ossian were valued, not merely for their intrinsic merits, but because they conjured up visions of the original spirit of a people in its most authentic and sublime aspects. Similarly with the pre-Romantics' revival of Dante and Shakespeare; they were inspired by those aspects which were both picturesque and primordial, which uncovered the pristine sources of a culture's energy and vigour.[13]

This pre-Romantic concern with purity of origins, with genius and with the worship of *natura naturans*, may be construed, in the first place, as a revolt against the levelling effects, the pettiness and bureaucratic rationalism of absolutism, and the standardising tendencies already apparent in secular thought and urban commerce. But, in raising the banner of diversity against political regimentation and social uniformity, the pre-Romantics stumbled upon a type of relationship which might cut clean across those which both the political regimes and social processes were creating, namely the ethnic bases which continued to align and divide European populations, even though this cultural substratum had played a secondary, even marginal, role in their social and political life.

In speaking thus of an 'ethnic substratum' of nationalism among the European populations after the Reformation, I refer to certain cultural ties and sentiments which persist in given populations over generations. These include:

(1) a myth of common origins and historical traditions, such as those contained in the Icelandic sagas or the chronicles of the Russian monks;

(2) the possession of common beliefs and customs or rites, which exalt a community in relation to its neighbours, more especially in its religious status, as among the ancient Persians or Jews;

(3) an individual cultural profile, manifested in common laws and institutions, and especially in the possession of a common and distinct language; and

(4) an association of the population with a particular geographical location, and with a distinctive constellation of neighbours.

The combination of such ties has in the past often furnished a basis for movements of cultural restoration or 'ethnic messianisms', particularly when the ethnic group has been threatened and its way of life undermined. On such occasions, indeed, the restoration involved not merely a repudiation of other ethnic groups and their mores, but also a sense of mission and a programme of self-purification which drew its inspiration from a visionary image of a pristine past and a transfigured future. It is this use of the past and attitude to the future on the part of ethnic messianisms which, more than anything, has led many to trace in millenial movements the roots of nationalism.[14]

Nationalism, however, differs in important respects from millennial movements, and the aims and inspiration of the pre-Romantics who unwittingly rediscovered the ethnic bases were quite alien to those of the messianic prophets. The pre-Romantics were concerned with a return to Nature; their interest in cultural diversity was an offshoot of their fidelity to Nature; and their revival of history was also derived from their understanding of the organic life of Nature. This close link between organic nature, historical growth and cultural diversity received its most elaborate expression in the work of Herder; but we find it equally in that whole medievalising trend in thought and art which made its appearance in the 1770s. 'We rather deprive nature of her wealth than agree to alter our System', complained Justus Möser in his defence of German particularism and her different historical traditions. Similarly, Goethe eulogised the Gothic builders of Strasburg Cathedral in the 1770s, even though he dismissed the Teutonic myths and Serbian songs in his old age. And from the 1770s, too, there dates that vogue for historical paintings of medieval themes, such as Vincent's *President Molé and the Fronde* (1779), and Fuseli's *Die*

Eidgenossen (1781), painted significantly for the Zurich Rathaus and depicting, not a universal theme of classical antiquity, but the Swiss Confederation's Oath of the Rütli in 1307 against the Austrians.[15]

It was out of this idealisation of the Middle Ages, from this cult of ethnic origins and purity, that there was fashioned the German Romantic doctrine of 'historicism', whose chief category is neither virtue nor citizenship but organic growth and becoming. German 'historicism', which treated the cultural community as a process of self-development, as a composite whole superior to the sum of its parts, merely extended and elaborated the pre-Romantic return to Nature and ethnicity. The themes of the pre-Romantic writers and artists were no longer part of Europe's sacred or classical heritage; the youth of Europe they extolled and explored was not the Greek spring, the model of the neo-classicists, but the primeval state and early development of each of Europe's ethnic groups. And, accordingly, the regeneration of which the pre-Romantics dreamed was modelled less on the severities of Lycurgan or Mosaic codes than on the spirit, institutions and myths of ancient tribal hordes in their localised landscapes, whose vigour and colour the pre-Romantics hoped to recapture.[16]

V

After 1800, under the influence of the Christian revival and the conservatism of political Restoration, neo-classicists and Romantics came to view each other as philosophical and artistic rivals, as mutually exclusive schools and conceptions. Before 1800, however, the position was much more fluid. Fuseli, for example, saw no contradiction in translating Winckelmann and joining the first group of Romantic painters; Goethe went through romantic and neo-classical phases; David's architectural ideas, as a member of the Convention, were symbolic and Romantic in their grandeur – even the Romantic hero paraded in neo-classical décor, when Napoleon patronised the neo-classical *Empire* style. These and other examples attest to the overlapping and complicity between what were later to be regarded as antagonistic conceptions and styles.[17]

The fact is that neo-classicism and early Romanticism shared a number of important features, and it is these elements that were vital for the rise of nationalism, rather than their much-vaunted differences. It is not just that neo-classicism may be seen as the first stage of the Romantic revolt, or that what inspired Winckelmann's listeners was his rhapsodic yearning, sensuous attitude to classical antiquity rather than his more formal precepts.[18] Nor again is it just that many writers and artists exhibit elements from both traditions. What all this indicates is the common basis of the rival movements' inspiration, and the proximity of their ideals.

One basis of this similarity is, of course, a rejection by neo-classicists and Romantics alike of the political status quo and, as important, of all authority that is external and imposed. There are, it is true, important differences of emphasis here, particularly between the English and American pre-Revolutionary traditions and the more radical Continental, especially French, thinkers. While Bolingbroke, Burke and Jefferson emphasised moderation, rationality and checks on individual and communal rights of self-assertion, Rousseau, Fichte and Schlegel turned increasingly away from such rationalist and liberal norms and paved the way for a cult of collective will, particularly after 1806.[19] Moreover, American and English thinkers did not glorify violence or justify rebellion as an end in itself. Nor did they reject politics as such, as some Romantics were later to do. There is nevertheless more than a purely temporal relationship between Anglo-Saxon and Continental neo-classical political thought. For, like their romantic counterparts, they desired a truly 'representative' form of government, one which embodied, if not the general will, at any rate the opinions and desires of educated urban strata, and not merely of an aristocratic clique or appointed officials. Hence the cry of liberty from personal tyranny and from existing bureaucratic despotisms was also a rejection of all constraint which was not self-imposed and freely negotiated.[20]

Second, neo-classicist and Romantic alike share a common quest for the inner springs of solidarity. It is these secret sources of life and vigour they hope to tap. In this respect, Herder's concept of *Kraft* has its neo-classical counterpart in the dynamic tension of David's three Horatii brothers, as well as in the thematic tension of sonata form developed by Haydn and Mozart in the 1770s and 1780s.[21] The idea that such internal, self-generated energy is the source of social solidarity and unity was to be taken over by nationalism in its emphasis upon moral struggle, will-power and self-determination.[22] The source of these notions is the treatment by neo-classicists and early Romantics alike of energy as a force that wells up from within; just as in natural bodies there is a vital power which, in the words of Lavater writing in 1778, 'continually acts from within to without, from the centre to the circumference', so it is with men and communities; if they can discover their roots, they can release the force that lies deeply embedded and concealed within.[23]

Closely related to the notions of self-discipline and internal energy is that of social regeneration through education. Education here stands for more than mere enlightenment. It is a process of self-development, of drawing out of oneself hidden and suppressed potentialities, until full self-realisation has been attained.[24] Such education is closely linked to the elevation of culture as the source of politics. Both neo-classicism and Romanticism turn to morality and culture, in a word, to Nature, against external artifice and political rules. It is from the genuine and sacred realms of culture and ethics that neo-classicists draw inspiration for their reform of politics, while Romantics wish to go further and revolutionise politics, or in some cases turn their backs upon it, in the name of Nature. In this way, both movements grope towards a non-political theory of politics, one which draws its categories from the untainted bonds of culture.[25]

Finally, both traditions are united in their respect for genius and the sublime. In this, they echo the early Baroque reverence for the hero which Rococo despotism had shackled in the toils of rational bureaucracy and courtly frivolity. It is exactly this frivolity and administrative mediocrity that genius can transcend. As the repository and exemplar of everything that is pure and original, the genius is as much revered by the neo-classicist as by the Romantic, even if the later Romantic cult of extravagance for its own sake exceeded the wildest dreams of neo-classicists. Burke's essay, *A Philosophical Enquiry into the origins of Our Ideas of the Sublime and the Beautiful* (1756), exerted an early influence in this direction,[26] but writers and artists like Goethe and Fuseli, Kant and Blake, in other ways at variance, echoed this theme; and it was a radical neo-classical architect, Ledoux, who complained of administrative timidity and incompetence, which must always try to extinguish diversity, strangeness and purity of design and 'the pure rays which flash from the dawn of Genius' (1790s).[27]

These beliefs in self-imposed authority, internal energy and will, regeneration through education and culture, and the sublime quality of genius, which were common ground for neo-classicists and Romantics alike, proved highly influential in the formulation of nationalist doctrines. If the absolutist state and tradition provided the nationalists with their goal and framework, neo-classicism and early Romanticism together supplied them with the conceptual armoury and motivation for their onslaught. The essential feature of this whole period of gestation is the drive to restructure the social and political life of the existing units in terms of ideals drawn from the realm of culture and morality. In this process of regeneration, the neo-classicist contribution is decisive. Not only did it supply the subsequent nationalisms of the French Revolution, Helvetic Republic and German War of Liberation with an ethic of autonomy involving inward purification and political activism, but it also crystallised a conception of rising social strata as constituting a homogeneous 'educated public', summoning them to form a new kind of community, a popular nation. For such a community, no self-sacrifice could be too costly; for no power and no loyalty could override that of the republican nation.[28] The idea appears most boldly, in terms of the concept of popular sovereignty, in Sieyès's pamphlet; but it also held a strong appeal for the classicising German intelligentsia before 1806.[29]

I have emphasised the role of neo-classicism as a cultural precondition of early European nationalism, partly because there is still a tendency to see nationalism as an essentially Romantic outgrowth, and also to suggest a different interpretation of early European nationalisms from that of Kohn, who makes a sharp dichotomy between what he terms the civic, rationalist and associational type of nationalism prevalent in France (and also England and America), and a more traditional, organic, even mystic, kind of nationalism found in Germany, Italy and Eastern Europe.[30] Certainly, before 1806, German, Swiss and Italian nationalism owed as much to civic, rationalist neo-classicism as to early Romantic notions of the organic community of language or culture. However much German intellectuals – in particular, men like Lessing and Winckelmann – reacted against French cultural leadership, they owed the educational and renovating thrust of their national conscious-ness (not to mention specific concepts like 'autonomy' and the 'public') to a general Western-European and American movement which sought a return to the austere republican virtues of classical antiquity for its impulse and model of social regeneration. For, in its aims and methods, neo-classicism was a universalist movement, even if its emotional impact and political ramifications were oriented to the nation-state. Herein lies an unresolved contradiction, both in neo-classicism's cultural programme and in its political consequences. On the one hand, neo-classicism espouses a universalist belief in nature and the antique as its noblest embodiment. The duty of artist and writer is to preach through a simplified and purified art the eternal lessons of morality and duty to the common weal. Politically, this meant that liberty was indivisible and republicanism universally applicable. In that context, the fact that man's rights happened to be regulated in historic nation-states was secondary, even accidental. On the other hand, the universal religion of liberty and moral virtue was felt by the participants as most keenly applicable to their particular political or ethnic communities, since the opponents and obstacles to its realisa-tion, i.e. the despots, aristocrats and bureaucrats, possessed definite territorial power bases. Besides, neo-classicism originated as a cultural movement directed against French cultural leadership in its Rococo forms, and even in France took on immediately a strongly collective colour, a return to Poussinism and the Grand Siècle.[31] The doctrines of civic participation and equality and of popular republican govern-ment of neo-classical political theory also reinforced the national character of the Western despotic states, since they provided it with a new and powerful source of legitimation and rationale for centralisa-tion, as Tocqueville argued. This is also why we meet considerable variation in neo-classical art and theory in different states of Europe, a variation which Romanticism was to glorify and exaggerate after 1800. From England to Russia, both neo-classicism and Romanticism are found side by side in the writings, music, art and architecture of the various states and nations from about 1760 to 1850, each state emphasising different elements of this dualism and in very varying degrees.[32]

On the whole, the neo-classical contribution prevailed over the Romantic before 1800. In a sense this was due to the continuing influence of Rome, Italy and the excavations at Pompei and Herculaneum. Even Scottish and English artists and noblemen felt the neo-classical pull of Rome; and though England's nationalism was less marked than those of its Continental neighbours during these years, the rise of national sentiment in England throughout the eighteenth century went hand in hand with a return to Nature and the antique. At the same time, England moved faster towards a high Romanticism, in flight from incipient industrialism rather than absolutist bureaucracy after 1780.[33]

Early European nationalisms, then, arose as a political precipitant of the confluence of the three major eighteenth-century cultural traditions – a Baroque absolutism, neo-classicism and early Romanticism. Both neo-classicism and early Romanticism, in turn, represent rival, but overlapping, revolts against the dominance of state absolutism; and they provide nationalism with its ethic of autonomy and its conceptual content. But nationalism's success was due not only to its ability to give concrete political expression to various themes and aspirations of the two cultural traditions, but also to its capacity for harnessing the machine and framework of bureaucratism by appropriating to its own ends the absolutist concept of sovereignty.

At the same time, the rivalry of neo-classicism and early Romanticism has left its mark upon the structure of nationalist ideals and programmes. Indeed, the subsequent history of nationalism in France and Germany, as well as further afield, testifies to this growing divergence which springs, not only from specific social conditions in each area, but from the ultimately incompatible models of social and political organisation to which neo-classicism and Romanticism aspire. The ideal of neo-classicism stems, after all, from an image of antique republican city-states, a small-scale *polis* of politically involved and educated citizens. Idealised and universal in principle, such an 'archaeological' cult fosters civic exclusiveness and bourgeois pride. The Romantic ideal, though even less precise and factual, envisages the resuscitation of tightly-knit ethnic communities resembling the kinship and tribal organisation of pre-feudal but post-Roman Europe (often confused with an idealised vision of the more evolved guild and estate organisation of feudal Europe). The two historicist cults are, in turn, bound up with the new social processes, with the impact of commerce, urbanisation and secularism, and with the persistence of ethnic ties in eighteenth-century Europe. Until 1800, however, the profound differences between historicist cults, and the conflict between social processes and ethnic bases, were subordinated to an overriding revolt against artifice, absolutism and bureaucratic regimentation. Hence early Romantics could embrace a neo-classicist ethic of virtue and will, while neo-classicists could accept early Romantic concepts of nature and genius. In the ferment of revolutionary enthusiasm which swept Europe between about 1770 and 1815, such 'historical mobility' and conceptual eclecticism appeared both natural and desirable.[34]

In such a period of fluidity and experiment with historical revivals, neo-classicism and Romanticism could for a time merge. It was this dynamic but momentary fusion which nationalism inherited, and which it has tried to synthesise ever since.

5

Nationalism and Language in Switzerland and Canada[1]

T. Rennie Warburton

The German and Italian nationalist movements of the nineteenth century, which played such a central part first in the unification of the two nations and later in the rise of Nazism, owed much to the thought of Herder who placed special emphasis on language as a central part of a people's identity.[2] In the search for 'natural' characteristics of peoples who were to live together within the same state, language, often together with religion, common historical traditions and other symbols, has been identified by intelligentsias in emerging nations as a national distinguishing mark.[3] But Hobsbawm and Lemberg have both acknowledged that a language community can be a consequence as well as a precondition of nation-building.[4]

The fallacy of identifying nations with language groups *per se* has been clearly demonstrated, for example by Sulzbach and Smith.[5] Independently they have pointed out that the possession of a common language by people in different states does not grant them a common nationality, that those who speak the same language within the same state can belong to different nations and that language groupings are not easily separated from each other. Smith has also suggested that the degree of language differences bears little relation to linguistic strife or to nationalism.[6] But Hobsbawm has claimed that language is today put forward by most nationalist movements as a criterion of nationhood and that it is *de facto* the commonest criterion, even though many rival nations, for example in Latin America, share the same language.[7] Certainly the designation and use of 'official' languages in new nation-states of the twentieth century suggests a continuing preoccupation of nationalist movements with language.

Gellner has pointed out the artificial, constructed aspect of nations. He claims that the use of vernacular languages in the growth of literacy encourages nationalism and that decisions have to be made by emerg-

For Notes and References to Chapter 5, see pp. 166–71.

ing nation-states about whether to make the vernacular the vehicle of education, to borrow an existing literary language that may already be in use among more educated groups, to revive a dead language or to use a regional *lingua franca* for this purpose.[8] The first of these choices, made by the Dutch for example, implies that language will have a special place in a nation's identity.

Language then is frequently a nationalistic symbol. It is also a vital medium for relating education and citizenship, which are central to nationalistic purposes and essential for the existence and operation of modern nation-states.

Smith has demonstrated the value of regarding nationalism as a social movement, defining it as 'an organized collection of individuals putting forward demands and pursuing activities designed to promote self-rule, integration (or the other corollaries) for the group which they conceive to constitute the "nation"'.[9] This approach overcomes difficulties presented by one-sided definitions like those which centre on strivings for economic independence, as well as tendencies to shift the discussion from one phenomenon to another, for example from national sentiment to nation-building to characteristics of nations.

What follows here is an attempt to extend our knowledge of the role of language in nationalist movements, including what Weber called 'genetic conditions' and 'consequences', by examining two examples, Switzerland and Canada, which have received only passing attention in previous comparative studies of nationalism.[10] They have usually been cited as evidence against scholars who see nationalism in terms of common culture, ethnicity or language. Multicultural and multilingual nationalisms provide excellent opportunities for studying the interplay of language, political institutions and economic changes which are associated with nationalist developments.[11]

Economic aspects of nationalism were stressed by Znaniecki when he cited the unifying efforts of nationalist leaders who eliminated tariffs and other economic barriers and made products accessible to inhabitants of all parts of the 'nation'.[12] He did not suggest that many of these leaders also obtained considerable economic benefits from these changes. Nor did Hobsbawm, but he noticed the role of liberal capitalism and its stress on the pursuit of self-interest in stimulating the defensive nostalgia for older collectivities which nationalism expressed.[13] Another group of scholars concluded that 'the rise of industry and the growth of national feeling went hand in hand' and saw economic causes of the demand for self-government on the part of Canadian, Australian, New Zealand and South African nationalists reflected in their use of tariff protection in reaction to Britain's free-trade policy to enable them to gain the 'profits and prestige of industrialization'.[14] Smith's observation that nationalism involves the recasting of the competitive ethic on a collective plane, and the search for dignity in terms of wealth and power, is partly a recognition of its close relationship to economic development.[15]

In both the Swiss and Canadian cases the expansion of modern capitalistic enterprise played a major part. Already in the eighteenth century an industrial revolution and the emergence of scientists and technologists accompanied the rise of Swiss nationalism.[16] The establishment of modern Switzerland in 1848 was advocated by many nationalist leaders on the economic grounds that it would facilitate growth, prosperity and internal and external trade. It was accomplished by astute politicians with strong attachments to industrial, commercial and financial circles.[17]

In Canada the link between nationalism and the growth of industrial capitalism can be traced to the aftermath of the war of 1812.[18] And the architects of Confederation in 1867 were political representatives of powerful business interests and many of them reaped benefits, as shareholders and in other economic positions, from the formation and expansion of the new nation-state.[19]

Concerns for the provision of modern school systems also figured prominently in both cases. For many years the Swiss debated proposals for a national university and in the Helvetic period of Napoleonic occupation vain attempts were made to set up a nation-wide school system.[20] The co-presence of French Catholic and English Protestant segments in Canada made proposals for a national education system unlikely, but within the provinces common systems, with provisions for religious minorities, had been built by the mid-nineteenth century.

As far as the influence of economic growth and a preoccupation with education are concerned, the two contexts are similar. It will be shown below that politically and linguistically, however, the Swiss and Canadian nationalist phenomena have taken very different courses.

THE SWISS CASE

Weilenmann has shown how the position of the Swiss Confederates in the German Reich from the fourteenth century onwards led to the replacement of Latin by German in official communications, thus granting them a degree of political liberty by aligning their written and spoken language.[21] Two important agreements, those contained in the *Pfaffenbrief* and the *Sempacherbrief* of the late fourteenth century, were written in German. The Swiss were dependent for the next three centuries on the goodwill of the French kings, and the Eternal Peace of 1516 supported the French position that the German language had become an essential feature of Swiss nationality.[22] In the seventeenth century linguistic ethnocentrism was accentuated by chroniclers who attempted to distinguish the Swiss from their German neighbours by tracing their historical origins. Tschudi even suggested that the Swiss were of Celtic ancestry and that the German-speaking Swiss were originally immigrants from as far away as Scandinavia.[23] Valerius Anshelm observed that the good language of the Confederates was used by them after the Pope, in 1509, had misunderstood a badly translated Latin text. From 1513 onwards even papal communications to the Confederates were in German.[24]

A similar increase in the use of the local language for official communication occurred in the small neighbouring Italian- and French-speaking communities, some of whom, like Geneva, were eventually to join the modern Swiss nation-state.[25] The respect which the old Confederates showed for the alien languages of their colonies, notably Ticino and Vaud, greatly encouraged these regions to join the Confederation as full members in 1803. This situation has been succinctly summarised by Mayer:

> German remained the only official language of the Swiss Confederation down to the end of the eighteenth century. However, around the Confederation proper were grouped from the sixteenth century onwards a number of Alpine valleys, cities and principalities of French, Italian and Romanish speech which were allied with the Confederation by treaties and looked to it for protection. In the course of the centuries the Confederation had also wrested sizeable territories from the houses of Austria, Milan and Savoy, some of which were French- or Italian-speaking. These territories were administered separately or jointly by the Swiss cantons as subject provinces. By their own tradition of localism and particularism the ruling cantons were induced to respect their local autonomy and linguistic diversity. The populations of the subject territories were always allowed to use their own language in the courts and local administrations.[26]

There is, therefore, no evidence of the dominant German-speaking Swiss group attempting to impose its language on others as a means of extending its territorial borders or political control.[27] In the development of ethnic identity, however, the Swiss-German dialects served for most member-states as a significant common cultural bond that united the otherwise loosely knit confederacy, and, as we shall demonstrate, became a central component of the early nationalist ideology.[28] Schwarber, in his summary of pre-eighteenth-century national sentiment, refers to language as a major unifying factor in Swiss culture.[29] But there had been difficulties in Fribourg, the only member-state that was not entirely German-speaking.

The admission of Fribourg into the Confederation in 1481 marked a crucial point in Swiss history. For the first time a fully-fledged member of the alliance was an area where an alien language was in extensive use. Fribourg entered the Confederation by choice, a curious decision for those who would maintain that language is a basis for national consciousness, since its leaders preferred to join the Swiss alliance rather than accept a subordinate relationship, despite a common language, with Savoy.[30] On the Confederates' side much reluctance was expressed about the possibility of admitting Fribourg, partly because of the difference of language. But when its soldiers chose to fight for the Swiss in their war against Burgundy, its acceptability was greatly enhanced.[31] After entry, the ruling groups of Fribourg immediately embarked upon a process of Germanisation, employed a town clerk (*Ratschreiber*) and a city school principal who were German-speaking. Preaching in the cathedral was in German from 1481 to 1511. Other measures taken included the closing of French schools in the city.[32] Members of the nobility began to use the language of the Confederates and some changed their French names into German ones. Only when a reaction set in around the middle of the sixteenth century were both French and German retained. It is noteworthy that these efforts at Germanisation were not initiated by the Confederates but were merely an attempt on the part of the ruling groups in Fribourg to conform to the norm in the hope of gaining fuller acceptance.

At the outset of the eighteenth century the Swiss-German dialects of nearly all the cantons were fully developed. German was used as the official language of the *Tagsatzung*.[33] French-speakers predominated among the patrician class in most of Fribourg and all of Vaud which since 1536 had been a colony of Bern. Italian was spoken in the Southern colonies of the Confederacy and parts of Grisons, which was still one of its associates (*Zugewandte Orte*). Although Switzerland was still a long way from becoming a unified nation-state, there were no problems regarding languages.

In the rhetoric and ideology of the eighteenth-century nationalist movement, Swiss-German dialects were stressed to distinguish the Swiss from the Germans. Efforts were made to try to elevate them into a national language, as had been done in Holland.[34] Bodmer, the leading Swiss nationalist intellectual at this time, engaged in prolonged debate with the Leipzig scholar Gottsched about the distinctiveness of Swiss-German. He stressed that it was the language of all social strata, not just of a cultured and influential élite. It bound all inhabitants of the nation together and put them, at least in this respect, on an equal footing.[35]

But language was only one of several elements in early Swiss nationalism. Other expressions of it included the use of traditional folk costumes, the establishment and care of national monuments, the holding of fairs and dances. A national education system was advocated and Balthasar called for a teachers' seminary where national sentiments would be cultivated.

The study of Swiss history as a search for virtues and moral lessons was encouraged by Bodmer but it was Johannes von Müller with his *History of the Swiss Confederacy* who made the greatest impact in this area. He was deeply influenced by Montesquieu's stress on the ethical roots of republican political systems, which he applied to his own account of the development of Switzerland.

Political reforms, including the abolition of subject territories and the granting of voting rights to the people, a system of proportional representation of cantons according to population size and the respect of citizens' rights in a 'firmly articulated state of democratic character' were also part of the ideology. Although many nationalists wanted to expand the powers of the *Tagsatzung* to bring about a centralised government, others thought the loosely allied Confederacy would remain basically sound if the virtues of citizenship could be cultivated and the powers of the *Tagsatzung* extended to include foreign politics and a firmer control of defence. The growth of a bourgeois ethicalism which stresses respectability and responsibility in communal affairs has frequently been associated with nationalistic movements.

Another key feature of this early Swiss nationalism was its opposition to foreign, that is French, corruption of the Swiss nation. French manners and customs, ranging from linguistic expressions to the aristocratic finery of balls, music, luxurious costumes and elaborate forms of transportation, were contrasted with the earthy, rural Swiss alpine heritage.

Various organisations and publications became the vehicle for the spread of this ideology. An intelligentsia of academics, lawyers, physicians and scientists who had travelled and been educated abroad, published books and pamphlets and made speeches. Many of them helped establish the Helvetic Society in 1761 to foster patriotism and the ethics of good citizenship. It became the organised core of the nationalist movement.

These eighteenth-century ideological and reformist developments in Switzerland were similar to those occurring elsewhere in Europe. Part of the optimistic and future-orientated ideal of progress, they were interpretations of social change that led to direct intervention in the flow of economic, social and political events.[36]

The linguistic diversity of modern Switzerland is directly traceable to the Napoleonic invasion of 1798 and the choice on the part of both French- and Italian-speaking colonies of the old Confederation to remain within the Swiss alliance.[37] A few years earlier an independence movement within the Bernese colony of Vaud resulted in the proclamation of a new Republic of the Léman. But its leaders, especially La Harpe, were intent on retaining Vaudois independence by implementing the ideals of the French Revolution within the Swiss political

system.[38] Their hopes were embodied in the liberating intentions behind the arrival of Napoleonic troops, and the French-speaking regions
eventually became or joined others as equal partners in the Confederation, much to the chagrin of many Bernese aristocrats and other
political leaders.

At the same time, the Italian-speaking people of Ticino also demonstrated that nationalism can transcend barriers of language and physical geography by opting, in certain districts by a plebiscite, not to join
their Italian kinsfolk. They, too, preferred independence within the
Swiss alliance, despite the subject status they had previously held in it.[39]
Consequently, the constitution of the Helvetic republic gave equal
rights to all three languages. Frei has claimed that this was more the result of practical exigencies of communication than an attempt to implement principles of inter-cultural understanding or the solution of the
problem of minorities.[40] It was opposed by some, and attempts were
made by both German- and French-speakers to have their language
designated as official. But there were a few members of the legislative
assembly who saw multilingualism, and the cultural exchanges it
afforded, as a value in itself.[41]

The ideals of the French Revolution regarding equality of citizens
were embodied in the Helvetic constitution. There was a requirement
for all official government reports, agenda, minutes and so forth to be
printed in German and French. Italian was included later.[42] According
to Weilenmann the educated executive, the Directorate, conducted its
business in French but many of the elected popular representatives in
the legislative assemblies could communicate only in their German dialects. The inviability of the Helvetic constitution was partly due to the
impact of multilingualism on representatives of conservative central
cantons who saw threats to their independence in a unified state in
which French-speaking areas would have considerable power. It took a
further half-century to bring about such a state and to subdue their
stubborn demands.

But an important outcome of the period of Napoleonic occupation
was that the cantons secured the right to preserve the languages spoken
within their boundaries. Four of them – Aargau, Thurgau, Ticino and
Vaud – had secured their independence after 1798. Another new
canton, Grisons, included three linguistic communities, German, Italian and Romansch. With only three cantons, two of them French-
speaking and one mixed French and German, to be added by the Congress of Vienna in 1815, the base of the polyethnic nation-state had
been firmly laid.

The Helvetic period led to the entrenchment within large sections of
the country of the ideals of modern republican democracy and,
although these did not eventuate in a modern nation-state for another
fifty years, their proponents initiated a programme for developing

Swiss national consciousness, thereby carrying the nationalist movement forward into the nineteenth century.[43]

Frei has shown how this was based, not on concepts of language, culture or ethnicity, which neighbouring peoples stressed, but on the concept of political community, which was projected back into the Confederation's history and related to a land whose natural beauty and diversity were unique.[44] An elaborate national propaganda was used to try to realise the wish for unity.[45] Cantonal particularism was condemned as egoism, an obstacle to national unity. Federalism was attacked and centralisation defended. Patriotism was hailed as a Christian duty, and according to Zschokke only a unified state could make for the spiritual happiness of all citizens. Concepts of national rebirth were used to portray contemporary developments as revivals of the Confederation's late medieval battles for freedom and political autonomy.[46]

The Helvetic government, mainly through its Minister of Education, Stapfer, and his 'Office for National Culture' had tried to evolve a nation-wide programme of national education. Magazines and pamphlets appeared, among them the *Helvetische Volksblatt* which Pestalozzi edited and Zschokke's *Schweizer Boten*, both of which included many exhortations to national unity and attempted to inculcate national pride in the less educated people.[47]

The Mediation of 1803 was a federalist compromise which enabled the cantons to preserve their autonomy. The attempts to develop a nationalistic consciousness and a national unity had been unsuccessful. But the spirit and ideology of the nationalist movement were carried forward into the Mediation period and beyond by people like Pestalozzi, Zschokke, La Harpe and Usteri. The Helvetic Society began to flourish again and attracted many republican liberals who were to take part in the movement towards the modern nation-state in 1848. Public education systems began to emphasise national history. The question of a national university became a burning one. All these developments can be traced clearly from the mid-eighteenth century onwards.

Although attempts in the constitutional proposals of 1803 and 1815 to make German the national language were not officially approved, it did effectively become the official language of the Swiss *Tagsatzung* and central authorities, except that representatives of Ticino used French. But communications with individual member-cantons were in their own official language. Of the linguistically mixed cantons, only Valais, which joined the Confederation in 1815, retained both French and German for official purposes, the others, including Fribourg after 1815, preferring German.[48] Weilenmann has stressed that the people generally were unaffected by these developments since court proceedings and local official matters were conducted in the local languages. Although there is evidence here of a reassertion of Swiss-German ethnicity, the preservation of territorial linguistic rights in the cantons, their enjoyment of political autonomy within the Confederation and the admissibility of the use of French when necessary all guaranteed that linguistic tensions would not prevent the survival of the Confederation. Weilenmann has claimed that there were no protests against the reinstatement of German from the French-Swiss areas.

The surge to the establishment of the modern Swiss nation-state in 1848 was marked by a number of significant developments. The election of liberal governments in ten cantons at the outset of the 1830s and the approval of new cantonal constitutions were vital turning-points. These events and, according to Rappard, the French July Revolution, led to a strengthening of national sentiment.[49] Already in 1833 there was an abortive attempt to get a constitutional revision of the Pact of 1815 approved. By the time they eventually secured a majority in the *Tagsatzung* in 1847, the Liberal leaders of the nationalist movement were ready to push through centralising political reforms.[50] They only managed to do so, however, after the army of the *Tagsatzung* defeated the Sonderbund alliance which the conservative Catholic cantons had formed in the hope of receiving foreign assistance from certain European powers. But the revolutions which several of the latter were experiencing prevented them from reacting.

The Pact of 1815 and the rejected proposals of 1833 were studied by a committee that included representatives of all cantons, although one or two from defeated Sonderbund cantons missed all but the last couple of meetings.[51] It is noteworthy how the victorious liberals, although they assigned governors to each of the defeated cantons to try to persuade their leaders and people to accept the idea of a centralised state, granted them full participatory rights in the constitutional deliberations. The new constitution received a 70 per cent majority when voted upon by all enfranchised Swiss, and $15\frac{1}{2}$ of the 22 cantons approved it. Although it was 1891 before the first Catholic conservative was elected to the seven-member executive Federal Council, all cantons reconciled themselves to acceptance of their position in the modern Swiss nation-state. The Council of States (*Ständerat*), where each canton whatever its size or population has two seats, was a concession to cantonal autonomy. It is the Swiss version of the United States Senate and its adoption was facilitated because certain prominent Swiss Liberal leaders, notably the lawyer Rüttimann, had visited the United States and perceived it to be a convenient way of accomplishing federation. All legislation has to be approved by the Council of States and by the National Council (*Nationalrat*), a body of popularly elected representatives from throughout the entire nation. These two assemblies combine to elect the executive seven-member Federal Council which may include no more than one member from a given canton.

The nationalist ideology that was developed after 1830 stressed national unity despite cultural, religious and linguistic diversity.[52] A nation based on the will of the people (*Willensnation*) was called for. Comparisons were made with France, Italy and Germany, all of which were striving towards unity during this period but none of which, despite the position of Alsace and the linguistic diversity within Italy, were as culturally heterogeneous as the Swiss. But Switzerland was a small nation with a long history of independence and the respect for territorial rights expressed in the policy of neutrality. It did not aspire to heights of political and military power. One of its deepest impulses has been to oppose power, except that which was necessary for self-defence.[53]

The report of the first committee to study revisions of the 1815 Pact included a statement about the national identity. It claimed that the Swiss were recognised by others as a nation, that their history, their flag, their troops, the feelings of belonging together and the bonds of brotherhood made them distinctive. Franscini referred to monuments and memories of battles, to culture heroes like Tell, Winkelried and Waldmann as symbols of Swiss nationality.[54] Switzerland was the federal country *par excellence*. He also claimed that the hand of Providence was working for Switzerland.[55] Ochsenbein, as President of the last *Tagsatzung*, spoke along similar lines to that body after the Sonderbund War, when he made a strong plea for the practical solution of problems of national unity and cantonal independence.[56] The more radical aspects of this national ideology were upheld by people like Troxler, who stressed the nation as an expression of popular sovereignty.[57]

One of the best-known Swiss authors of the period, Gottfried Keller, who associated frequently with leaders of the Liberal movement, claimed that the will and spirit to become a nation were more important than blood relationships and language.[58] The association of the ideals of freedom with the Alps was made. It was part of the legendary attitude towards the independent outlook of the early cantons (*Urkantone*), all of which were opposed to national unification at this time. They had all joined the Sonderbund and strongly resisted centralisation. That they eventually took their position in the new federal state was due to the efforts of those like Bluntschli who argued in writings and public speeches that the new federal constitution with its bicameral system would protect a common Swiss nationality as well as local cantonal independence.[59]

Among the vehicles on which this national ideology was carried was the press, which Hunziker has shown to have been used by intellectual leaders of the nationalist movement to disseminate their reformist ideals.[60] Many societies and unions, including the

New Helvetic Society which carried on the activities of its eighteenth-century predecessor, were formed for nationalistic purposes.[61] In 1835 Troxler helped found the National Society which sought to defend the rights of a free nation and to bring about its genuine federation by means of a popularly elected assembly, a free press and political equality.[62]

Language played no part in the controversies leading up to 1848. There were some minor disagreements in this field in Valais and Fribourg, but they were resolved amicably after the middle of the century. The decision to adopt three official languages at the Federal level was taken without dissent. By that time the non-German-speaking members of the Liberal movement had become very powerful, and a nationalism which stressed German at the expense of the other languages might have led to external interference to protect the minorities.

In the 1874 constitutional revision, representation of all three languages among members of the supreme Federal Court was stipulated. Already the informal practice of having at least two and frequently three non-German-speaking representatives on the Federal Council had begun. It continues today. Since 1848 one-third of its members have been in this category.[63] Although Italian has been rarely used in parliamentary debate, practical reasons having made it and the Federal Civil Service effectively bilingual, all approved legislation and all Federal communications to Italian-speaking areas and individuals are written in that language.[64] The Swiss army is almost entirely composed of linguistically homogeneous groups.

The fourth language, Romansch, which is spoken in three separated parts of the canton of Grisons, is anomalous. There were protests from leaders of these communities as early as the 1890s about the possibility of Romansch dying out as a result of infiltration by German-speakers. When it was made a national, as distinct from an official, language in 1938, and thenceforth received Federal financial support for its preservation, essentially nationalist forces were at work. Strengthening the multicultural diversity of Switzerland was a means of thwarting the threats to Swiss independence of the German and Italian Nazi regimes and of increasing the determination of the Swiss people to resist. Suggestions in the 1930s that Swiss-German should be elevated to national language status were also part of this nationalistic upsurge.[65] Concern still exists on the part of the Romansch communities, nearly all of whose members combine use of their native tongue with German or Italian, that the Romansch culture and language are in danger of being overwhelmed. Similar anxiety is expressed by Italian-speakers of Ticino.

The dialects of Swiss-German, which are used in informal everyday work, family and leisure contexts, and which are clearly a very important component of the national and cultural identity of many Swiss, have enabled them to barricade themselves against excessive German influences. German itself, used for nearly all reading and writing, and certainly all educational and official purposes, is not their mother-tongue but a language they learn in school and, according to Lüthy, one with which the majority of German-Swiss do not feel entirely comfortable.[66] It is also worth noting that many French-speaking Swiss have recognised that the preservation of Swiss-German dialects has been a guarantee of protection against Germanisation.[67]

Apart from the Swiss-German dialects, there has never been a way in which one language could become a national symbol since the three official languages were shared with larger neighbours. The preservation of political independence, of peculiar types of local, particularistic communal culture (of which the Swiss-German dialects themselves are a prime example) and a long-standing tradition of broad participation in political decision-making – a kind of democratic decentralisation – have been more significant symbols of Swiss nationalism than language. Schmid has described the Swiss nationality as the interweaving of cultural objects and subjective feeling into a consciousness condition, reflecting a deep, complex relationship between political and cultural actualities.[68] In Switzerland, liberty has included the right of large and small regions of the country to be linguistically and culturally different, as well as the franchise, legal protection and freedom of economic transactions. That the sexual restriction on voting persisted so long reflected, in a different way, the same, strong conservative streak in Swiss culture that is embodied in the integration of local communities. In his account of Swiss nationalism, Schmid refers to the small circle (*Der Kleine Kreis*) which lies at the basis of cultural and political organisation and is reflected in concepts like *Hof, Gemeinde, Talschaft, Kanton* and *Sprachgemeinschaft*.[69] It is decentralisation in the sense that larger and higher forms of political organisation are believed to be dependent on the sound operation of smaller ones. The adage '*Im Hause muss beginnen was leuchten soll im Vaterland*,'[70] which the peasant writer Jeremias Gotthelf developed, and which has become part of the lore of many German-speaking Swiss, is a good example of this point. The respect of the Swiss for decentralised particularism explains partly why they look disdainfully at colonising peoples and take pride in their country's neutrality.

But the linguistic and national stability associated with Switzerland has one major point of tension. The Jura situation is one where a Catholic, French-speaking, minority occupies economically under-developed rural districts within a region where the Protestant, German-speaking majority of an industrial area carries greater economic and political weight.[71] In 1815 the Jura region was placed in the canton of Bern by the Congress of Vienna, partly as compensation for its loss of what are now the cantons of Aargau and Vaud. Although

Bern recognised French as a second official language as early as 1830, and places were later reserved for two Jurassiens on the cantonal executive, there were those who already wanted a separate Jura canton. Catholic–Protestant rivalries, particularly during the *Kulturkampf*, heightened dissension.

In the early twentieth century a language problem developed with a large influx of German-speakers to the Northern Jura, where the French Catholic minority is located, and tensions worsened during and after the two World Wars. Bern made concessions in 1950 by legalising the two Jura seats on the cantonal executive, making French the official language of nearly all the Jura districts and permitting the Jura flag to be flown alongside that of Bern. Demands for a separate canton were growing, however, and led in 1959 to an unsuccessful canton-wide referendum on the subject of separation. In the three northernmost French-speaking Jura districts there was a large majority in favour. After guerrilla bombings and other protests in the early 1960s, further heated discussion ensued and a plebiscite on separation, held among voters in all seven Jura districts in 1968, was defeated. But in June 1974 a majority voted in favour and the Swiss weekly, *Die Weltwoche*, hailed this vote, which will create a new canton out of the French-speaking Northern Jura districts, as a lesson in Swiss federalism. The Southern Jura districts have voted (March 1975) in favour of remaining in the canton of Bern. Although it looks as if a major barrier to permanent linguistic and political stability in Switzerland will soon be removed, the Jura separatists have said that they will not rest until they have won over the Southern Jura districts to their cause. Whatever the outcome, from the standpoint of the Swiss political authorities and most of the Swiss people, the process whereby the Jura question is being gradually resolved illustrates the strength of their national political culture. By means of plebiscitarian voting, the Swiss people take important decisions directly, even when they may result in significant changes in the composition of the nation. On the other hand, from the viewpoint of the Jurassiens it has been unfortunate that peaceful democratic settlement came only after drastic steps had to be taken to demonstrate the seriousness of the problem and the strength of independentist attachment to the concept of the Jura as a distinctive cultural entity.

The French language is an important component of this concept of Jurassien sub-nationalism. As Mayer has pointed out, 'it is the French character of the Jura which is stressed predominantly in the separatist propaganda as contrasted to the German character of the old parts of the canton' (that is, Bern).[72] He stressed the relations between the Jurassien movement and the internationally active *Ethnie française*, which incidentally has had an influence on Quebec. For Mayer 'such intense, self-consciously nationalistic conceptions' which the Jurassiens use to attract support are 'entirely untypical of Swiss traditions'.[73]

It is certainly true that since 1798 there have been no other movements for the establishment of new cantons or for cantonal independence. But the Vaudois liberation movements of the eighteenth century were similar to the Jura ones in several respects. The demands for political autonomy and for freedom from Bernese domination were the most prominent. Others were the use of local cultural symbols like language, flags and patriotic songs. Since Vaud was not religiously different from Bern, Catholic–Protestant antagonisms were absent.

Yet Mayer's comment on typical Swiss traditions, as distinct from the tensions and struggles that accompanied the emergence of the modern Swiss nation-state, has validity. It is not contradicted by the current move towards Jura autonomy within the Confederation. This process itself indicates that the Confederation of Switzerland is still evolving and that its multilingual nature is not threatened by the recalcitrant demands of one segment.

Although the traditional political culture and neutrality of Switzerland have been more central features of its nationalism, the Swiss take pride in the admiration that they receive from others for their capacity to accommodate four linguistic groups with equal rights within a stable democracy. Writers like Zinsli have stressed the idea of the 'multilingual homeland' and its tolerance of linguistic particularism as examples to Europe and the world.[74]

THE CANADIAN CASE

There are four aspects of the situation of Canadian nationalism that make it quite different from the Swiss experience. Canada is a product of British imperialism and, partly for this reason, has experienced considerable difficulty in asserting its independence – culturally, politically and economically. It is also dualistic. The relationship between Quebec and English Canada has been a tense one for over two hundred years and remains the central problem of Canadian history.[75] A third element is that the position of the United States in relation to Canada has been altogether more powerful than that of Switzerland's neighbours in relation to it. Finally there are the Canadian native peoples: Nationalism in Canada has always had to confront these four conditions. The last one has been completely ignored.

The relationship between language and nationalism in Canada is also complicated by the coexistence of several types of nationalism and by the changing attitudes of the English towards the French throughout Canadian history, seen in terms of legal pronouncements and regulations as well as the actual social and economic position of these two linguistic groups.

After the conquest of New France in 1760 the British government

first considered a policy of anglicisation for Quebec but this was
deemed impractical by its administrators in Canada. French culture
was too firmly entrenched in the local population and this was recognised by granting them rights to their legal system and Catholic religion. All proclamations and ordinances were published in both
French and English, although neither had been in any way designated
'official'.[76]

Ambitions for the assimilation of the Canadians continued to be
held, however, and even some of their own leaders saw the adoption of
the English language as 'the sole means to banish the antipathy and
suspicion which the diversity will maintain between two peoples'.[77] But
bilingualism was recognised in fact in the Parliament of Lower Canada
in 1792, although it was not to gain full legal status until 1867. This did
not prevent further efforts at anglicisation: for example, Governor
Craig in the first decade of the nineteenth century accused French-
Canadian leaders of trying to define Quebec as a separate nation and to
impede 'the Establishment of a Canadian nation'.[78]

More than thirty years later, in the aftermath of Lord Durham's
missionary efforts to resolve the problems of Canadian dualism,
English was proclaimed the official language of the new Parliament of
the united provinces of Upper and Lower Canada. But the goals of the
badly informed and ethnocentric metropolis were again frustrated by
practical political problems, and motions, minutes and private bills
were all required to be presented in both languages. For the twenty
years prior to Confederation the Parliament was bilingual.

With regard to language the British North America Act, the major
written part of the Canadian Constitution, is virtually silent. Compared to religion and education, language was never an important issue
for the nationalist movement of the time. The Act says that English or
French may be used in the debates of the Federal Parliament, the
Legislature of Quebec and before any Court of Canada or Quebec. The
Acts of the Canadian and Quebec Parliaments must be printed in both
languages. The recent Royal Commission on Bilingualism and Biculturalism has rightly observed that, at best, this 'represents embryonic
concepts of cultural equality'.[79] It goes on to point out that Belgium,
Finland, South Africa and Switzerland have established a more fundamental principle of equality than the British North America Act. A
leading Canadian historian has said that there was 'nothing in the
British North America Act that remotely approached a declaration of
principle that Canada was to be a bilingual and bicultural nation'.[80]
The greater significance attached to religion was expressed in the provisions within the Act for Protestant and Catholic minorities within the
four provinces at the time of Confederation to preserve their own de-
nominational schools. Except for the English in Quebec no such provisions were made for linguistic minorities.

The nationalistic proclamations at that time did not stress Canada's bilingual structure as a major feature of the Canadian nationality. Compared with the British connection as embodied in Parliament and the monarchy, it was insignificant. The deliberations of the Charlottetown and Quebec conferences from which the opposition in Lower Canada was excluded were carried on in English.[81]

As Ryerson suggests, the absence of any declaration of principle that Canada was to be a bilingual or bicultural nation gave grounds for 'suspicion in French Canada that the "federalism" was somehow strangely flawed'.[82] Macdonald's statement that the 'nationality' of Lower Canada should be respected was at best only partially embodied in Confederation. Ryerson's succinct comment that its historical reality lies in the fact that it was 'the joint work of the dominant Anglo-Canadian bourgeoisie, its French-Canadian subordinates and the semi-feudal church' is very much to the point. Its authors 'evaded the binational reality'.[83]

But this reality did not take long to reassert itself. The Quebec Parti National was formed 'to protest against denial of full recognition of the national character of French Canada'.[84] The rebellions in the Northwest led to an Act establishing the province of Manitoba in 1870 in which French language rights were upheld. The rebel leader, Louis Riel, became a patriotic hero in Quebec.[85] Mercier, later Premier of that province, lauded him as a victim of fanaticism and treason. For the present study he stands as a tragic reminder of the triumph of English-Canadian imperialistic nationalism and of the cultural devastation heaped upon the native peoples. They and others were considered unfit to become citizens of a new nation whose leaders and their supporters arrogantly assumed themselves to be products of the most advanced level of human civilisation.

For, despite the ideals of ethnic co-operation and understanding that Cartier and others had expressed at the time of Confederation, a nationalism emerged which stressed the identity of Canada within the British Empire. Beginning with the 'Canada First' movement in 1868 it can be traced down to the First World War and is even present among conservatives in Canada today.[86] It was patronising to all non-British elements of the population and drew upon Social Darwinism and theories of racial superiority to justify the mission of the British to develop and civilise the Canadian nation.

In order for Quebec to continue within the Canadian Federation, it chose to maximise its provincial rights and powers, and it has been assisted in this respect by the rulings of the Privy Council in London in upholding those rights at the expense of the Federal government.[87] Successive Premiers of Quebec have advocated the pursuit of 'nationalist' objectives within the provincial context. But the strengthening of provincial autonomy alone was not enough to hold the country together and it has taken much ingenuity on the part of successive Federal governments, mostly Liberal, to manage the national social system of Canada to its present stage. From Confederation onwards, French-speaking Canadians have received heavy representation within Federal Cabinets. The office of Speaker in the House of Commons alternates between French- and English-speakers. Positions like those of Governor-General and Prime Minister have not been dominated by anglophones. Federal legislation has been carefully calculated not to alienate support for the Federal system in Quebec. Organised separatism has not gained a foothold there among federal parties. All of these developments have been helped by national economic growth and increasing prosperity in a North American context where growing consumption opportunities have developed into the central political and economic goal.

But Quebec has never been without strong movements of protest and opposition to British domination and the federal system. The crises surrounding conscription in the two World Wars and the youthful Laurentian movements in the 1930s were noteworthy predecessors of the current nationalist separatist movement.[88] The social, economic and educational reforms initiated by the Liberal provincial government in 1960 led to the formation of the several nationalist parties, including militant F.L.Q. movements, the latest of which became the centre of controversy in the October 1970 crisis. In order to deal with this, the Federal government of Prime Minister Trudeau used the War Measures Act and strong police tactics.[89]

Despite obtaining 30 per cent of the popular vote in the most recent provincial election (compared to 23 per cent in 1970) the socialistically inclined separatist Parti Québecois receives only half-a-dozen seats in an assembly of 110 because of the way seats are distributed. It has emerged to a position of single opposition party to the powerful and ingenious Liberal government. One interesting feature of the Parti Québecois is that it appears directly to reflect protest against real or imagined restricted occupational mobility, in line with Smith's interpretation of nationalist movements.[90]

In 1974 the Quebec legislature passed Bill 22 and made French the official language of Quebec. In its preamble it describes French as 'a national heritage which the body politic is in duty bound to preserve'. A major change is the insistence that it become the 'language of labour relations'. For many years the anglophone (that is the British, English-Canadian and American) control of industry has meant that many workers in Quebec have been forced to use English to communicate with their superiors. Bill 22 has produced a storm of protest in the rest of Canada where English has as a matter of course been the only effective official language. Controversy rages in Quebec because of threats to the education rights of the English minority which has in recent years been augmented by immigrants from neither French- nor English-speaking countries who have chosen to join the English-speaking community. Federal law will protect these minorities, but future immigrants will find it difficult to avoid learning French.

The move is clearly a gesture to pacify separatist claims. It may produce an exodus of a large portion of the English minority. The separatist organisations strongly oppose it on the grounds that it does not go far enough and is aimed at keeping Quebec within Federal Canada.

The history of language rights in provinces outside of Quebec illustrates other typically Canadian problems and tensions. In Manitoba, for example, in spite of the educational protections afforded in the founding legislation of 1870, separate (Catholic and French) schools were abolished in 1890 in the aftermath of the Riel controversies and as an assertion of provincial educational rights over those of minorities. Tc the consternation of many people in Quebec, the then Prime Minister, Laurier, refused to intervene. The province of Ontario placed severe limitations on the use of French in schools in 1912, while New Brunswick, despite having over one-third of its population whose mother tongue is French, did not recognise French as an official language of the province until 1969. Although there have traditionally been French-speaking schools and since 1963 a French-speaking university, French was not regularly used in the courts of that province until very recently, and although the provincial legislature is formally bilingual, English continues to be the language of debate.

In the past decade or so the bilingual and bicultural nature of Canada has been a matter for considerable public discussion. The Royal Commission set up to investigate this situation produced a number of reports and research studies. It led directly to the Official Languages Act of 1969 which provided for bilingual notices, signs and communications in all departments and nation-wide branches of the Federal government and the establishment of bilingual districts where a minority of 10 per cent of the population speak one of the official languages. The Royal Commission also led to a programme of bilingual education being introduced into the Federal Civil Service – with consequent difficulties for many middle-aged anglophones. For even in 1962 the Glassco Royal Commission on Government organisation pointed out that the Federal Civil Service was mainly staffed by unilingual anglophones and that French-speakers were frequently obliged to use English when communicating with the Federal government.[91] But since the Bilingualism and Bicultural Commission's activity the proportion of newly hired civil servants who are bilingual has increased considerably and there is currently talk of awarding higher salaries to bilinguals. In Ontario and throughout the rest of Canada increasing numbers of people are learning French and reflecting concern to develop a genuinely bilingual state.

The Federal government has also embarked on a policy of multiculturalism according to which ethnic and immigrant communities are encouraged to apply for financial support to develop their culture and an appreciation of their history in Canada. But bilingual and multicultural policies have little appeal for Quebec nationalists.

What Jones has called the Quebec 'minority complex' could only be alleviated within the present Federal system not only by the development of a more positive national consensus, but also by a genuine willingness on the part of the dominant political authorities to face the issues seriously and negotiate in good faith. But the type of nationalistic ideology which has dominated the Anglo-Canadian majority has made it difficult for it to view minorities as having rights to cultural distinctiveness and preservation or to full and meaningful participation in all levels of economic and political decision-making that concern them. Even a Canadian nationalism which is confined to the two charter groups, the French and the English, whom Professor John Porter – in one of the most remarkable and revealing slips of the tongue ever made by a sociologist[92] – once described as having occupied 'previously unpopulated territory', may not guarantee national unity and stability.

Ossenberg has optimistically argued that 'the common goal of repatriating Canada's economy and culture overshadows the traditional sources of disintegration', and that most regions of Canada are becoming increasingly aware of their hinterland economic relationship to the United States.[93] Yet he asserts that there has not been a period since Confederation when pan-Canadianism has reached its present level. He may be justified in making such an observation with regard to Ontario. But in other parts of the country, notably in Alberta, British Columbia and the Maritime provinces, there are deep regional sentiments that become accentuated with the discovery of rich local oil and natural gas reserves, or by what are seen as large concessions to the province of Quebec – which they incorrectly but stubbornly perceive as merely a province like the other nine. Canadians are very much aware that separation on Quebec's part could mean the beginning of total national disintegration.

The situation of Canadian aboriginal people remains uncertain. Although he acknowledged the problems for national integration in New Zealand presented by the Maori people, Akzin's reference to the Canadian native people as 'remnants of the original inhabitants' reflects a certain lack of familiarity and empathy with the Canadian situation. Not only do these peoples have the highest population growth rates, but their demands for aboriginal rights to expropriated land have become stronger as the discovery of rich natural resources in Northern Canada and elsewhere proceeds apace. They have well-organised political representation and are developing concepts of nationalism in which language figures prominently. The probability of violent turmoil over these issues in the next five years is high. It is one of the bitter fruits of colonial expansionism and imperialistic nationalism. Despite the liberal and egalitarian rhetoric of modern Canadian nationalism, the social and ethnic inequities in Canada persist. It will require considerable redistribution of land and resources before the aims of native peoples are satisfied.

In advocating the abolition of the Indian Act in its 1969 White Paper, the Federal government was attempting to extend full citizenship rights to all Canadian people, hoping thereby to complete the membership of the Canadian nation.[94] The abrupt negative reaction which it received from Indian political leaders came as a shock. Extending rights and duties of citizenship, admitting native people to full participation in the Canadian political and economic culture, looked like a further series of paternalistic concessions to people who had been given child-like status by nineteenth-century Canadian nationalists. They demand more than the extension of 'civilised' rights and duties, having suffered economic misery and cultural devastation while non-native Canada has prospered. The confrontation reminds one of what Marshall has called the war between 'twentieth century citizenship and the capitalist class system'[95] and Carstens has analysed the 'Indian question' as a conflict between deprived and privileged classes.[96] The political consciousness of Canadian native peoples is both that of a proletariat and of a sub-nationalist movement. Completion of the growth of the Canadian nation can only occur when it is taken seriously and they are given a place of dignity and recognition as partners in the national experiment. Until they are able to secure not merely citizenship, voting and legal rights but also a fair economic stake in the land, resources and wealth of Canada, their protests and demands will grow more vociferous and they will resort to guerrilla action to make themselves heard. Canadians may eventually have to recognise that their country consists of several, not merely two, nations in a single state. One possibility is the recognition of aboriginal languages as 'national' in a way that parallels the position of Romansch in Switzerland.

In his discussion of multicultural nation-states Watts has said that 'the development of a federal political framework which provides significant cultural minorities with an enduring sense of security for their distinctiveness, and which, at the same time, continues to generate a sense of community among all its diverse groups' is necessary for equilibrium.[97] The interests of a single provincial or cultural group must not dominate the political or economic process. In Canada the unresolved problems of the native peoples and of Quebec suggest that this equilibrium has not been reached. This is partly due to the failure of Canadian nationalism to develop that 'positive consensus' to which Watts refers, as well as the dominance of Quebec by anglophone, and of the aboriginal peoples by non-native, economic and political interests.

Canada's economic, political and cultural relationships with the U.S. economy and government cast a big shadow over these internal tensions. Contemporary nationalist groups like the Committee for an Independent Canada and the leftist Waffle wing of the New Democratic Party aim, in different ways, for independence.[98] Even the Federal government has recently shown signs of being eager to take a more independent line towards the powerful neighbour to the South. But given the system of world capitalism in which these states are deeply interlocked, and the expectations that most North American people have about retaining a high material standard of living, any serious reduction in dependency seems improbable.

The growth of multinational corporations which transcend the legal boundaries of modern states and, operating on a kind of neutral, international ground, control the lives of millions of people, make goals of national independence seem peculiar. Unless widespread disaffection with the international capitalist system sets in, its oligopolistic tendencies will strengthen these corporations. Something more than just nationalism may be necessary to control their influence.

CONCLUSION

In conclusion, while the economic contexts of these two nationalisms show remarkable similarities, their political and linguistic situations were quite different and have had contrasting consequences. Akzin was unjustified in viewing the situations of Swiss and Canadian pluralism in the same light.[99] The vast majority of French-speaking Canadians live in one province and the political symbols of Canadian nationhood reflected and fostered a type of imperialistic nationalism that was developed by people who sought to maintain a Canada that was essentially British. (The only alternative they thought possible was annexation by the United States.) Consequently, in Quebec the English-speaking minority has rights that are not extended to linguistic minorities in other provinces. This situation, as well as anglophone control of most of Quebec's economy, and the persisting economic deprivation of the native peoples, has resulted in Canada's being, as Akzin has put it, 'farther on the road to polarization, with fairly dangerous consequences for the overall unity of the State'[100] than Switzerland.

There has really been only one kind of Swiss nationalism. In Canada there have been several, and the ethnic nationalism of Quebec is opposed to the territorial one of federated Canada.[101] So far the latter has not been able to define itself in such a way as to satisfy the goals of the former, as well as those of the native peoples. Unless it can, the federated state of Canada will remain precarious.

In the Swiss case there was an old and distinctive political, and a younger multilingual, tradition for nationalism to draw on. Swiss national unification was possible because the particular identities of regions, cantons and significant linguistic groups were preserved. The dominant language group had at no time tried to impose itself on the minorities. Politically it was never a strongly united group. Although religion divided the Liberal and Conservative factions at the time of the Sonderbund, and later threatened to do so again during the *Kulturkampf* years, it proved not to be divisive except for the Jura situation, mainly because it cut across regional and linguistic boundaries.[102]

But the greater stability of the Swiss system, and its current flexibility with regard to the Jura problem, owes much to the capacity of its bourgeois leaders to implement many of the Enlightenment goals of equality and human rights, at least as far as ethnic communities are concerned.[103] It has also developed an efficient and respected multilingual civil service that facilitates communications between the state and its citizens with few language difficulties. The institutions of the popular referendum and the initiative, as well as the policy of external neutrality, have also minimised tensions.

Federal nation-states by their very nature are prone to tensions. These tensions are more acute in those multilingual contexts where wealth, property, living standards and political rights are unevenly distributed among the component groups. In both cases examined here there is unevenness. But this is less in Switzerland than in Canada, and the ultimate integration of the Jura into the system is closer than that of Quebec and the native peoples in Canada. Compared to that of Quebec, the Jura question has never really been a threat to the survival of the Swiss nation-state and neither are the fears of Germanisation held by the Romansch-speakers and the Ticinese. In Canada the possibility of a Quebec nation-state, perhaps in an associate relationship with a smaller Canada, remains feasible, unless the federal system can make accommodative adjustments in time to prevent it.

The tensions of multilingual states cannot be resolved if the unifying instruments, that is the political institutions and the ideologies of nationalism, do not grant a self-respecting, secure, economic and political position for self-conscious linguistic minorities. The Canadian federal nation-state has not done this. It has not developed fully 'a political concept large enough to embrace all the factors and stimulating enough to command the allegiance of widely differing communities'.[104] Meanwhile it remains in a position of economic dependency in relation to the United States, including the control exerted over vital sectors of its economy by multinational corporations. Given the nature of contemporary world capitalism, therefore, nationalism seems to be an almost anachronistic method of gaining independence.

6

Nationalist Movements
and Social Classes

V. Kiernan

'What ish my nation? Who talks of my nation?' peevishly exclaimed
Captain Macmorris, at Fluellen's innocent allusion to the Irish. In
Shakespeare's Europe, nationalities were coming more in contact,
often painful contact, and growing more conscious of how they were
thought about by others. What they felt was only at the beginning of
turning into a political idea. A 'nation' meant those born of a common
stock, and sharing a common character. Fluellen's own Welshmen
could be panegyrised by Milton as 'An old and haughty nation, proud
in arms', but they had never been a state, and he certainly had no wish
to see them one. Today there is a Welsh nationalist movement, one of a
bewildering variety of such movements sprawling over modern history.
A paradoxical difficulty in the way of any effort to unravel them is that
they could only fully develop after national states and nationalism were
established facts in a certain number of countries. Nationalism was a
creation mainly from above, the outcome of state power exercised over
long periods in the special conditions of early modern Western
Europe.[1] Yet among these conditions was the prior existence of
national feeling, rough and half-formed like Captain Macmorris's
though it might be. State and nationality constantly interacted, each
requiring the other for its full development towards the point where
they could help to inspire nationalist movements in other lands, further
and further afield.

Medieval society and its jarring classes were held together, so far as
moral cement was wanted, by religion, as in Asia. But towards the end
of the Middle Ages a number of feudal monarchies were acquiring
something of the quality of the true state, as an entity felt to be somehow representative of all its subjects collectively, and entitled to an allegiance different from mere submission to a ruler of the moment.

For Notes and References to Chapter 6, see pp. 171–6.

England led the way, and helped to provoke a similar spirit in France by repeated attacks on its neighbour, as France was to do in turn with Germany. In the sixteenth and seventeenth centuries when the strengthened state of the 'absolute monarchies' took shape, it some-times coincided, if never more than approximately, with the bound-aries of nationality or language. In this case, centralised authority and quickening currents of economic circulation made for a closer linkage between state and public feeling. In all this process urban middle classes figured prominently. Patriotic feeling could bolster their self-esteem and confidence, and by identifying themselves with it they could the better aspire to a leading place in a changing pattern of society. A national revolt like that of the Netherlands – or, less conclusively, that of Scotland about 1640 – was at the same time a kind of bourgeois revol-ution. Conversely, the bourgeois revolutions in England and then France had a markedly nationalistic tone.

Modern capitalism came into being in Western Europe very slowly indeed.[2] Tools and techniques, and ideas too, often lay long unused. We can reckon four centuries of preparation for the big leap of the In-dustrial Revolution. Nationalism can be seen growing up along with it, also very gradually and fumblingly, and linked with it in many complex ways. By dissolving traditional social structures and substituting fresh ones, the national market that capitalism made for itself brought classes into sharper confrontation, requiring a potent ideology as well as a firm administrative apparatus to keep it within bounds. More and more functions or services of a positive kind had to be undertaken by the state, which enmeshed all classes in its activities. Always a big employer, it became far the biggest employer. Given this increasing in-volvement, growing cities were a fertile breeding-ground for national feeling; this, with religion declining, was the readiest emotional com-pensation for the strangeness of urban and industrial life to the first generations of incomers from the countryside. At the same time, news-papers and other means of spreading the nationalist spirit proliferated.

Renan called the nation 'une grande solidarité', a communion of memory and purpose.[3] It was also, however, a combination of classes, and the state was built not on the nation as a community but on the divisions within a community which it was itself welding into a nation. It learned to do so increasingly, as time went on, by deliberate indoc-trination, through mass education especially. Haydn is said to have thought of composing a national anthem for Austria because of the in-fluence he saw exercised in England by *God Save the King*. Full-blown nationalism was worked up out of old elemental ties of neighbourhood and dislike of strangers, much as rival religions have been organised by Churches out of man's plastic primitive religious sense. Nothing can be further from the mark than the oft-repeated maxim that nationalism is natural and proper, whereas communism is unnatural and improper.

Prophets of nationalism have usually been 'very remote from the economic and class interests of the period'.[4] This abstraction was part of what made their ideas acceptable to all classes within established states, but with diverse meanings for each class; and similar diversity of meaning was to show itself in nationalist movements endeavouring to set up new states. On the whole, nationalism was least congenial to the highest and lowest strata. From the aristocratic point of view it was an invasion of the sphere of public life by plebeians. John Chester, the cynical man of the world in Dickens, prided himself on his aloofness from its 'intensely vulgar sentiments'.[5] When such men 'loved their country', they were thinking of it as a glorified private estate owned by themselves and their friends. About most of its inhabitants, and their wants, they preferred not to think: instead they idealised the 'sacred soil', the territory inalienable as an entailed patrimony. A landowning peasantry could share this sensation in its own way. In the towns it was the lower-middle-class groups, made up (like the peasantry) of a mass of individuals with little corporate organisation, to whom the thought of nation as 'family' had most appeal. Industrial working classes, far more antagonistic to those above them, and busy building their own forms of organisation, had much less emotional need of it, and shared in it chiefly because the state touched their life at more and more points.

In a few countries state nationalism was already old by 1789, but this date may be taken as a starting-point for modern nationalist movements of opposition. They were ushered in by a flurry of revolts in the Habsburg Empire, provoked by the bureaucratic reformism of Joseph II. These were, in the main, conservative regional reactions against change, though in both Hungary and Belgium their social composition and temper were very mixed,[6] their affinity was with the aristocratic intransigence of 1787–9, the initial phase of the French Revolution. In 1808–14 the Spanish War of Independence against Napoleon was prophetic of many later ones in containing another jumble of class ideas and interests, with clerical conservatism dominant but two tendencies opposed to it emerging, a middle-class Liberal programme and peasant discontent against landlord exactions. It was the hope, quickly dashed, of seeing patriotism wedded to progress and reform that made Wordsworth so enthusiastic about the Spanish resistance, and inspired his *Convention of Cintra*, as profound and imaginative a eulogy of the Nation as any ever written.

Within Spain, not long after the Napoleonic wars, there was reviving an old regional separatism of Catalonia. It is instructive as displaying what has been repeated in the history of many lands, a shift from an earlier stage of conservative withdrawal to a later, more progressive one, introduced by industrial growth, and then pushed on by the contradictions this brought with it. At the time of the first Carlist War (1833–9) rural Catalonia, along with the inner Basque area, was the mainstay of the reactionary Carlist cause. These areas were turning away from the alien modernity, the new fangled administration and the secularism, of Liberal Spain, and fighting to regain or preserve old local rights. But their coastal fringes, with the stimulus of French nearness and capital, were before long becoming Spain's chief workshops, very unlike Brittany in France or Ireland in the British Isles. After the middle of the century a new, less archaic, though still socially conservative *Catalanismo* was developing, to the accompaniment (as in all such cases) of a cultural revival.

Simultaneously industrial growth was generating acute conflicts of capital and labour. Spain had been little touched, but was none the less alarmed, by the revolutions of 1848; and these had made men of property everywhere look to 'national unity as a miracle worker which would prevent class warfare and a popular rising'.[7] A home-rule movement was encouraged by employers as a means of diverting working-class resentment away from them and against Madrid. Several right-wing groups coalesced in 1901 in the *Lliga Regionalista*. It won electoral successes, as did a broader combination formed in 1906, the *Solidaritat Catalana*, which in 1914 secured a regional au'hority of its own, the *Mancomunitat*, with very limited powers. All this could not exorcise class conflict. Barcelona's lower-middle strata remained faithful to their old Liberal tradition, travestied now by the anti-clerical demagogy of Lerroux and his Radical Party. Because this was also anti-separatist, Madrid winked at its inflammatory talk.[8] More serious, the workers persisted in organising militant trade unions and waging a chronic warfare of strikes and sometimes bullets against their employers. After the Great War many of these were in a mood to welcome the right-wing dictatorship of General Primo de Rivera, who in 1925 abolished the *Mancomunitat*. On his fall, and that of the monarchy, the Catalan movement resumed its advance, but with the Left now in the lead, and the workers marshalled in their own *Esquerra Republicana*.

Just a century earlier, in 1831, Belgium gained its independence from Holland very largely by dint of foreign backing. Industry was coming in, sufficiently to stimulate the country and to make the national rising, in part, a bourgeois revolution; it had not gone far enough to set up too many class contentions, and it was monopolised by the Walloon half of the country and gave this a certain solidarity as against the economically backward Flemish half – today strongly autonomist, and insisting on its belated fair share. Norway, transferred in 1814 from Denmark to Sweden, moved during the century from an insulated peasant society's resentment of change towards a modern national consciousness. Economic growth here took the form of worldwide shipping activity, ideally suited to promote a sense of distinct national interests without causing too much class division: after the days of wooden sailing ships, Norway was buying most of its vessels from abroad, not setting up a big shipbuilding industry at home. It was after universal suffrage came in 1898 that a demand for independence became insistent. Class solidarity in support of it was not tested too severely, because the Swedes – especially their trade unions[9] – were too civilised to try to preserve the union by force.

Ireland, that museum collection of historical miscellanies, went through many experiences before the later 1870s when the home-rule movement led by Parnell sought a mass social basis by joining hands with a militant peasant movement. It could afford to do so because the landlords were so largely Anglo-Irish and (like Parnell) Protestant; for the same reason the British government could not afford to go on relying on them for support, as it could in some other colonies, but had to quieten the agitation by buying them out. Nationalism recovered, with underemployed urban lower-middle strata for its chief carrier. There was no big industrial bourgeoisie as a counterweight, and the small working class played little part, in spite of the Socialist Republican Party founded in 1897 by James Connolly.[10] England paid a penalty for its policies in earlier days of hindering industrial development: a bigger Irish bourgeoisie would have seen its interest, sooner or later, in an English partnership against its workers, and (like the Scottish) in a share of empire profits – an important consideration for Catalan businessmen too, so long as there were any Spanish colonies left. Ireland, unlike Catalonia, thus escaped the Scylla of capital-and-labour deadlock, though not, later on, the Charybdis of an undeveloped economy and a sterile social outlook. This sterility was worsened by the movement having too much of a religious complexion, and, like sundry others, too many of its roots abroad. Irish-American sympathy and subsidies did much to keep the desire for freedom alive, nothing to kindle a progressive programme.

National ideology, like a theology such as Calvinism, could take shape only in a very specific social environment, but could then be adapted to a wide variety of others. Middle and Eastern Europe entered the post-1815 age shaken by the recent political upheavals, and now by the accelerating march of the industrial revolution, as an odd medley of large multinational entities and small fragments of divided peoples. Much of the time from then on was to be devoted to rectifying these anomalies, and establishing the national state, by revival or fresh creation, as the common norm. Britain and France by their success had raised its prestige very high. The endeavours of the rest of Europe to emulate them were to be very often a pursuit of red herrings hidden in holy grails. Still, history has never moved in straight lines, and the more complex and contradictory European society became, the more devious its advance was bound to be, and the fuller of illusions and delusions.

East of the Rhineland, industry was making its appearance only spasmodically, here and there. But while successful risings could take place in regions still pre-industrial,[11] it is to be remembered that capitalism exerted novel pressures even on districts still agricultural: on Rumania, for instance, where demand for food in the urban West offered bigger profits for landlords, and incited them both to desire greater autonomy from Turkey and to take away land from their peasants while exacting all their dues from them in full.[12] They were not averse to taking land away from their neighbours as well. Widening horizons, geographical and technological, made for aggressive self-assertion as well as progress, and a climate in which nationalism meant a claim not only to exist, but to expand. Acquisitiveness as well as romantic irrationality often helped to fix a people's ambitions on a territory larger than itself, though arguably belonging to it once upon a time. Again, as in industrialism, Britain set the example. Its own 'nationalist movement' was imperialism, to which patriotism came to be so closely tied that 'Little Englander' was a term of reproach. Tolstoy lamented that small oppressed peoples were catching the infection of nationalism from their oppressors, and were ready in turn 'to perpetrate on other peoples the very same deeds'. He saw realistically how this perversity was fostered by all privileged classes, because their position depended on the possession or favour of state power.[13]

For the outcome of a nationalist movement and the quality of its future state, the vital question was the extent to which different classes participated in it. There was no simple equation between mass involvement and success, since classes once aroused might collide; moreover, foreign opinion always counted, and foreign governments or respectable publics abroad were always averse to the common people taking the bit between their teeth. As a rule only quite small minorities were actively engaged, though they might have the approval, warmer or cooler, of larger numbers. At one end of the scale, in Russia, it might be said that the tsar himself was the standard-bearer: Nicholas I, 'the policeman of Europe', was in some ways, and prided himself on being, very Russian, and his official version of Russian nationalism[14] was only a caricature of what the Western state taught its citizens. At the other end, support was nearly always forthcoming from the loose bundle of lower-middle-class groupings – teachers, small traders, artisans and many more – which have been lumped together as the 'petty bourgeoisie'. This clumsy as well as un-English term fails to express what is most characteristic of the sector it covers, namely that it is made up of unattached, unanchored individuals or clusters. They are not *individualists* by nature or choice, though they may be made so by circumstances. An individualist requires a firmer footing in society, to sustain as well as to repel him. As a rule these irregulars of history ask nothing better than to be relieved of their non-attachment, incorporated into some union, whether body politic or *corpus mysticum*. They improvise all kinds of minor fraternities of their own; they cannot invent the nation, but they welcome it more emotionally than any other class. To their scattered ranks have belonged most of the intellectuals who have done the work of adapting and spreading nationalist ideas and illusions – both ideas and illusions being, more than with other men, a part of their daily bread.

'Un nom devenu terrible, le nom du prolétaire':[15] so a student of the new working class wrote, two years before the *Communist Manifesto* and the June days of 1848 in Paris which displayed it as a rebel against the social order, not against any mere government. No peoples had yet gained their freedom except the Belgians, and, less completely, some in the Balkans, and in all these cases foreign assistance counted for much. Other movements had mostly lacked mass participation, but their revolutions in 1848–9 failed largely because, now that masses of men were beginning to be aroused, their class divisions were more evident; a dilemma equally fatal to the bourgeois revolution needed, above all, by Germany. After the collapse nationalism persisted, and often achieved its aims, but not by force of popular enthusiasm as idealists had hoped; it was being taken up by governments and shepherded into safe conservative ways. National states were again, as previously in the West, though more rapidly now with the aid of modern administrative resources, being built from above.

Germany's first patriots, in the late eighteenth century, often looked forward to a peaceful nation taking its place in a free and fraternal Europe.[16] They were men of the Age of Reason, which was very much an age of amiable fancies, nowhere more than in such blindness to the Manichaean dualism of the Nation. Twenty years of war, ending with the Prussian army recovering its laurels at Leipzig and Waterloo, deepened a harsher note which had been audible from the first in the admiration felt for Frederick the Great.[17] In a country with few industries and many governments, the educated middle class was more than usually addicted to official service. A considerable part of it was made up of semi-hereditary bureaucrats and clergymen; a multitude of malcontents failed to find places, and might – until their luck changed – be very loud on behalf of the twin causes of Liberalism and nationalism. The intelligentsia was too weak to challenge aristocratic privilege; it could find consolation in calling on fellow Germans to rise and take their rightful place as masters of Europe. In the cloudy bombast and megalomania of German nationalist ideology can be recognised the frustrations and aspirations of all these plebeians.

In this ideology there was from an early date a note of economic nationalism and capitalist method amid romantic madness. Germans dreaming of a united Fatherland were dreaming also of building up their industries and challenging a hated Britannia on the seas.[18] Economic growth, quickened by the Zollverein, strengthened the bourgeoisie and its claim to a share of political power, but it also sharpened class tension lower down, as the rioting of hungry Silesian weavers in 1844 revealed. More perilous in the long run, industrialism was bringing with it that fatal Siamese twin of capitalism, the proletariat. French events in 1848 sounded a thunderous warning against any stirring up of the masses: there was no foreign oppressor in France to unite the classes, but Germany's foreign oppressors were more imaginary than real, and the bourgeoisie now spreading across the continent was always highly sensitive to the European atmosphere.

Industrial expansion continued, and with it the Liberal threat to autocracy in Prussia; but as Bismarck – in power from 1862 – was shrewd enough to observe, the working-class and socialist threat to the bourgeoisie grew at the same rate. His solution for the difficulties facing conservative rule and its institutions was to give Germany the unification it hankered for by force of Prussian arms. Instead of Prussia being merged in Germany, as Frederick William IV – temporarily reduced to demagogy – proclaimed in 1848, Germany was merged into Prussia. The capitalist wing of Liberalism was relieved at getting so much without a hazardous appeal to the masses, and from now on was content to cultivate its industrial garden, leaving state affairs to the conservatives. Economic growth had already gone so far that political unification scarcely seems to have been necessary for its further increase. It was needed rather for political and social reasons. The function of the new Reich was to provide means of harmonising or holding in check the animosities of rival classes, as the Western state had done, but as now required to be done far more hastily and forcefully because industrialism was growing so much more rapidly. Chauvinist and militarist indoctrination accompanied by universal military service was an essential part of the process.[19]

Gramsci's mind was always coming back to the problem of the Risorgimento and its hollowness or inconsistencies, thanks to which his Italy had succumbed so easily to fascism. Regional particularism, attachment to Venice or Sicily more than to Italy, was one of the most palpable obstacles. Devotion to Italy came easiest to small groups of enthusiasts, many of them exiles like the old Garibaldians in South America who dreamed nightly of their native land and were buried with their faces towards it. Distance has often lent enchantment to a patriot's view of his fellow countrymen. One of the earliest and most determined struggles for liberation was that of Corsica against Genoa, only defeated when the Genoese sold the island to France in 1768. Ordinary Corsicans were emboldened by hatred of outsiders, an élite leadership by desire for power or by literary patriotism. General Paoli explained his motives to Boswell by quoting Virgil – 'Vincet amor patriae.'[20]

Paoli was anything but a leveller, as another remark recorded by his admirer shows: 'a diffusion of knowledge among the people was a dis-advantage, for it made the vulgar rise above their humble sphere.'[21] His words were ominous of too much Italian nationalism of the next century, and class division was a much more deep-seated impediment than regionalism. In poverty-stricken Italy a social programme to rein-force the romantic dream of union and independence was all the more requisite because religion was both powerful and anti-national, Rome and Vienna as thick as thieves. But any pledge of concessions to the masses, to draw them into the struggle, would mean sacrifices for those who lived at their expense. Ardent young men of the middle classes might be ready for periodical conspiracies and risings, but they were likely, as in Asia, to have too many ties with the landowning system to dream of invoking the land-hunger of the poor cultivator.

Commercial enterprise was damped by the rooted preference for investment in land,[22] in a country where land – in the North at any rate – had always been a market commodity. In the North some industrial development was taking place by the 1840s, and in Lombardy, where it attracted an active younger section of the aristocracy as well as the wealthier middle class,[23] it was the business interests that suffered from Austrian rule, acceptable enough to most of the big landlords and to the peasantry under clerical tuition.[24] It was complained that the tariff system sacrificed local industry to the interests of Austria and Bohe-mia, and with Mediterranean trade expanding it was felt that Italy ought to have a better place in it.[25] There was very little revolutionary fervour among the businessmen however. Liberal publicists, so far from representing 'an aspiring and self-conscious bourgeoisie', were often landowners or intellectuals with upper-class connections, 'exerting themselves to rouse a timid and lethargic bourgeoisie to a con-sciousness of its interests'.[26] And whatever capitalist development took place, in Lombardy or Piedmont, added as always to bourgeois tim-idity about any breach of law and order that might endanger property as well as government.

Of social and economic facts, Mazzini, living on coffee and spinning his pipe-dreams and plots in London, understood very little. Workmen did themselves no good by clamouring for their rights, he told them, and ought to think of their duty instead. All he had to offer as a social programme was that a free government would welcome 'labour associ-ations . . . of proven morality and capacity', and turn unused common lands into smallholdings.[27] Cavour knew all about economics, but from the angle of a landowner and businessman, and with him as with Bismarck national unity was a secondary consideration. His concern was to fortify established interests in Piedmont, where he took office in 1852, which could only be done by enlarging the principality. It could then beat off the peril of 'red republican' anarchy sweeping Italy, a peril he made use of to frighten European governments and win their approval.[28] Piedmont's army was too small to play a Prussian role; a French army was brought in instead. Napoleon III wanted prestige and scraps of territory, but he also wanted to forestall social agitation in Italy which might infect his own kingdom.

He was disappointed by the few volunteers who came forward in 1859, and by his army's poor reception in rural Lombardy.[29] Realities lurking under the tinsel phrases of patriotism showed themselves in the harsh suppression of peasant mutiny during and after the unification, chiefly in the south.[30] A nation's duty lies in 'supporting and not hindering the actions of the elect minority',[31] as Croce, a true representative of the élite, was to write. A very inorganic Italy emerged, which its rulers set to work to mould into a national state, as in Germany but less successfully, by compulsion. Young men would be made to feel Italian by being made to wear Italian uniforms; jingo propaganda would usurp the place of the fraternal relations with other peoples that Mazzini had looked forward to. Thus speeded up, the state-building which in the West had been the slow work of centuries could not hide its artificiality. Poverty continued to drive swarms of Italians abroad in search of work. When a gang of these labourers were asked by a traveller whether they loved their native land, one of them smiled and said 'Italy is for us whoever gives us our bread.'[32]

In the West, nationalism had an urban habitat, close to the traditions of the old city-state or chartered town. In Eastern Europe it was taken up – like the Reformation earlier – in default of an energetic burgher class, by the landed gentry, that 'middle class' of feudal society. An archaic body like the Polish nobility could acquire some degree of moral justification by leading the defence of a subjugated country, and deflect social discontent away from itself. Only a minority of the gentry ever took up arms, and a good proportion of those who did may have been younger sons or men of broken fortunes, although the number of estates confiscated by the Russian authorities is proof that not all were so. Whatever their individual motives, their sacrifices conferred merit on the whole body. Religion supplied a buttress, but also a further blockage against progressive social thinking. Poland, not the Polish people, was the theme of patriotic rhapsodising, and served to keep social realities out of sight. Mickiewicz, the poet in exile, carried the theme furthest with his mystic concept of Poland as the martyred Christ among the nations.

Mysticism usually means mystification; the real martyr was the Polish peasant, his persecutor the patriotic gentleman. 'Congress Poland', the separately administered kingdom under the Tsar Alexander I after 1815, was free of serfdom, which had been abolished there in the Napoleonic era, but agrarian relations in their essentials were little altered. Gentry patriotism, moreover, was strongly tinged with the feudal imperialism which had ruined Poland in former times: its demand was not for simple freedom within Polish ethnic limits, but for the old Eastern marches as well, with their non-Polish inhabitants and Polish landlords.

Agitation in 'Congress Poland' burst out in the revolution of 1830–1. This was initiated by secret societies and students who seized control of Warsaw. Women took an active part, a symptom as in so many other national movements of new ideas reaching a depressed stratum. Not many peasants, and not all districts, joined in. Tsarist reprisals fell heaviest on the gentry, while the province lost its constitution and was incorporated in the Russian empire. Another rising was quelled in 1846, and in Galicia, the Austrian share of Poland, the government gave a demonstration of how easily the tables could be turned by allowing a peasant *jacquerie* against the landlords. This hint was not thrown away, and in 1848 most of Poland was quiet. It was time for a new class to come to the front, and by mid-century a fairly strong bourgeoisie was present, with industry (besides coal-mining), sprouting at Warsaw, Lodz and other centres, impoverished peasants providing the labour force. Industrial depression helped to launch the second big revolutionary outbreak, this time in 1863. All classes were represented in the long-drawn, mainly guerrilla struggle, but unevenly; there was still no united front of the whole nation.[33] Warsaw workers and artisans were prominent. There were divergent views as between progressives, who wanted to set the peasantry in motion by promising it land, and landowners, who demurred. They and the bourgeoisie pinned many of their hopes on foreign intervention, which did not come. Sometimes peasants profited by the confusion to rise against their landlords, as they had been doing on and off all the time, and handworkers to smash machinery.[34] Indirectly the peasants did benefit when the Russian government, after regaining control, carried out a partial agrarian reform in order to draw the gentry's teeth.

Industry went on growing in the later nineteenth century, but politically speaking it was growing up too late, when the Commune had sounded its tocsin to capitalists everywhere, and the German Liberals had taken refuge with Bismarck. It benefited too by the large Russian market for its goods, as Catalan production did by the Spanish. For the working class there was likewise an alternative, between nationalism as presented by Pilsudski's 'Polish Socialist Party' and class alignment with the workers of Russia. This latter, and eventual federation, was what Rosa Luxemburg, a very much more genuine socialist than Pilsudski, advocated; she maintained – forgetting, Kautsky objected, the intelligentsia – that no class in Poland now identified itself with the struggle for independence.[35] Some other 'unattached' strata may have been exceptions. It has been shown that in Eastern Europe generally national feeling was strongest not in industrial zones but where artisans carried on small-scale production for township and village requirements.[36]

At the time of the 1905 revolution in Russia, the Polish propertied classes came to terms with the weak Russian Liberal party, for fear of being swept away by the tide of social revolt. This may have helped to push the workers in the opposite direction. In 1913 Stalin was lamenting that a good many of them were 'still in intellectual bondage to the bourgeois nationalists'.[37] When the latter got power after the Great War they made a temporary discreet pretence of socialist sympathies,[38] until it was safe to throw off the mask and seize the disputed Eastern lands from Soviet Russia. How the better-off classes really thought of socialism, and of their poorer fellow countrymen, can be judged from the white terror in Finland when it gained independence under German auspices in April 1918, and a quarter of the working class may have been massacred or jailed.[39]

'The nobility was bound to be everywhere the principal champion of Hungarian nationality',[40] as of Polish; a landowning gentry, or middle nobility, with some distinct qualities, being partly Calvinist, and having along with its dour religion a more tenacious political tradition and hold on local institutions than the Polish gentry. Down to 1848 the peasants, unlike the Italian and most of the Polish, were still serfs, and by agreeing to emancipate them, as the progressive leader Kossuth advocated, the nobles could make an impressive-looking sacrifice which cost them little. Serfdom was out of date and dangerous, as had been shown very recently in Galicia: to abandon it was to deprive Austria of a weapon.[41] With some overstatement an English admirer of Kossuth asserted that this gesture gave the country 'a greater unity of class than any other in the world'.[42] It did at any rate facilitate an alliance of gentry, peasantry and urban middle class, and enabled Hungary to set on foot a regular army – as the Poles were never able to do – and offer a prolonged resistance. Aristocratic officers, it is true, could not conceal their dislike of Kossuth as an upstart[43] – he belonged to the poorest gentry by birth, to the professional middle class by vocation. On the other hand, these nationalists, like the Poles, were not prepared to renounce their claims on borderlands inhabited by other nationalities, where the landowners were often Magyar. They had therefore to fight their Slav underlings as well as their Austrian overlords.

Hungary was finished off by a Russian army instead of being rescued by a French army. Revolutionary ferment went on, and might have broken out afresh in 1866 when the Habsburg Empire was being defeated by Prussia, if Deak and Andrassy, two spokesmen of the nobility who fought in 1848, had not held their friends back.[44] They preferred to accept instead the *Ausgleich* or 'Compromise' of 1867. They may have shrunk from summoning to action again peasants whom emancipation had left still land-hungry. They undoubtedly realised that only by agreement with Vienna could they win back control of their non-Magyar borderlands. To the misfortune of Magyar peasants and workers, and of the national minorities, the empire was turned into the Dual Monarchy. Down to 1918 all the Hungarian wing was lorded over by the Magyar oligarchy.[45]

Slavs in the empire were peasant peoples, within which evolution of classes had been cut short by foreign dominion and alien landlords, Magyar or German. Modernity reached them mostly at second hand, furnishing them as time went on with spokesmen who were often teachers or other educated middle-class individuals. Railways, newspapers, wider markets and their ups and downs, all did their work in shaking up old habits of mind. National and class consciousness could then be very close together, as in the Croat Peasant Party founded by Stepan Radic in 1904. Countryfolk were going to the towns in search of work, and very often working for employers of alien stock:[46] the same underlining of social by national antipathy took place as in the countryside, but in the hothouse urban atmosphere. It is in the town that the newcomer finds he has been talking prose, or feeling patriotic, all his life.

It was the Czechs who were proving the most energetic and hopeful. They too were mostly peasants, ever since the Habsburg conquest of Bohemia in 1620 and the replacement of much of its old nobility with Germans. Besides landowners and officials there was a considerable German minority in Bohemia, and in Prague, and a nationalist mood takes on a special character when there is an intrusive population to be envied and resented, with reason or without. Industry and commerce were to a great extent in German hands, so that government service was the first ambition of the burgeoning Czech middle class, whose championing of its own language was at the same time a scuffle for jobs.[47] Control of, or access to, the state machine is all the more vital to a class or community lacking economic strength. But it is from their enemies or rivals that nations learn most, for good or ill, and Czechs had lived side by side with Germans long enough to develop talents for business and practical organisation as well as for music. They were pushing their way now into modern economic life, and a Czech bourgeoisie was coming forward, desirous of a national market of its own. The fact that so many employers were German must have done much to avert or soften the collision of interests between Czech employers and workers. Here again émigré patriots, in Western Europe and the United States, led the way in aspiring to full independence.[48]

In the Balkan peninsula Rumania was exceptional in its feudal structure, akin to that of Poland or Russia. Its largely absentee nobility had always enjoyed an autonomous status under the Turks. Elsewhere the situation was akin to that of the Habsburg Slav lands. Towns were chiefly Turkish garrison centres, and in the countryside conquest had eliminated native landlordism, except where, as in Bosnia, owners of estates turned Muslim in order to keep some of their acres, or, as in Greece, the district headmen through whom the rude administration was carried on acquired small properties. A barbarous Turkish feudalism grew up to fill the gap, and oppression was compounded by the weakening of central authority, which allowed an anarchic mode of local misrule and extortion to flourish. By the later eighteenth century the peninsula was coming to look more like a region undergoing foreign invasion than one under settled foreign occupation – which comes in time, like home-bred class rule, to be submitted to as part of the order of things.

What might grow into national rebellion, and was always likely to be mistaken for this by Westerners, was usually at bottom agrarian revolt. Social relations, most democratic in the Slav-speaking areas, could give this the strength of tribal simplicity, and draw in the masses far more than any movement in a divided society like Italy's. Resistance which broke out in Serbia in 1804 was a protest against local conditions with no sort of 'national' intention in view.[49] In its ranks, however, were some men with wider horizons, village headmen or dealers engaged – as the partisan chiefs Karageorge and Obrenovich both were – in the country's principal trade, export of pigs. Such individuals were in contact with Serbs outside the fighting area, traders belonging to prosperous colonies in neighbouring Hungary, smaller groups further afield. It was among them that newspapers, modern commerce and town life, could kindle national ideas, which would find their way, along with material aid, into the homeland. Much the same can be said of the Bulgars later on: their homeland contained only peasants, but their migrants in towns like Bucharest and Odessa sprouted a merchantry and an intelligentsia. In such a dislocated social structure, classes in the making were scattered about instead of being perched one on top of the other; a state of affairs helpful in lessening class friction during the struggle for independence, but making for lack of equilibrium later on.

Far the most complex structure was that of the Greeks, whose national rising was correspondingly confused. Something of Byzantine power had survived under the Ottoman aegis. The Church was prompt in rendering to the Sultan what was due to Caesar, and its Greek hierarchy held sway over religious life in both Serbia and Bulgaria until they won their freedom: in fact a desire for native prelates was one of the focal points of Bulgar peasant nationalism. Greek traders and tax-farmers held a big place in Ottoman affairs, particularly the wealthy Phanariot community of Stamboul, members of which had been for a century the well-hated governors of the Rumanian provinces. Greek revolt began at the top, instead of as elsewhere at the bottom. Greek shipping and trade had windfall opportunities during the Revolutionary and Napoleonic wars,[50] but all business activity in the decaying empire suffered from arbitrary exactions and general insecurity. Merchants who sent their sons to school in Paris, and were in touch with Greek traders all over Europe, were bound to feel the stirrings of the national idea. Characteristically, those who were willing to run the risks of challenging authority, in the first phase at any rate, were not the most prosperous, but those whom success had eluded and who were ready to blame the Turks for their disappointments.[51] This very fact may have lent their schemes a touch of extravagance; they dreamed of something like a restored Byzantium, as the Polish or Magyar gentry aspired to the recovery of their colonies as well as their freedom.

It was in the narrower theatre of the Morea, or Peloponnese, that the real battle had to be waged, and in the islands with their shipping fleets. Shipowners too wealthy to be eager to risk their possessions were pushed on by their militant seamen. Tensions between the two were frequent, but there was something to draw them together in the cooperative arrangement by which a crew as well as a capitalist held shares in a cargo and benefited by the success of a voyage.[52] As the contest went on, the merchant class gave important support, more than the propertied classes on *terra firma* where lives as well as goods were at stake. These were owners of estates, few by comparison with the Turk feudatories; 'primates', or district headmen; and the higher clergy. They had little fault to find with Turkish rule, except that those with land wanted more, and as things were could not hope to get it.[53] Village priests were ardently on the popular side, as village priests unlike prelates so often were in olden days in the West. Another gulf separated agriculturists from hillmen, half shepherd and half brigand. Very much as in the Spanish War of Independence not long before, there was only bad and quarrelsome leadership, or none at all, but this reflected not only personal faction but a chaos of jarring social interests. Such a war, against an opponent almost as undisciplined, could only lead to stalemate, until foreign intervention grudgingly established in 1833 a small Greek state, furnished with a Bavarian king. In the century and a half since then it has grown in size, but has proved quite unable to reconcile the internecine hatreds that accompanied it into the world.

Of the two Rumanian provinces Moldavia, closer to Russia, was the more purely feudal and inert. In Wallachia, which included Bucharest, there was more of an urban middle class, and in 1848 a rising and a provisional government.[54] This quickly ran aground on antagonism between progressives who wanted agrarian reform and recalcitrant nobles, and the Russian intervention was far less needed to restore 'order' than in Hungary. Rumania slid into independence in 1858, when both Russia and Turkey were crippled by the Crimean War, and the two provinces united. It was the only Balkan country to start its career with a ready-made ruling class, one of the worst imaginable. To the peasants whose efforts counted most towards freedom in the other lands, the notion of a ruling class, or of a state, was incomprehensible. What they wanted was to be left in peace in their villages; the Serbs, for instance, whom their first ruler Milosh Obrenovich had to dragoon heavy-handedly into acceptance of regular government.[55] The élites which could provide a civil and military apparatus were a motley and unsatisfactory set: expatriates returning from abroad, local vested interests, others thrown up by the struggle itself. All these could savour the prospect of a state of their own, with patronage to be dispensed and power to be wielded. Obrenovich's rise from pig-sty to palace left him with an unquenchable greed for money as well as power. In Greece during the fighting the bigger men were amassing land and plunder;[56] when it was over they were ready to coalesce with the merchants and shipowners and form a dominant bloc. Foreign enterprise was active in setting an example of greed, under cover of the monarchies supplied by the Concert of Europe to three of the new states – royal families themselves keenly interested in dividends, and in saving up for a rainy day.

A good deal of territory was still Turkish at the end of the century, and ethnic boundaries were indistinct. Everything conspired to make the Balkans a hotbed of irredentism. Bad governments were in chronic need of alibis; army men were prominent in politics; exporters wanted access to the Black Sea, the Aegean or the Adriatic. Calls to liberate downtrodden brethren met with a ready response from peasant peoples with strong ties of family and clan. They could be set against each other as easily as against the Sultan, and their naïve patriotism was soon inflamed by the ruling groups into a peculiarly vicious chauvinism. Many other governments with little taste for social reform and progress were finding a convenient alternative in irredentism. A fresh bout of tub-thumping about Alsace-Lorraine was one of the most effective expedients of French conservatism before 1914, faced with the socialist menace.

Patriotism was becoming the last refuge of reaction, and nationalist labels were favourites with right-wing parties. They were to be utilised most grotesquely by Franco's 'National' movement, conquering Spain with Moorish, Italian and German forces, and Chiang Kai-shek's 'National' government, retreating before the Japanese and then trying to reconquer China with American guns. Irredentism and fascism both owed their names to Italy. The latter represented right-wing nationalism in intensified form, and carried furthest the false simplification of class society into a community of *Volksgenossen*. There was implicit in the nation from the outset, it has been said, a recognition of society's responsibility for all its members.[57] But if so, this has far oftener been its 'recessive' than its 'dominant' characteristic. Once harnessed to the state, national feeling was distorted, and its prime function was to obscure class issues instead of finding healthy solutions for them. With fascism the cycle was complete.

Beyond Europe, nationalism continued to prove itself an idea adaptable to very diverse needs. Western goods, machines and books were subverting old patterns of life, and making a vacuum. Communism has spread in Asia, it has been pointed out, thanks not only to poverty but to the groping of bewildered multitudes for new ideals.[58] In many ways nationalism too has met this need: inadequately by itself, but the two creeds have often converged, as in Europe they could very seldom do. Hence nationalism in this century has proved a more constructive force in Asia than in its European homeland, where its mission has long been exhausted. Outside Europe it has had the freshness, the inspiration, of a new faith, and by coming later it has been able to profit by Europe's later and better social thinking. China, far bigger and more slow-moving than Japan, was fortunate in the long run in taking so much longer to assimilate modern nationalism, but imbibing it in the end in a far more mature and progressive form.

Any social stratum resembling the old Western bourgeoisie – a political as well as economic construct – was even harder to find in Asia than in Eastern Europe. What could be found everywhere was some kind of urban middle-class intelligentsia, becoming acquainted with Western thought and serving as a *conductor* for it. What more powerful sponsors could be enlisted depended on the environment. In the Ottoman Empire, where trade had been left to non-Turks as an inferior concern, only the army was available to deputise for a bourgeoisie. For a few years before 1914 its leaders were seduced by the pan-Turanian fantasy, which constituted a stepping-stone at least between the old Islamic outlook and a Turkish national one. This came to life suddenly when defeat in the Great War swept away the Sultan-Caliph and the rebellious Arab dependencies. With Allied occupation and partition looming before the country, a successful general, Kemal Pasha, raised the banner of national defence, and patriotic enthusiasm swept the towns where Turk and non-Turk lived side by side on chronically bad terms. But the new idea had to be forced on the sluggish rural masses, whose mentality was still Islamic, not Turkish. Only foreign invasion compelled it to accept the new leadership, much as it was compelling the Russian masses to accept that of the Bolsheviks.

Kemal's utterances during the conflict reveal much of the thinking of his party, with its somewhat mystic image of the nation, that half-digested foreign idea, and its highly élitist attitude towards the illiterate commonalty. In his opening address to the congress at Erzerum on 23 July 1919, he declared that centuries of torpor had blunted the Turkish mind. 'Therefore, those who had penetrated into the inner depths of human affairs and had recognised the truth, must regard it as the highest duty on earth to enlighten and educate the people as far as possible and guide them on a path that leads them to their goal.'[59] In all such pronouncements echoes of older religious axioms can be heard. Kemal's goal was an equivocal one, for Turkey like Asia at large was trying to throw off European shackles in order to be free to Europeanise itself, or its whole outward life at any rate. In non-communist Asia this meant an equivalent of bourgeois revolution, with a bourgeoisie taking shape during the process and cornering most of the gains. Turkey's village masses have been left to stagnate, and the nationalist cycle from progressive to reactionary has been gone through rapidly. Today, with semi-military rule, there is a right-wing 'Nationalist Front' bloc, and a neo-fascist 'Nationalist Action Party'.

At the other end of Asia the Far East is a continent by itself, as distinct as Europe is from the rest of the Eurasian land-mass, and cut off from it by sea, mountain and desert far more definitely than either Europe or Asia is divided from Africa. Islam, that obliterator of nations, scarcely reached it, and all its historic states were, to some degree, 'nations' many centuries before European ideas arrived. Even China's early stage of primitive mass protest against Western intrusion, culminating in the Boxer rising of 1900, was more than mere xenophobia. Clearly the Boxers had a sense of China as a fatherland, of belonging to Chinese tradition and civilisation; it came to them through the favourite tales and dramas that were always the conduit between upper-class and plebeian culture.[60] This was confusedly mixed up with a far older, still lingering, anti-foreign feeling against the reigning dynasty, descended from Manchu conquerors of the seventeenth century. Attachment to the memory of the old native Ming dynasty was an example of how men at odds with the present, but unable to envisage a better future, will idealise a vanished past. In Peru as late as the 1920s the Amerindian peasantry struggling to regain the communal fields that once belonged to it went on rebelling in the name of the long-defunct Incas.[61]

Among younger sections of the intelligentsia and what may roughly be termed China's middle classes, especially in the more volatile South, Western civilisation was having by 1900 its familiar attractive as well as repellent effect. A nationalist movement sprang up which was also a pallid, prematurely born bourgeois-revolutionary movement; the 'foreignness' of the dynasty and its subservience to foreign imperialism made a linking factor. As with so many stirrings further West, its earliest vantage-points were abroad, among Chinese emigrants under Western rule who gave considerable aid to the rebels at home. This always had its drawbacks; reliance on aid from outside may have made Sun Yat-sen's party less eager to look for popular support at home. There were some contacts with the sporadic mutinies of peasant and worker,[62] but the fall of the monarchy in 1911 found the progressives still few and isolated.

After the Great War, the 'August 4 Movement', starting among the students, found a broader basis. Years of warlord anarchy and then Kuomintang tyranny and corruption had the happy result of compelling Chinese nationalism to remain in opposition, instead of being imprisoned in an official cage as in Japan or Europe. It had to identify itself with the cause of reform, progress and modernisation deeper than any technological change. United action against foreign pressures, with Japanese invasion in the 1930s for climax, was impossible. Rather than share with the masses, the propertied classes preferred collaboration with, or virtual surrender to, the outsiders, like the Manchu regime earlier. It fell to the communists to organise national resistance. Their recruits came from the humbler ranks of the intelligentsia, artisans, petty-bourgeois[63] – those familiar 'unattached' elements, electrons easily detached from their social nucleus, that have so often furnished the priming for mass movements. They had done so already in modern China's two biggest outbursts, the Taiping rebellion and the Boxer rising.[64] Through these recruits communism had access to the masses. It could not rely on the working class, which was small and concentrated in coastal areas where the Japanese hold was strongest. Apart from this, modern weapons and conditions of warfare have been everywhere unfavourable to urban revolutionary forces – as Engels was recognising near the end of his life.[65] Instead there was the peasantry, goaded into action by indiscriminate Japanese brutality.

There is much in the thesis that the peasants came under communist guidance because they had to wage a guerrilla struggle against the invaders, not because they wanted to be led against the landowners and their Kuomintang government.[66] But it leaves out of account the agrarian protest, the egalitarian sentiment, that were part of the peasant mind all through the ages. By disrupting the old order, silencing the claims of legitimacy, the war set the peasantry free – like the intelligentsia before it – to follow its natural bent. In the Northern regions where communist strength was greatest and most of the guerrilla fighting took place, numerous landlords and officials absconded, or fraternised with the enemy. It was hardly to be expected that they would be allowed to return and resume their sway when the war was over. It must be recalled, too, that in North China a surprising proportion of peasants, as many as three-quarters perhaps, were not tenants, but had somehow managed to hold on to their small ancestral farms.[67] This had formerly made the North, like the countryside of Northern Spain, conservative and loyal, but now as in the time of the Boxers gave it added readiness to stand firm against foreign attack. So too Northern Spain had done, but the Chinese resistance had vastly superior political direction. Victory would fulfil not only the present aim of expelling the intruder, but age-old dreams of expelling hunger and oppression as well. By an odd freak the same thing was happening in a corner of the Balkans, Yugoslavia, where the old revolt of the countryside was being repeated, but now on a far higher plane.

India had no past as a nation, and had to grow into one for the first time under the spell of Western ideas and institutions, more firmly implanted here and over a lengthier period than anywhere else in Asia. The National Congress, founded in 1886, represented a standard blend of idealism with the desire of educated professional groups for entry into higher government posts.[68] Within the nationalist ranks were members of sub-castes which in past times served the Mughal government, or, like the Chitpavan Brahmins, administered the Maratha empire. To these latter especially, with their instincts of a hereditary governing class, memories and myths of bygone days, and a more conservative attitude than that of the westernisers, were congenial.

It was not long before wider public support was found necessary to put pressure on the British, and disarm their stock argument that only a few self-seekers and cranks were concerned. Regional and caste barriers hindered the formation of *classes* as understood in Europe. But there it was the poorer urban middle strata – petty traders, lower government employees, discontented clerks – that were the most ready to react to changing times, and to join in. Linking them with the higher grades were the students, a swelling host with diminishing prospects of a livelihood, and a swarm of lawyers – a race ubiquitous in the politics of Europe, unknown in Asia until called into being by British rule. One of these, Gandhi, with a background of struggle for Indian rights in South Africa, worked out a philosophy to meet the needs of a country striving towards advance, but still heavily entangled in the past and all its ways. It diluted cautious reformism with old-world religious views: it allowed conservatives to be mildly progressive, and restrained radicals from being too progressive. It admitted that India must fit itself for independence by some degree of social reconstruction for the benefit of the unprivileged, including women and Untouchables, but insisted that traditional Indian life and thought contained treasures not known to the materialistic West. Under Gandhian tuition, in short, a hesitant India could take up its bed and walk without having to feel that it was leaving home.

This made Gandhi acceptable also to the small body of industrial capitalists, self-preserving men who did not mean to get into trouble with the government but were prepared to give subsidies and newspaper backing to Congress. In return they stood to gain by its pressure on the British, which compelled London step by step to concede tariff autonomy.[69] Nationalism was stimulating industry more than industry was stimulating nationalism. Indian millowners in the epoch of the Third International were more nervous of their workers than querulous about the government, and had a common interest with British businessmen in strong police protection. But to hoist the patriotic flag, at half-mast if no more, might shelter them from some opprobrium, and

Gandhi with his theories about the rich being trustees for the poor could be a mediator, or buffer, between them and the working class.

On its side the working class, desperately poor and exploited, could see little advantage in a transfer of power to a Congress hand in glove with its masters. More often than not these were men of different speech as well as class: in Bombay mills, Maratha and many other workers were employed by Gujerati capitalists; in Calcutta, Bengalis and Biharis worked for Marwaris. On the whole labour was little drawn into the national struggle, but fought its own industrial battles, though through these, and harsh experience of the British-officered police, it was coming to a national consciousness of its own. In the countryside the big feudal landlords were solidly pro-British,[70] but Congress could not attack them squarely, or call out the peasantry against them, because too many of its own adherents had an interest in the soil. This was above all the case in Bengal, with its peculiarly morbid agrarian structure, the outcome of the Permanent Settlement.[71] Here the educated Hindu groups which were the first in India to absorb Western ideas, and pioneered the opening phases of the national movement, dropped out of the lead after the Great War, because they were too deeply embedded in the rotting countryside.

There was the danger also that agrarian agitation would invite communism into the countryside, and might worsen unrest among millworkers whose ties with the village were still close. Gandhi's trusteeship principle, or fable, which he extended to landlords and princes as well as capitalists, could reassure them that they had little to fear from Congress, even if Nehru's radical talk gave them uneasy moments. Gandhi's religious phraseology could impress rustics, but talk of 'Ram Rajya', the coming reign of God on earth, was better calculated to keep them away from the socialist-inspired Kisan Sabhas, or peasant unions, than to draw them actively into the national movement.[72] During its spells of civil disobedience, Congress thought of summoning peasants to refuse tax-payments, but boggled at the proposal. Refusal of taxes might too easily lead to refusal of rents, and a general breakdown of social discipline.

Altogether Gandhi might be said to be pursuing united-front tactics, and superficially with success. But the result left British power intact, though at times embarrassed, able to go on running the country by means of officials, soldiers and policemen, most of whom were Indians. It is a commentary on nationalism at large that Britain could rule India and Ireland through Indians and Irishmen, Russia ruled Poland through Poles, and so on, and a reminder that nationalism is only fully itself when stiffened by state power. Congressmen and office-holders came from the same circles, the same families, and got on very well together after India gained independence. It owed this to the enfeeblement of British power in Asia by the Second World War. Independence was accompanied by partition, and the breakaway of Pakistan – one consequence of the shallowness of the national movement and its reluctance to draw in the masses except as a stage army of 'extras'.

This left the Muslim masses vulnerable to religious propaganda. Jinnah and the Muslim League after 1936 maintained that Indian Muslims met all criteria of nationhood,[73] but religious passion was what really counted, along with the economic grievances that fed it. In the consciousness of the more genuine zealots, nearly all belonging to the urban lower-middle classes, the two things were fused. Muslims resented Hindu economic and educational superiority just as Hindus resented the British ascendancy, and pride in a superior religion was both compensation and protest. More gradually, League propaganda could penetrate the countryside too, and in fact achieve more success there than Congress, because it denounced tangible enemies of the Muslim peasantry in the form of Hindu usurers in the North-west and Hindu landlords in East Bengal. Of Muslim landlords it had no criticism to make.

Once again the roots of separatism were partly external. The word 'Pakistan' was invented by a student at Cambridge, and the campaign got its start among the Muslim minorities in regions like the United Province only later gripping the Muslim majority areas which eventually formed the national territory. When this happened, a Muslim bourgeoisie, lacking in those areas, flitted from Bombay to Karachi and set up as an industrial–financial oligarchy, in partnership with the feudal landlords of the western Panjab. Their flimsy ideological backcloth, the Muslim League, promptly disintegrated. Pakistan was a hotch-potch of nationalities each better able to meet Jinnah's tests of nationhood, and one of them has already broken away. It has been observed that the separatist movement in East Bengal followed precisely the same lines as Jinnah's,[74] under stress of the same middle-class and petty-bourgeois anger at being kept out of a due share of loaves and fishes, and at being looked down on as inferior.

In other colonial regions the counterpoint of class and nationality was repeated with endless variations. Where no élite was ready to take the lead, a national movement could not start, but where classes were well developed they were liable to cancel each other out. During the inter-war years the new Third International was always scratching its head over the choice of tactics, and generally inclined towards the united fronts prescribed at the outset by Lenin and challenged at the outset by M. N. Roy.[75] National freedom was to be won first, like bourgeois democracy in Europe, social revolution to follow – though the Left, Lenin insisted, must preserve its own distinct organisation.[76] But as in Europe (in Marx's Germany of 1848 for instance) mass participation could only be secured by pledges of social reform going beyond what the propertied classes were willing to endorse. They were always

nervously aware, even without studying the *Communist Manifesto*, of an
executioner standing at the door. Communist parties were so much
more likely to divide than to unite subject nations that it was foolish of
colonial governments to be so anxious to suppress them. Their search
for a 'national bourgeoisie', ready to join in a struggle for independence
and fight it out with its left-wing allies later, proved elusive. On their
side the masses, wherever they were sufficiently aroused to turn against
foreign dominion, were apt to be in a mood to turn against their own
parasites as well – 'the Eaters', as they were expressively called in
Burma. And while men of property often made common cause with
foreign power against their own people, the masses might rejoice, as a
Puerto Rican nationalist has said, to see their masters knocked about
by the more powerful foreigner.[77]

The collision of empires in the Second World War liberated a great
part of Asia, and led towards liberation (or promotion to neo-colonial
status) for Africa. Élites were ready to take over in Asia; in Africa, as in
the more primitive Balkan countries, they developed very much in and
through the national movement, and after independence were further
built up by foreign interests and influences.[78] Tribal or regional discon-
tents have been rampant, and seem to turn very easily into 'movements'
of a sort wherever two or three job-hunters are gathered together.[79]
These are men of some education, often Christian converts. Intellectuals of all grades have regularly oscillated between nationalism's
two poles, the ideal and the sordid, under the sway of a complex of historical circumstances. Where imperialism refused to withdraw after
1945, Marxism was often on the scene, able to supply guidance as it had
lately done in China, and local intelligentsias were among its first adherents. Of all social types the intellectual has it in him more than any
other to be a man of action, but only when history compels him.

'A nation is not merely a historical category, but a historical category
belonging to a definite epoch, the epoch of rising capitalism.'[80] Stalin's
formula appears in many ways close to the mark, but it applies much
better to the handful of original nation-states in the West, and their
nearest neighbours, than to their imitations further afield; it applies far
less well still to the majority of nationalist movements, as distinct from
nations. Marxism has often slurred over the distinction between these
two things, and made modern nationalism, as well as the classical
nation-state, an *alter ego* of capitalism.[81] Capitalism required a homogeneous population, a single language, for its market, Lenin wrote:
'Throughout the world, the period of the final victory of capitalism over
feudalism was linked up with national movements.'[82] In the world at
large 'final victory' for capitalism has been as rare as for socialism;
Lenin was thinking too schematically in terms of a universal advance
from feudalism to capitalism and thence to socialism – though it was he
who excised the stage of full-blown capitalism from Russian history.

In effect, Marx, Engels and Lenin wanted to see national states established, as good for economic development, but had no liking for nationalism. Like religion, however, or any other great emotive force, nationalism is ambivalent, and can escape very completely from a prescribed political channel. Even in its origins it was a complex phenomenon, deriving both from the solidarity and from the divisions of society. It would have astonished Marx to see socialism owing so much to partnerships with nationalism, in Afro-Asia and in the Soviet Union during the Second World War, but this was a nationalism in which the populist element, instead of the class complex, was uppermost. It may be said indeed that just as the national state of the nineteenth century led logically, by way of the sovereignty of the nation and people, towards bourgeois democracy or republicanism (and hence underwent pathological strains in a country like Bismarckian Germany), nationalism in opposition in the twentieth century has led logically towards socialism.

7

On Attaining Sovereignty

Peter Calvert

'And after independence, what then?' That is the question to which some of the best brains of our century have chosen not to address themselves. Not, that is, before independence has actually been achieved. The fact is that though the act of attaining independence is a necessary condition for attaining the ability to govern oneself, it is not a sufficient condition. Why is this so? Basically, it is because the ideal of sovereignty, which alone sustains the leaders of independence movements through their darker hours of struggle, is an absolute one. One is either independent, or one is not. And it is therefore very hard for leaders of independence movements to appreciate how far sovereignty today has become merely a fiction. Not that it ever was very much the fact; there must have been few countries, even in the most remote periods of time, which did not share boundaries with some neighbour, and engage in some kind of relationship with that neighbour involving some degree of predeterminacy.

But even if it were not so, independence would still carry disillusion. For the most elementary fact about politics, and consequently, it seems, the most difficult for politicians to remember, is that their capacity to satisfy the demands that are, and will be, made upon them, is always strictly limited. Limited, that is, not by human antagonism, but by the facts of their countries' material position, human and non-human resources, and potential for development. It must be particularly galling, when you have accepted for so long that your country is so desirable that a major state wishes to retain possession of it, suddenly to discover that it is not so wonderful after all.

Perhaps the colonising country, in the first instance, was mistaken in its belief that the country it colonised contained immense resources which would be of benefit to it. Perhaps, on the other hand, it was never interested in material resources as such, merely in a strategic location, or in a simple desire to deny a strategic strong-point to some other power. In fact, all other things being equal, it may be taken as very probable at least that the more desirable a colony is, the less likely it is to be relinquished without a very hard fight. Such a battle will sap the human, if not the material, resources, and at the same time leave it in a state of potential dependency upon any other power that may offer to help. In this enfeebled state, even if it is only temporary, the new government has to cope with the mammoth tasks of organising a system of public administration, the collection of revenue, the establishment of credit, and the creation of a new system of law and order in circumstances most unlikely to be propitious to it. It is not surprising, therefore, that nations as politically mature as Algeria and Ireland have had to undergo a period of internal political turmoil and even violence before settling down to reorganise their government in something approaching a permanent form.

It follows, then, that one of the first tasks of most governments, when they have won independence, is to take it away from someone else. When I describe these people from whom a second level of independence has to be won, I would refer to them generally as 'minorities'. However, minorities vary in size considerably, and, as we shall see, in certain locations they may in fact constitute majorities. Nevertheless, the usefulness of the term in this particular context is too great for it to be set aside easily. I will divide these minorities into four main groups. In order of urgency they will be: those within the state who have been actively opposed to independence, those minorities within the state that have been incompletely suppressed by the government of the colonial power in the past; related minority groups in other neighbouring states; and groups resisting independence in other countries generally.

The most urgent problems are those that directly affect the internal stability of the government. Hence, those who have been actively opposed to independence constitute the most urgent problem; that there will be some is almost inevitable. In the ebb and flow of division and reunification which constitutes the theme of human history, the goal of unification and cumulation is, in the long term, as significant as the goal of independence. Indeed, if we are looking for a primitive motive force in human societies, as characteristic of advanced ones as of primitive ones, we need seek no further. In biological terms, it is not possible to imagine human societies without the urge for cumulation and unification, since without it the goal of the reproduction of the species can scarcely be attained. If, on the other hand, there is a primitive urge to independence, it stems partly from a psychological need for the young to grow up and to realise the fact, partly from the social necessity of space in which to live without the urge to conflict with one's neighbour, and partly from the economic constraints of territory which determine the amount of space each member of the community must occupy in order to earn a living.

I am not of course suggesting that these psychological motivations can be transferred to the macro level and applied directly to the state seeking independence as to an individual. But men govern states in accordance with their personal psychological habits; hence, in any community, newly independent or not, the urge to cumulation, to solidarity and to the assurance of past patterns of cumulation and solidarity dominates the ideology of government. Furthermore, in revolutionary war, whether purely internal or for purposes of secession, a common theme is the division of families across party lines. One needs only to recall how the fateful, decisive vote of the execution of Louis XVI was cast by his cousin Philippe Égalité, whose son was to succeed the deposed Charles X. Suspicion at the most personal level is thus present from the first. The politically conservative, those who had been the best citizens of the colonial regime, are those that are most likely to incur suspicion, and the fact of their relationship, where applicable, to those known to be loyal to the successor government only creates a higher degree of tension in the minds of the insecure successors. In fact the politically conservative may well be the best citizens of the new regime too, in that they are the least likely actively to oppose it. 'What is treason?' asked Talleyrand, and answered: 'merely a matter of dates'.

Then, too, we must have regard to the international dimension of independence. One can barely conceive of independence as a purely internal phenomenon, and the fact is that both the leaders and the opponents of independence movements are formed in the wider cultural awareness of the international setting of the metropolitan countries' sphere of influence. The fact that leaders of revolutionary movements, and in particular of movements of independence, have frequently undergone formative political experiences while travelling abroad, is something that is well known. But no less important are the culturally aware members of society who accept the international culture without political implications that it may carry – they may be republican believers in self-government – without necessarily applying it to their own condition. Indeed, the most distinguished of them, those who have attained international reputations in literature and the arts, or those who are simply conscious of the interest and excitement that attaches to a unifying culture, are likely for many years to be seen to be the most serious potential enemies of the infant state. One needs only to think how the Russian Revolution, which began as a rising of a regional grouping of a depressed class in the name of the world proletariat, was transformed under Stalin into a movement for Russian independence from Europe and in particular from Germany, to see how those elements within society who have transcended the narrow chauvinism of their fellows are most likely to fall victim to them in the years after their success has been achieved.

No one is more likely to be aware of the narrow boundary line between loyal opposition and treason than the leaders of independence themselves. They have lived with it, waking and sleeping, for years. They have learnt the arts of dissimulation, of infiltration and of manoeuvre; they have been trained to think in secret and to carry their thoughts with them wherever they go. They expect as a matter of course that others will do the same. They will be aware that a frank profession of loyalty may mask infidelity, and silent acceptance be tinged with dumb insolence. Above all, they will have to struggle within themselves against that psychological urge for positive and constant reassurance, something that even the most loyal followers may choke at giving. Frequently they will not struggle very hard. They will instead find it easiest, as well as most reassuring, to regard and designate all manifestation of opposition as treason.

Hence the vast majority of independent states which have achieved their independence through force tend to fall into the hands of those who will seek to make them as oppositionless as possible. In the euphoria of independence it is particularly easy to present the oppositionless state as an ideal which has actually been achieved momentarily. Only its immediate transformation into permanent, institutionalised terms, so the argument runs, can prevent it from being stolen from the newly independent citizens. So in the late 1950s and early 1960s, one after another of the newly independent African states, from Ghana onwards, threw off the notion of legal opposition. Frequently, in doing so, this was accompanied by a measure of force, most dramatically in Uganda where President Milton Obote used the device of a military coup to rid himself of his opponents. In Ghana itself, President Nkrumah did not go quite so far; in mobilising the vastly superior force of the Convention Peoples Party (C.P.P.), however, so that it threatened any political opponent who did not profess instant and total obedience to the leader of the state, he was channelling towards them a degree of implied force that stood only one degree short of actuality.

For the removal of the opposition is not simply an administrative act. Generally it accompanies a degree of mobilisation centred upon the personality of a single individual. The phenomenon is known most commonly in Latin America under the name of *caudillismo*. The *caudillo* is a charismatic leader in the Weberian sense. He is a hero, a man of outstanding personal qualities, a man who has had the special favour of fortune shown him by his success in attaining leadership and rank. He claims to be the guardian of the state, and the state is expressed by him. He shapes the state to the needs which he conceives for it, and he interprets the will of all the citizens in their name in the way that Robespierre interpreted the words of Rousseau. In the presence of his claim to leadership, all other claims to leadership are melted down. Thus Nkrumah, who effected the paraphernalia of a chief within his state,

destooled the traditional tribal chieftains. A more restrained personality, President Kenyatta, carries the traditional fly-whisk of high rank
and has made it his personal attribute. Though a few megalomaniac
South American dictators, such as Santa Anna in Mexico or Melgarejo
in Bolivia, have proclaimed their supremacy with the panoply of monarchy, the charismatic leader of independence frequently affects intense humility, dresses simply as befits one who is merely the servant of
his people, and stands out among his followers by the modesty of his de-
meanour and dress.

The emergence of this single figure of outstanding personal qualities,
whether he is the actual leader and director of the armed struggle for
independence, or whether he is one who distinguished himself during
that period and so inherits the claim to power, is of crucial significance
in the formation of nationhood. The nation is a personification of the
state. There is no easier way to create a personification than through
attaching it to a person. How can we imagine the United States without
the figure of George Washington, Venezuela without Bolivar, Ireland
without De Valera, or India without Nehru. Conversely, the absence of
such a prominent national figure in the early years of independence is
clearly a substantial bar to the creation of national identity. Without
such a figure, nationalism becomes, as it will become in the mature
state, a much less definite thing, a sentiment attached to an abstraction, to a flag or to a phrase.

This sort of nationalism is not a single feeling of loyalty, but a combination of things, incorporating a sense of national separateness, a
sentiment of some degree of ethnic or linguistic unity with other people
within the same formally independent country, and perhaps a degree of
aggressive assertiveness towards the inhabitants of neighbouring
states. Since it is not one sentiment or phenomenon, it is very difficult to
generalise further about its relationship to the process by which
independence was gained, except to say that the most powerful feelings of nationalism seem to occur where the struggle for independence has been the most prolonged, but then such conditions are
those in which the element of personal leadership is likely to have
been of the highest significance.

When we turn to the status of minorities incompletely suppressed
by the colonial government, we encounter a second set of problems.
Much depends on the circumstances of the original act of colonisation. But, generally speaking, the most successful and long-lived
acts of colonisation have not been those involving the direct application of military force by a colonising power. They have been those
in which colonising powers entered, or were drawn into, a colonial
territory by the use of the forces of that colonial territory. The most
successful empires are those that use their subjects to hold down
themselves. Since this is a piecemeal process, there is often no need

for a colonising power to establish actual control over regions or districts inhabited by minorities. And, even if such control is established, it may well be of an entirely separate nature to that established over the districts inhabited by the majority, as for example in Malaya, or combine dissimilar elements on an equal plane which were previously entirely separate, as in the British decision to administer Burma from India. Thus, in Vietnam, for example, under French rule it was possible for the Meo to coexist with their lowland neighbours without any interpenetration of their social and political structures. British actions on the frontiers of India, though they had for Britain a real military purpose in seeking to anticipate the advance of Russian or Russian-supported forces, were nevertheless in the main concerned only to provide a *modus vivendi* and not to establish direct political control. In fact British colonial administration, like British domestic administration, has always been characterised by a delight in the elaborateness and complexity of its administrative arrangements, and the attractive little local differences between one system and another. Even where extensive cultural interpenetration occurred in key areas, as, for example, in the case of the Spanish conquest of Mexico and Central America, there continued throughout colonial times to be substantial minorities enjoying nearly complete autonomy, as in the case of the Maya of the Yucatán peninsula, or the Indians of Panama.

For a newly independent country, the administration of a minority presents no new problems. But the nationalisation of a minority is a very different question. The minorities may well acquiesce in separate, independent status which they enjoyed under the colonial regime. They are scarcely likely to view with enthusiasm their forcible incorporation in a pattern of cultural and social behaviour which they may well find totally alien. Additional complications arise in a few other cases. Some states, notably Nigeria in Africa, Outer Mongolia in Asia and the Spanish viceroyalties of South America, were originally delimited by purely administrative considerations. An additional consideration arises where boundaries of originally purely administrative convenience become national boundaries through secession, as in the case of the break-up of the Central American Republic. The defence of these, and of similar boundaries, generates a need for nationalism which may well not previously have been felt, at least on that level. Thus, for example, in Central America the primary loyalty of a citizen will still tend to be to his native town or village. Only secondarily does it focus on the national unit. And there is no logical end to the process of secession; the fact of a minority means the risk of an attempt at secession, and even if that attempt is not made, the possibility remains.

In recent years the campaign of the Indian government against the Nagas, the attempt of the Ibo to secede from Nigeria, and the successful secession of Bangladesh, all mark different degrees of success in the achievement of secession. And recent developments in Ethiopia, where Eritrean nationalism is receiving immense impetus from the circumstances of its repression by the Ethiopian army warn us that the creation of such new nationalisms results more often from testing in the crucible of suppression by a superior government than from the mobilisation of the population from below. Minorities subjected to persistent discrimination, particularly where this is accompanied by arbitrary misgovernment or brutality, quickly develop a desire for independence.

Hence, to take an example, the Indian campaign against the Nagas must be seen in a very different context from the Indian campaigns in Hyderabad, Kashmir or Goa. The struggle for Kashmir was seen by the Indian government as the act of claiming their rightful share of a bargain. It stemmed therefore from the circumstances of an international agreement, which had very little to do with the actual wish of the inhabitants of the area concerned, and nothing whatever to do with a sense of nationalism within Kashmir itself. Kashmir, however, lay on the edge of the Indian territory, and therefore secession was an option easily open to it. No such option, effectively, was open to Hyderabad, the annexation of which was a social gesture against the independence of the Princes. The lesson, since fulfilled, was that the spirit of Indian nationalism required not only a powerful state bent on the unification and ruling of its national territory, but, more importantly, the social equality of the classes and castes before the Nation, and the overriding demands which the nation was to make on the individual. It was an act, therefore, which was necessary to the maintenance of a sovereign state in the rest of India. Lastly, the seizure of Goa was not just the seizure of a very small piece of territory by a relatively very large country which had no particular right to it, and the rulers of which were well aware that the inhabitants were not particularly keen on the idea. It was a diplomatic gesture to the invading Chinese forces in the North that India was an independent, sovereign state; to potentially rebellious minorities within India (for example Kerala), that the power of the government was adequate to secure internal obedience; and, in a paradoxical sense, to the rest of the world that India was a power that supported independence for small nations. It may well be asked how the act of taking independence away from a small piece of territory proves that you support independence? But this question is at the root of the understanding of nationalism, as opposed to an act of state. Nationalism is its own self-justification; a nationalistic act cannot be imperialistic, unless it is practised by an imperialistic power, and if one is not an imperialistic power, then one cannot be practising imperialism; so runs the argument.

Nothing could be more disquieting to the rulers of newly independent states than to see related ethnic or religious groups in adjacent states leading comfortable lives under alien rule. Their contentment, if accepted or recognised, would subtly undermine the whole logical foundation of independence. For independence, to be real, must involve a certain degree of adversity. In national terms, adversity, austerity, and in extreme cases (such as Cuba) a kind of puritanical delight in self-denial, form a satisfactory theme for the coercion of the individual by his or her fellows. Not only has this economic advantages for the government, it also strengthens their hand immeasurably against the will of the individual. In individual terms, this involves a single will and a single decision. In the case of the community it implies, necessarily, the likelihood of internal divisions. And neighbouring groups can then easily come to form a focus for disaffection.

In theory the 'threat' can be met by annexation or by an act of federation. However, in modern times annexation outright seems impossible for practical reasons in all but the very smallest target states. Goa is one example, but the number of very small states where annexation has not, so far, been practised, such as Macao, Gibraltar, the Falkland Islands and Belize, reminds us that not only are the costs high for the annexing power, but there is no real glory to be won that way either. Hence in the majority of cases such action is limited to diplomatic gestures used to serve as statements of a case for future legal settlement. Thus the new state of Guyana received an unwelcome birthday present from its neighbour Venezuela when it was announced there that over half its national territory rightfully belonged to the larger country. In fact, threats of annexation appear to relate in no way to the degree of intransigence shown by the neighbouring state – the Goans could hardly have been more pacific.

Lastly, by a supreme flight of illogic characteristic of our age, all other groups not yet independent appear to be seen, at least by some independent states, as a potential threat to the justification of their own nationhood.

Minorities are, then, the principal targets of post-independence politics. But why is the treatment of them, and of political problems generally, more revolutionary in some states than in others? Clearly, the answer must lie to some extent in the decisiveness of the demands originally made. But it must lie, too, in the nature of the people who direct the movement and those who follow them.

We have already seen how post-independence leaders seem to establish a charismatic leadership which transcends all other forms of authority within the state. But it is not sufficient to have a charismatic personality; the formula for success is charisma backed by guns. Guns in themselves are useless unless they are pointing in the proper direction, and the key to the control of armed force in the newly independent state lies not just in charisma but also in organisation. The fact is, it is easier to build up an organisation around a single dominant personality than around a group. Group organisation necessarily implies indecisiveness. And as a tool for restraining power it is extremely valuable. But nationalists are not seeking to restrain the power of their new state. And even though their organisation may be led by a single man, its success will depend on the degree of its diversification and the efficiency with which it can be made to operate.

Independence, then, is the end of heroism and the beginning of politics. Politics is the art of building majorities, and the attack on minorities is only its negative, if in so many ways its most noticeable, aspect. Politics in this context means the mobilisation of resources. These depend on the human and non-human bases available, but their mobilisation always implies the co-operation of others, and the utilisation of resources is something on which people may legitimately have more than one view. It follows, therefore, that the organisation of the new state will rapidly be directed towards the safeguarding of majority opinion and its consolidation where necessary. Provided, that is, that the government does represent the will of the majority – it may well not, particularly where it owes its success to the desire of the former metropolitan power to surrender gracefully to the inevitable.

The government coalition is stabilised in three principal ways. First, organisation gives coherence and a sense of *identity*. Second, it enables the financial resources of the state to be marshalled and a due proportion of them skimmed off for the use of the government. The extent to which the government draws upon these financial resources will vary principally according to the scale of its ambitions and the way in which its internal politics permits individuals to extend their fields of competence. Since in most developing countries government is essentially multi-functional or transitional, there can be very considerable scope for such expansion. Third, organisation exists for its own sake, inculcating a common government code by which the government may, if it so desires, improve the efficiency of its operations by the simplification of tasks into clearly delimited spheres of activity and the improvement of communications links. This has the additional virtue, in government eyes, of strengthening the identity of the government within the state as a whole.

Now the degree to which each of these will receive attention in the first instance will depend directly on the method by which the national movement has attained power. There are four principal means by which national movements attain power in the modern world: the direct use of armed struggle, the indirect assistance of armed struggle, agitation and negotiation. We shall consider them in inverse order. There is also a fifth form, independence by attenuation, as in the cases of Canada, South Africa, Australia and New Zealand, but this will not be considered.

Where independence has been achieved by negotiation, as in the case of the Philippines, Ghana, the West Indies and the majority of states of the French Community, the new government has definite advantages. It not only inherits the legitimacy of the representatives of the colonial regime but it also engenders its own legitimacy as representing those who have stood up to colonial rule and been recognised by them. In organisational terms it has the advantage of being able to take over a basically autocratic system of administration in full working order, virtually unaltered. Opposition, where it exists, is already likely to be institutional in spirit and parliamentary in form, and to a considerable extent its distinctive programmes will have been subordinated voluntarily to the overriding demands of the negotiations for independence. The successor government in these cases has a high capacity for the mobilisation both of people and of resources. Its chief danger, indeed, is that it will be so successful at mobilising financial resources that it will become extremely corrupt. Corruption, though not necessarily antipathetic to the sense of national identity, rapidly erodes the sense of identity between the people and their new rulers. The possibility that this in turn may lead to some sort of intervention by the armed forces is ever present, as witness the twenty-eight successful coups in Africa between 1960 and 1975.

National movements that have attained independence by agitation, as in the case of Norway, India, Pakistan, Burma, Malaysia, Tunisia, Malagasy, and, perhaps, Guyana, have undergone a more testing experience; one which still has not been so severe as to be disruptive. Indeed the necessity for agitation has probably forced a much keener sense of solidarity upon the inhabitants as well as the government. In such states, political organisation is likely to be very strong, while the ability of the government to mobilise resources will to some extent be tempered by the awareness that those resources need to be intelligently safeguarded. States in this category seem to be the ones most likely to enjoy stable post-independence politics and to have the maximum potential, within the limits given them by their bases, for social and economic development, but the empirical evidence remains uncertain.

There are, however, some states in the third category which enjoy many of these advantages. This category consists of those states which, while not themselves engaging to any significant extent in actual fighting, have been assisted to independence by the presence of fighting in the international environment.

Examples are those states such as Brazil, Panama, Outer Mongolia, or in our own time, Rhodesia, which have declared their independence in circumstances in which the metropolitan power has been, through its own remoteness or inadequacy, incapable of the act of reconquest. Here the threat of reconquest, if serious, would naturally act as a strong consolidating factor.

A second sub-category consists of those states attaining independence in wartime, as an incidental part of the diplomatic and military manoeuvres of the contending powers, each intent on clipping off such parts of the other's empire as seem to be conveniently loose. Here there is no common factor. Iceland, on the one hand, whose metropolitan had been invaded and was only technically at war with the Allies, and which has the special advantages of isolation and prosperity, seems to have very little in common except legal personality with states such as Syria or the Lebanon, deficient in natural resources and deeply involved to this day as medium-sized pieces in the game of international conflict.

A third sub-group are those that achieve independence mainly as the result of an internal coup in the metropolitan state. These include some of the Spanish-American states, particularly Chile, Mexico, Colombia, Venezuela and Paraguay, the Central-American states and, more recently, Guiné, Angola and Moçambique.

The fourth sub-group comprises those states that achieve independence as the result of the defeat of the metropolitan state in a general war, though in most cases the inhabitants of these territories take part in the war themselves. Possible examples are: Argentina, Cuba, Hungary, Poland, Czechoslovakia, Egypt and Cambodia.

As will be seen, these form a very diverse group, and the division of the group into four sub-groups is attended by considerable difficulties of interpretation and classification. Though it appears, therefore, for the category as a whole, that post-independence politics does to some extent vary according to the origins of the state, other more individual factors are exceedingly important, and perhaps more important; these include leadership, population, the natural resources of the country concerned, its geographical location and the precise circumstances.

But if one factor stands out above the others, it is the extent to which reconquest seems to be a present possibility. Clearly in the majority of instances this has not been so, and the new states have rapidly assumed a distinctive international personality and even a degree of self-assertiveness which others do not have. Since they did not generally form the main theatres of destructive international or national wars, their economic resources were substantially untouched on independence, and, indeed, in many cases enhanced by an increase in demand from other states engaged in conflicts with one another. Others such as Mexico, Cuba and the Portuguese-African states have been less fortunate. However, with the marginal case of Brazil, interestingly enough, none of them has so far attained the position of being a power of the first rank in its own right. Nor has any of them in the immediate post-independence period become the theatre of social or economic experiments so distinctive or innovatory as to lead their acts of independence to be remembered as being among the more significant of the world's events, though it is only fair to point out that of those powers that have attained first rank, only the United States has had recent experience of colonial rule, for China had assimilated its alien dynasty and the dates of independence of France, Britain, Russia and Japan are historically meaningless to current events.

So we turn to the fourth category, those states that have attained power by fighting for it.

Those that immediately strike the eye are those who have achieved independence by a direct struggle against the metropolitan power, that is to say by an act of secession backed by armed force where external help was limited to diplomatic negotiation and the purchase of supplies. Such states include the United States and Ireland, Peru and Bolivia, Algeria, Haiti and Vietnam, Israel, South Yemen, Finland and some others. In the ambiguous case of Cuba, foreign help was of overwhelming importance, forestalling and reducing the impact of independence, and subsequently involving an unacceptable period of tutelage which bred disillusion and corruption. Otherwise it appears to be in these states that the keenest sense of national identity is felt, and the most extreme manifestations of nationalism have taken place. Almost all of them have been characterised in the period immediately following independence by enthusiasm for drastic social experiment. In each a considerable measure of continued violence appears to have been a feature of post-revolutionary society, with a degree of puritanism in official government policy, a sense of common commitment to abstinence which goes well beyond the norm for most ages and most states. In fact the politics of these secessionist states in the post-independence period has strong affinities with the policies of those states in which strongly nationalist regimes have attained power by revolutionary means, such as Russia or even Hitler's Germany.

The reconstruction of the state and of the social life that goes with the state has involved the same type of recreation of identity as is characteristic of the post-independence state. In a kind of mass therapy for a whole people, a conscious attempt is made to shed the old and put on a new personality, to eradicate old social vices and to manipulate symbols in order to construct a new social style which is to become habitual, and hence lasting. It has been the tragedy of many of them that their territories have been so ravaged by the wars of independence that permanent damage has been done, either (as witness Frantz Fanon) to their peoples, or, as we see now in Vietnam, to their material resources.

How then to create a sense of identity? Basically it is, in fact, a case of the manipulation of symbols. But which symbols, and how to manipulate them? Symbols cannot be chosen simply at random. There are three principal sources on which to draw.

The best, because the most 'real', is the historic past of the nation before colonisation. The effectiveness of this depends on the remoteness of that historic past. Many ex-colonial territories of today had colonial histories lasting a hundred years or more. But this is not a long time in the social consciousness, even if it were not so in all but a few cases that the actual social area extensively touched by direct colonisation is relatively small. Local government and the daily customs of the people are relatively untouched, except for those evolutionary changes in technology brought about by the reception of advances in the understanding of the physical world that are the common property of mankind, and, as such, politically neutral.

In the case of countries such as Mexico or Peru, where colonial status lasted for more than three hundred years, the vast bulk of the population continued at the end of that time to live in much the same sort of fashion as did their forebears. Such elements as were introduced into the socio-economic structure 'by the Spaniards' were in fact, with one exception (the chicken, which replaced the indigenous turkey), artefacts or goods which represented in some sense an improvement on what had been used previously.

With some states it is rather more difficult. Egypt was under foreign rule from 30 B.C. to A.D. 1922, a period long enough for all memories of the historical past to have been forgotten had it not been for the dry climate which preserved it for the reviving interest of the modern world. Politically, too, the revival was to some extent a consciously archaistic one, and one which could only have had meaning for a country with such a rare combination of archaeological good fortune. It is noteworthy that Libya, on the other hand, since the Revolution there, has determinedly ignored the visible heritage of its Roman past, as its symbolism clashes with that of the invading Italians of the 1930s.

Second, national symbols can be drawn from the less essential aspects of colonial rule. The introduction of cricket, for example, as part of the process of British colonisation and economic expansion in the nineteenth century, was probably of little or no economic value to the British. But it has offered a useful arena for the symbolic defeat of the former metropolitan state, not only in those states such as Australia and New Zealand that achieved independence by attenuation, but even in India and Pakistan. Football, introduced into South America at a further remove, has today been completely purged of its association with imperial power, and become a living source of nationalistic pride in Brazil and Uruguay, where the absence of historic conflicts and legacies of historic bitterness would otherwise have made national identification rather difficult. It has the dual advantage of being cheap to play, so cutting across potentially divisive class lines, and offering immediate access to a wider international role.

Last, with the customary imitativeness of human beings, national leaders tend to borrow preferred models from any state or period that they may happen to admire. From Sarmiento's admiration for U.S. democracy to General Idi Amin's high regard for Hitler is a wide step indeed, yet both illustrate the way in which personal predilections and individual experiences may influence the most fundamental aspects of political and social behaviour. Few Argentinians in 1868 had any first-hand knowledge of the United States, and Uganda's experience of Germany ended in 1915. As with ideas, so with symbols. Both can be transplanted into foreign soil with some chance, if the circumstances are right, that they will take root. Whatever their origin, the symbols of identity combine certain critical elements.

First and foremost are the emblems of authority. It is here that the duality of origin becomes most obvious, because emblems have to be chosen both with regard to the approval of the international community and of peer states, and for compatibility with the traditions of the country concerned. Thus the stool of the chieftain may support a man who calls himself a 'President' in the standard mode of today, and the flag in the usual tricolour pattern originated from the French Revolution, adopted by the Spanish successor states, and now almost universal, may bear a cryptic symbol, such as the wheel of India or the man of Mali, deemed particularly applicable to the region over which it flies.

No such duality exists in the case of language, the most powerful tool of the nationalist because it is most omnipresent and governs the reception of nearly every social action. Those states where a historic language is available for the purpose naturally tend to use it; where it is not widely accepted by a bilingual people its effectiveness may well be reinforced by other means, as in the case of the Gaelic League in Ireland, which encouraged not only the use of the language, but also a whole range of peculiarly Irish sports and activities which excluded, along with British influences, the generally prevailing international ones as well.

Such common activities, public rituals and, even better, the grand national festivals of which they may well form part, are essential occasions for the demonstration of physical presence and solidarity. By gathering together for a common purpose in one place, or at a series of centres on a common day, they make the individual more aware of the presence of a group, soothe his sense of separateness by presenting a collective identity, and offer a useful outlet for energy that might otherwise be expended in political opposition. It is symbolic that the one occasion for a national festival now used by all but a handful of countries is Independence Day. They have replaced the physical birthday of the monarch with the abstract birth of the nation. Rarely, on the other hand, are they not backed up with numerous other acts of public togetherness.

Lastly come badges of belonging, which may be worn (national dress, headgear, and so on), displayed (cockades, sashes, photographs of high dignitaries) or carried by individuals.

Effective as all these devices may be in creating a sense of solidarity, however, they do have one disadvantage. They exclude, and are no less effective in creating a sense of hostility towards 'others'. In the world of the nation-states of today, not all those offended will be minorities. This is dangerous enough. But what causes the most concern for the future of the human race is that the force of nationalism has almost universally, both in the East and in the West, superseded all other forms of integrative behaviour and given a rigidity to the concept of the nation-state which is quite new in world experience. It is not in fact the sentiment of nationalism that is new; it is its product.

In the old monarchies of Europe there was one valuable human foible which beneficially acted to counteract the tendency towards fission and disruption which is characteristic of twentieth-century statecraft. This was the custom of marriage between royal families. So Austria was created, so Brittany was joined to France, and England to Scotland. In the republican, independent states of today this human mode of unification cannot work; a president may marry whom he pleases, and only rarely does his choice have political consequences. The history of European unification since the Second World War has been particularly discouraging in this regard, as evidence that the marriages of states involve more complex legalistic debate and possibilities for conflict than the most formidable marriage settlement dreamt of by an Elizabethan lawyer. Together, the old nationalism and the new nationalism have given millions a chance of greater dignity in the collective enjoyment of the territories in which they live. We cannot believe that these benefits are completely outweighed by the sad stories of wars, massacres, atrocities and torture with which government and non-government agencies alike have sought to eradicate individual quirks and eccentricities from the world of nation-states. But we must also realise that if we do not find such mechanisms of unification, the twenty-first century will need to find them, if indeed it does not turn out to be the last.

Sovereignty is a means to an end, not the end itself. Historically it was a legal formula giving authority to act. But there are other possible formulae, and the fact that sovereignty is no longer in the absolute sense an attainable goal in the modern world need cause us no concern. Without it, governments may still look after their citizens, and their citizens look after themselves. By definition, municipal government never has sovereignty, but it still works. What gives rise to concern is the fact that the decline in the independence of municipal government, and the erosion of sovereignty, both relate directly to the increased coercive power of the state.

As long as there was a rather limited number of states, the management of the conflicts involved seemed to be capable of at least eventual solution by discussion and negotiation. One powerful transnational force, socialism, grew up indeed and became powerful under the protection of the sovereignty it affected to be opposing; in turn, other states strengthened their own sense of national independence in order to resist it the more effectively. What neither side saw was that the increase of new nationalisms might escalate to the point at which their multiplication was effectively out of control.

The end of nationalism, then, if it does not lie in co-operative effort to transcend the bitternesses of the past (as in Western Europe), will take instead the form of its *reductio ad absurdum*, as witness those politicians who in Northern Ireland call for the solution of 'an independent British Ulster'. It is a situation where the most serious obstacle to a reasonable solution lies in the faded hopes of the past; hopes which, as I have tried here to show, will never be wholly rational and which can never be achieved.

Notes and References

CHAPTER ONE

1. The literature on definitions of nationalism and the nation is extensive. See especially L. Snyder, *The Meaning of Nationalism* (New Brunswick: Rutgers University Press, 1954); E. H. Carr (ed.), *Nationalism: A Report* (London: Oxford University Press–Royal Institute of International Affairs, 1939) and R. Emerson, *From Empire to Nation* (Harvard University Press, 1960).

2. The assumptions and definitions adopted here are more extensively discussed in A. D. Smith, 'Nationalism, A Trend Report and Bibliography', *Current Sociology*, xxi/3 (1973) section 2.

3. On Ethiopia, see R. Hess, 'Ethiopia', in *National Unity and Regionalism in Eight African States*, ed. G. Carter (Cornell University Press, 1966). For the conflict between German nationalism and Prussian patriotism, see W. M. Simon, 'Variations in Nationalism during the Great Reform Period in Prussia', *American Historical Review*, 59 (1954) 305–21.

4. But, see H. Kohn, 'The origin of English Nationalism', *Journal of the History of Ideas*, i (1940) 69–94, for the view that the Puritan revolution embodied a religious nationalism, with the English as 'God's chosen people', and England as the 'new Jerusalem'.

5. H. Martins, 'Ideology and Development: "Developmental Nationalism" in Brazil', *Sociological Review Monograph*, no. 11 (1967) 153–72. On Canada see also G. Spry, 'Canada: Notes on two Ideas of Nation in Confrontation', *Journal of Contemporary History*, 6 (1971) 173–96.

6. For the 'racial' theory prior to the Revolution, see J. Barzun, *The French Race: Theories of its Origins and their Social and Political Implications prior to the Revolution*, Columbia University Studies in History, Economics and Public Law, no. 375 (New York, 1932).

7. N. Keddie, *Religion and Rebellion in Iran: The Tobacco Protest of 1892* (London: Cass, 1966).

8. For some current 'secession' movements, often called separatisms, see the *Journal of Contemporary History*, 6 (1971) entitled 'Nationalism and Separatism'.

9. On Black emigration movements, see H. Brotz (ed.), *Negro Social and Political Thought, 1850–1920* (New York: Basic Books, 1966), and T. Draper, *The Rediscovery of Black Nationalism* (London: Secker & Warburg, 1970). On Zionism, see A. Hertzberg (ed.), *The Zionist Idea: A Historical Analysis and Reader* (New York: Meridian Books, 1960).

10. On irredentism and nationalism in Eastern Europe and the Balkans, see the essays in P. Sugar and I. Lederer (eds), *Nationalism in Eastern Europe*, Far Eastern and Russian Institute, Publications on Russia and Eastern Europe, no. 1 (Seattle: University of Washington, 1969).

11. Rotberg's concept of 'nation of intent' is illustrated by his study of East and Central Africa; see R. I. Rotberg, 'The Rise of African Nationalism: The Case of East and Central Africa', *World Politics*, 17 (1962) 75–90. On Argentina and Latin-American cultural nationalism, see A. P. Whitaker, *Nationalism in Latin America, Past and Present* (University of Florida Press, 1962).

12. For fuller discussions of these 'mixed' nationalisms, see the political anthropology of 'primordial ties' offered by C. Geertz, 'The Integrative Revolution', in his *Old Societies and New States* (New York: Free Press, 1963); and A. D. Smith, *Theories of Nationalism* (London: Duckworth, 1971) ch. 9.

13. In fact, Corsican nationalism has remained below the surface since the mid-eighteenth century, always however weakened by foreign exploitation of vendettas between glens and clans; see P. A. Thrasher, *Pasquali Paoli* (London: Constable, 1970) pp. 23–5.

14. On Breton and Basque nationalisms today, see P. E. Mayo, *The Roots of Identity: Three National Movements in Contemporary European Politics* (London: Allen Lane, 1974) chs 2, 4 and 7.

15. On the Coptic Assembly of 1910, see P. J. Vatikiotis, *The Modern History of Egypt* (New York: Praeger, 1969) pp. 193, 196–8.

16. On Tito's Partisans, see R. Burks, *The Dynamics of Communism in Eastern Europe* (Princeton University Press, 1961) pp. 119–30. On the break-up of F.L.N. unity, see W. H. Lewis, 'The Decline of Algeria's FLN', *Middle East Journal*, xx (1966) 161–72. The growth of Israeli Yishuv institutions is documented in A. M. Hyamson, *Palestine under the Mandate* (London: Methuen, 1950) and B. Halpern, *The Idea of the Jewish State* (Harvard University Press, 1961) esp. ch. 6.

17. Patriotic mobilisation is first exemplified during the *levées en masse* of the French Revolution; see G. Rudé, *Revolutionary Europe* (London: Collins, 1964); and for its uses in the Vietnamese struggle, see D. A. Wilson, 'Nation-building and Revolutionary War', in *Nation-Building*,

ed. K. Deutsch and W. Foltz (New York: Atherton, 1963).

18. See G. Procacci, *History of the Italian People* (London: Weidenfeld & Nicolson, 1970) esp. pp. 324–8; and D. Beales, *The Risorgimento and the Unification of Italy* (London: Allen & Unwin, 1971) which emphasises continuing particularism and *campanilismo*. For Greece, see D. Dakin, *The Unification of Greece, 1770–1923* (London: Ernest Benn, 1972).

19. In many ways, the prototype were the *Burschenschaften*, first founded at Jena in 1815, and the *Turnershaft*, which Jahn and Friesen originated in 1811; see H. Kohn, *The Mind of Germany* (London: Macmillan, 1965) pp. 84–8. For the folk high schools of Grundtvig in Denmark, see J. Wuorinen, 'Scandinavia and National Consciousness', in *Nationalism and Internationalism, Essays inscribed in honour of C. J. H. Hayes*, ed. E. M. Earle (New York: Columbia University Press, 1950).

20. The point is forcefully made by E. Kedourie, *Nationalism in Asia and Africa* (London: Weidenfeld & Nicholson, 1971) 'Introduction', pp. 35–64, especially on Koraes and Banerjea.

21. For the cult of Brutus and Voltaire, see R. L. Herbert, *David, Voltaire, Brutus and the French Revolution: an Essay in Art and Politics* (London: Allen Lane, The Penguin Press, 1972) esp. pp. 52–5, 81, describing the translation of Voltaire's remains from Sellières to the Panthéon.

22. For Corsica, see Thrasher, *Pasquale Paoli*, p. 25; on the Yakuts, W. Kolarz, *Peoples of the Soviet Far East* (London: Philip Allen, 1954) ch. 4.

23. There is a political and historical rationale behind the size condition: nations require a minimum military capacity relative to neighbours so as not to create a vacuum; and France and England, the first real nation-states, were both large (in population and extent) and successful. For the range of national populations, see Smith, *Theories of Nationalism*, pp. 188, 322–3.

24. See B. Akzin, *State and Nation* (London: Hutchinson, 1964) pp. 55–64.

25. Salomon Gessner's alpine idylls are matched in Norway by Hans Bull's eulogies of the fjords, at the onset of Rousseau's influence; see H. Kohn, *The Idea of Nationalism* (New York: Collier, 1967) pp. 264, 382–92. For the Tyrol, see L. Doob, *Patriotism and Nationalism: their Psychological Foundations* (Yale University Press, 1964).

26. On Transylvania, see C. C. Giurescu, *Transylvania in the History of Romania* (London: Garnstone Press, 1967). On Poland, see O. Halecki, *A History of Poland*, rev. edn (London: Dent, 1955) pt IV, and R. F. Leslie, *Reform and Insurrection in Russian Poland, 1856–65* (Athlone Press, University of London, 1963).

27. J. Katz, 'The Jewish National Movement: a Sociological Analysis', in *Jewish Society through the Ages*, ed. H. H. Ben Sasson and S. Ettinger (London: Valentine, Mitchell & Co., 1971) and L. Greenberg, *The Jews of Russia*, 2 vols (Yale University Press, 1951).

28. J. Godechot, *France and the Atlantic Revolutions of the Eighteenth Century, 1770–99* (New York: Free Press, 1965) esp. pp. 3–7, 51–63, 127–30.

29. A. Cobban, 'The Enlightenment and the French Revolution', in his *Aspects of the French Revolution* (London: Paladin, 1971).

30. See H. Honour, *Neo-Classicism* (Harmondsworth: Penguin, 1968).

31. See Kedourie, *Nationalism in Asia and Africa*, pp. 81–90, esp. p. 85, where he cites Banerjea's reaction to his dismissal, namely that 'the personal wrong done to me was an illustration of the impotency of our people'; and A. D. Smith, '"Ideas" and "Structure" in the Formation of Independence Ideals', *Philosophy of the Social Sciences*, 3 (1973) 19–39.

32. See L. S. Stavrianos, *The Balkans Since 1453* (New York: Holt, 1961) ch. 3, esp. pp. 222–5, which emphasises Rumanian and Slav hatred of the phanariot merchant class and tax farmers, and Greek domination, with the Porte's approval, of ecclesiastical posts in the Patriarchate, especially after the abolition of the Serbian Patriarchate of Pec in 1766, and the Bulgarian archbishopric of Ohrid in 1767.

33. M. Weber, 'Ethnic Groups', in *Economy and Society*, ed. G. Roth and C. Wittich (New York: Bedminster Press, 1968) vol. I, ch. 5.

34. C. E. Welch: *Dream of Unity: Pan-Africanism and Political Unification in West Africa* (Cornell University Press, 1966).

35. J. F. A. Ajayi, 'Nineteenth Century Origins of Nigerian Nationalism', *Journal of the Historical Society of Nigeria*, 2 (1960) 196–210.

36. See such accounts as R. July, *The Origins of Modern African Thought* (London: Faber & Faber, 1968) and C. Legum, *Pan-Africanism: a Short Political Guide* (London: Pall Mall Press, 1962).

37. R. W. Seton-Watson, *A History of Czechs and Slovaks* (London: Hutchinson, 1943) and J. Armstrong, *Ukrainian Nationalism*, 2nd edn (Columbia University Press, 1963) chs 1–2.

38 Mayo, *The Roots of Identity*, ch. 5, esp. pp. 63 ff.

39. One of the best documented is the Zealot revolt in first-century Judea: see S. F. Brandon, *Jesus and the Zealots* (Manchester University Press, 1967) ch. 2.

40. For some varieties of this 'historicism' in art in the late eighteenth century, see R. Rosenblum, *Transformations in Late Eighteenth Century Art* (Princeton University Press, 1967) pp. 34–7, 48–51, 75–89.

41. See the essays in J. Fishman *et al.* (eds), *Language Problems of Developing Countries* (New York: Wiley, 1968) esp. those of Paden and Haugen.

42. S. S. Harrison, *India; the Most Dangerous Decades* (Princeton University Press, 1960).

43. On European nationalists in the eighteenth century, see A. Kemilainen, *Nationalism, Problems concerning the Word, the Concept and*

Classification (Yvaskyla: Kustantajat Publishers, 1964). For the religious element in Indian nationalism, see R. I. Crane, 'Problems of Divergent Developments within Indian Nationalism, 1895–1905', and M. Adenwalla, 'Hindu Concepts and the Gita in Early Indian National Thought', both in *Studies on Asia,* ed. R. K. Sakai (University of Nebraska Press, 1961).

44. On the Indonesian music-dramas, see J. L. Peacock, *The Rites of Modernisation* (University of Chicago Press, 1968). On the arts in Europe, see Chapter 4 above.

45. D. E. Smith, *Religion and Politics in Burma* (Princeton University Press, 1965) ch. 3.

46. On Islam as a political religion, see S. Haim, 'Islam and the Theory of Arab Nationalism', in *The Middle East in Transition,* ed. W. Z. Laqueur (London: Routledge & Kegan Paul, 1958); and A. D. Smith, 'Nationalism and Religion: the Role of Religious Reform in the Genesis of Arab and Jewish Nationalism', *Archives de Sociologie des Religions,* 35 (1973) 23–43.

47. On the Rumanian heterodox priests, see R. R. Florescu, 'The Uniate Church: Catalyst of Rumanian Nationalism', *Slavic and East European Review,* 45 (1967) 324–42.

48. See Smith, 'Nationalism and Religion', pp. 35–7, and G. E. von Grunebaum, 'Problems of Muslim Nationalism', in *Islam and the West,* ed. R. N. Frye (The Hague: Mouton, 1957).

49. For the secularising role of colonial bureaucracy, see W. Roff, *The Origins of Malay Nationalism* (Yale University Press, 1967), ch.2, and B. T. McCulley, *English Education and the Origins of Indian Nationalism* (Gloucester, Mass.: Smith, 1966) esp. ch. 4. British rule reinforced traditional authority formally, but also rendered it politically and spiritually impotent in the eyes of educated youth.

50. M. Weber, 'The Social Psychology of the World Religions', in *From Max Weber, Essays in Sociology,* ed. H. Gerth and C. W. Mills (London: Routledge & Kegan Paul, 1948) esp. pp. 269–70, 279–84.

51. G. C. Coulton, 'Nationalism in the Middle Ages', *Cambridge Historical Journal,* v (1935) 15–40; and G. Zernatto, 'Nation: The History of a Word', *Review of Politics,* 6 (1944) 351–66.

52. See Honour, *Neo-Classicism,* pp. 87–98, and F. Antal, *Classicism and Romanticism, with Other Studies in Art History* (London: Routledge & Kegan Paul, 1966).

53. W. Bruford, *Germany in the Eighteenth Century* (Cambridge University Press, 1965).

54. H. S. Reiss (ed.), *The Political Thought of the German Romantics, 1793–1815* (Oxford: Blackwell, 1955); and Simon, 'Variations in Nationalism', 305–21.

55. Beales, *The Risorgimento and the Unification of Italy,* 'Introduction'.

56. Cited in Simon, 'Variations in Nationalism', 305 ff.

57. For this vicarious patriotism of Lafayette, Mirabeau and the Girondins, see R. Palmer, 'The National Idea in France before the Revolution', *Journal of the History of Ideas*, I (1940) 95–111.

58. On early Arab nationalists like Abduh, Rida, Azoury and Kawakibi, see S. Haim (ed.), *Arab Nationalism; an Anthology* (University of California Press, 1962).

59. See J. H. Kautsky (ed.), *Political Change in Underdeveloped Countries* (New York: Wiley, 1962).

60. For the Sixth Pan-African Congress, see Legum, *Pan-Africanism* pp. 30–2, 135–7; for the Arab Students' Congress Manifesto, see Haim (ed.), *Arab Nationalism*, pp. 100–2.

61. E. Ramsaur, *The Young Turks: Prelude to the Revolution of 1908* (Princeton University Press, 1957); S. N. Fisher (ed.), *The Military in the Middle East: Problems in Society and Government* (Ohio State University Press, 1963); G. Lenczowski, 'The Objects and Methods of Nasserism', *Journal of International Affairs*, 19 (1965) 63–75; and A. P. Whitaker and D. C. Jordan, *Nationalism in Contemporary Latin America* (New York: Free Press, 1966).

62. See Burks, *The Dynamics of Communism*, and C. Johnson, *Peasant Nationalism and Communist Power: The Emergence of Revolutionary China, 1937–45* (Stanford University Press, 1963).

63. F. von der Mehden, *Religion and Nationalism in Southeast Asia* (University of Wisconsin Press, 1963); and J. Cady, *A History of Modern Burma* (Cornell University Press, 1958) esp. chs 5–6.

64. R. Kedward, *The Dreyfus Affair* (London: Longmans, 1965).

65. Cited in Stavrianos, *The Balkans since 1453*, ch. 9; for the klephts, see J. Campbell and P. Sherrard, *Modern Greece* (London: Ernest Benn, 1968) pp. 57–9; for clerical involvement, see C. A. Frazee, *The Orthodox Church and Independent Greece, 1821–52* (Cambridge University Press, 1969).

66. See T. Stoianovitch, 'The Conquering Balkan Orthodox Merchant', *Journal of Economic History*, 20 (1960) 234–313. T. Stoianovitch, 'The Social Foundations of Balkan Politics, 1750–1941', in *The Balkans in Transition*, ed. B. and C. Jelavich (University of California Press, 1963) analyses this alliance between merchants, haiduks and intelligentsias in the Balkans. For the stimulus of Norwegian timber traders to national consciousness in the eighteenth century, see A. Elviken, 'The Genesis of Norwegian Nationalism', *Journal of Modern History*, 3 (1931) 365–91.

67. G. McT. Kahin, *Nationalism and Revolution in Indonesia* (Cornell University Press, 1952) chs 2–3, esp. pp. 65 ff. for Sarekat Islam.

68. On the Tatar merchants and jadidism, see A. Bennigsen and C. Lemercier-Quelquejay, *Les mouvements nationaux chez les musulmans de la Russie* (Paris: Mouton, 1960) pt I.

69. L. Nalbandian, *The Armenian Revolutionary Movement* (University

of California Press, 1963) esp. on Emin and Bagramian.

70. A. Zolberg, *One-Party Government in the Ivory Coast* (Princeton University Press, 1964).

71. The Tatar merchants suffered particularly from the economic competition of their Russian counterparts in Central Asia; see S. Zenkovsky, 'A Century of Tatar revival', *American Slavic and East European Review*, 14 (1955) 15–41.

72. For a discussion of the Marxist thesis that nationalism is a phenomenon (or weapon) of early (or mature) capitalism, see Smith, *Nationalism, A Trend Report and Bibliography*, section 4.3.

73. On the creation of Belgium, see M. S. Anderson, *The Ascendancy of Europe: Aspects of European History, 1815–1914* (London: Longmans, 1972) pp. 16–17, and J. Droz, *Europe Between Revolutions, 1815–1848* (London: Collins, 1967) pp. 230–3; and on Greece, see ibid. pp. 223–8, and Campbell and Sherrard, *Modern Greece*, ch. 3, emphasising external events.

74. For Kurdistan, see C. J. Edmonds, 'Kurdish Nationalism', *Journal of Contemporary History*, 6 (1971) 87–107; and on Biafra, see V. A. Olorunsola, 'Nigeria', in his *The Politics of Cultural Sub-Nationalism in Africa* (New York: Doubleday & Co., 1972) esp. p. 39.

75. See E. Durkheim, *The Elementary Forms of the Religious Life*, trans. J. W. Swain (London: Allen & Unwin, 1915) p. 428; and Herbert, *David, Voltaire, Brutus and the French Revolution*, pp. 53, 81.

76. On Scotland, see H. J. Hanham, *Scottish Nationalism* (London: Faber, 1969), and in general, M. Hechter, *Internal Colonialism: the Celtic Fringe in British National Development, 1536–1966* (London: Routledge & Kegan Paul, 1974) and Mayo, *The Roots of Identity, passim*.

77. See M. Halpern, *The Politics of Social Change in the Middle East and North Africa* (Princeton University Press, 1963) pp. 290–1.

78. F. Fanon, *Les Damnés de la Terre* (Paris: Maspero, 1963), p. 123; see also the review of work on populism by Low, Kilson and others in J. S. Saul, 'Africa', in *Populism*, ed. G. Ionescu and E. Gellner (London: Weidenfeld & Nicolson, 1969).

79. See M. Matossian, 'Ideologies of "Delayed Industrialisation": some tensions and ambiguities', *Economic Development and Cultural Change*, VI (1958) 217–28.

80. Kautsky, *Political Change in Underdeveloped Countries,* 'Introduction', pp. 57 ff. argues that even the Russian (Bolshevik) revolution constituted an anti-colonial, modernising nationalism of the intellectuals; see also note 62.

81. On incipient class conflict, see P. C. Lloyd (ed.), *The New Elites of Tropical Africa* (Oxford University Press, 1966).

82. See W. B. Quandt, Fuad Jabber and A. Moseley Lesch (eds), *The Politics of Palestinian Nationalism* (University of California Press, 1973); and more generally, P. Wilkinson, *Political Terrorism* (London:

Macmillan, 1974).

CHAPTER TWO

1. I relegate to a note any claim for the United Nations to be an even more inclusive group. It is true that the rather elastic criteria I use for a 'corporate group' could be stretched to include this body, but there is a certain subjectivity in the application of such criteria and mine inclines me to doubt if the United Nations effectively meets them. I have no such doubts about at least some of the nations which are supposedly united in it.

2. E. E. Evans-Pritchard, *Kinship and Marriage among the Nuer* (Oxford: Clarendon Press, 1951) p. 5. See also his *The Nuer* (Oxford: Clarendon Press, 1940) p. 194.

3. P. J. Bohannan, *Social Anthropology* (New York: Holt, Rinehart & Winston, 1963) pp. 171, 168.

4. M. G. Smith, *Corporations and Society* (London: Duckworth, 1974) p. 177.

5. Ibid.

6. Not only to me: the anonymous reviewer of Smith's book in the *Times Literary Supplement* of 21 June 1974 (p. 662) calls 'corporate category', 'a preposterous misuse . . . of an indispensable concept'.

7. A. Cohen, *Custom and Politics in Urban Africa* (London: Routledge & Kegan Paul, 1969) p. 4.

8. A. Cobban, *National Self-Determination* (University of Chicago Press, n.d.) p. 50.

9. Carleton J. H. Hayes, *Essays on Nationalism* (New York: Macmillan, 1926) p. 5.

10. See E. Kedourie, *Nationalism* (London: Hutchinson, 1966) p. 120.

11. 'Wallach' was one form of 'Vlach', the Slav word for Rumanian, which was widely used at this time, even by Rumanians themselves, though it soon afterwards became part of the nationalist programme to use 'Rumanian' instead.

12. R. W. Seton-Watson, *A History of the Roumanians* (Cambridge University Press, 1934) p. 177.

13. Ibid.

14. The early date is especially interesting in view of the common tendency to date the origins of modern nationalism from the second half of the eighteenth century or even later, at the opening of the nineteenth. From my point of view, it 'begins' with the Bishop, if not before him.

15. Cited in R. Portal, *The Slavs* (London: Weidenfeld & Nicolson, 1969) p. 374.

16. H. Kohn, *The Idea of Nationalism* (New York: Macmillan, 1945) p. 544; and C. A. Macartney, *National States and National Minorities* (Oxford University Press, 1934) p. 93.

17. The spelling of all Slav and Magyar names in this paper follows that of the most recent sources available to me, except that I have omitted the diacritic marks which I judge are unlikely to mean more to most readers than they do to me. No serious confusion should result from the omission.

18. Seton-Watson, *A History of the Roumanians*, pp. 176–7.

19. C. A. Macartney, *The Hapsburg Empire, 1790–1918* (London: Weidenfeld & Nicolson, 1968) pp. 76n., 90n.

20. See Macartney, *National States and National Minorities*, p. 93; and Kohn, *The Idea of Nationalism*, p. 544.

21. W. Kolarz, *Myths and Realities in Eastern Europe* (London: Lindsay Drummond, 1946) p. 30.

22. Seton-Watson, *A History of the Roumanians*, p. 177.

23. Kohn, *The Idea of Nationalism*, pp. 534–5.

24. Macartney, *National States and National Minorities*, p. 93.

25. O. Jaszi, *The Dissolution of the Habsburg Monarchy* (University of Chicago Press, 1971) p. 265.

26. Ibid. p. 265; and H. Kohn, *Nationalism* (Princeton: Van Nostrand, 1955) p. 156.

27. Cited in Macartney, *The Hapsburg Empire*, p. 139, his brackets.

28. Seton-Watson, *A History of the Roumanians*, p. 289.

29. Cited in R. J. Rath, *The Viennese Revolution of 1848* (University of Texas Press, 1957) p. 263.

30. Jaszi, *The Dissolution of the Habsburg Monarchy*, p. 262.

31. R. W. Seton-Watson, *Racial Problems in Hungary* (London: Constable, 1908) p. 43.

32. Cited in S. Z. Pech, *The Czech Revolution of 1848* (University of North Carolina, 1969) p. 86.

33. One of the most bizarre of all was provided by a Magyar nationalist who complained about the ingratitude of the Slavs in Hungary who were 'breathing Magyar air' – a truly remarkable extension of the category.

34. Macartney, *The Hapsburg Empire*, p. 219.

35. Jaszi, *The Dissolution of the Habsburg Monarchy*, p. 264.

36. Macartney, *The Hapsburg Empire*, p. 218.

37. Translated and cited in Kohn, *Nationalism*, p. 156.

38. H. Kohn, *The Habsburg Empire, 1804–1918* (Princeton: Van Nostrand, 1961) pp. 118–22.

39. He could not have declared it in Czech, since that language has only one word for both 'Czech' and 'Bohemian'. This fact made the definition of the 'Czech' category even more problematical than that of other categories.

40. Pech, *The Czech Revolution of 1848*, p. 30; and Kohn, *The Idea of Nationalism*, p. 721.

41. Macartney, *The Hapsburg Empire*, pp. 215, 350n.; and Pech, *The*

Czech Revolution of 1848, pp. 74, 107, 136.

42. Pech, ibid. pp. 264–5.

43. Kohn, *The Idea of Nationalism,* p. 559.

44. G. Barany, *Stephen Széchenyi and the Awakening of Hungarian Nationalism, 1791–1841* (Princeton University Press, 1968) p. 219. Cf. 'the great masses of the peasantry were not [previously] members of the nation': Jaszi, *The Dissolution of the Habsburg Monarchy,* p. 241.

45. See Seton-Watson, *A History of the Roumanians,* pp. 271–2; Kohn, *The Idea of Nationalism,* p. 530; and Macartney, *The Hapsburg Empire,* p. 91.

46. Carleton J. H. Hayes, *The Historic Evolution of Modern Nationalism* (New York: Macmillan, 1949) p. 294.

47. Macartney, *The Hapsburg Empire,* pp. 245, 251.

48. Barany, *Stephen Széchenyi,* p. 213.

49. C. A. Macartney, *Hungary: A Short History* (Edinburgh University Press, 1962) p. 138.

50. Ibid. p. 131.

51. D. Wilson, *The Life and Times of Vuk Stefanović Karadzić* (Oxford: Clarendon Press, 1970).

52. I here allude to, but do not actually employ, the techniques for the analysis of 'social networks' developed by a number of social anthropologists in recent years.

53. Barany, *Stephen Széchenyi,* p. 284.

54. Pech, *The Czech Revolution of 1848,* p. 31.

55. M. B. Petrovich, *The Emergence of Russian Panslavism* (Columbia University Press, 1956) pp. 148–9.

56. Barany, *Stephen Széchenyi,* pp. 168–9.

57. Pech, *The Czech Revolution of 1848,* p. 28.

58. Barany, *Stephen Széchenyi,* pp. 150, 168.

59. Pech, *The Czech Revolution of 1848,* p. 28.

60. See Barany, *Stephen Széchenyi,* p. 168.

61. Ibid. p. 150.

62. Ibid. p. 310.

63. Ibid. p. 170. f.n.

64. Pech, *The Czech Revolution of 1848,* pp. 30–1.

65. Ibid. p. 29.

66. Ibid. p. 27.

67. Ibid.

68. Jaszi, *The Dissolution of the Habsburg Monarchy,* p. 262.

69. Ibid. p. 249.

70. Kohn, *The Habsburg Empire,* p. 63.

71. Pech, *The Czech Revolution of 1848,* p. 25.

72. A. J. May, *The Hapsburg Monarchy, 1867–1914* (Harvard University Press, 1951) p. 347.

73. Seton-Watson, *A History of the Roumanians,* pp. 281–2.

74. Pech, *The Czech Revolution of 1848*, p. 27.
75. Ibid. p. 314.
76. Macartney, *The Hapsburg Empire*, p. 304.
77. Pech, *The Czech Revolution of 1848*, pp. 293–5.
78. See Macartney, *Hungary*, p. 158; *The Hapsburg Empire*, p. 387n.; Pech, *The Czech Revolution of 1848*, pp. 153–4; Seton-Watson, *A History of the Roumanians*, p. 221; and Kohn, *The Habsburg Empire*, pp. 33, 60.
79. Pech, ibid. p. 114.
80. Ibid. pp. 151–20.
81. Ibid. pp. 293, 302.
82. Cited in May, *The Hapsburg Monarchy*, p. 51.
83. See Cobban, *National Self-Determination*, p. 23.
84. Whether they have all gone through the process of converting a national category into a nation-state is a matter which I cannot here pursue, but that they can exist as *states* surely implies that they might equally exist as *nation-states*.
85. G. C. Abbott, 'Size, Viability, Nationalism and Politico-Economic Development', *International Journal*, vol. 25, no. 1 (1969–70) 56–68.
86. K. W. Deutsch, *Nationalism and Social Communication* (Massachusetts Institute of Technology Press, 1953).
87. M. Olson, *The Logic of Collective Action* (New York: Shocken, 1971) p. 2, original italics.
88. Macartney, *The Hapsburg Empire*, p. 83.

CHAPTER THREE

1. Hans Roos, *A History of Modern Poland* (London, 1966) p. 48.
2. *Ethics*, ix, ch. 10 (Harmondsworth: Penguin, 1953) p. 281.
3. *Politics*, ed. Ernest Barker, iii, ch. 9 (Oxford, 1946) p. 120.
4. *Leviathan*, ch. 21, Everyman edition (London, 1973) pp. 113–14.
5. *Considerations on the Government of Poland*, ch. 2.
6. *Sunday Times* (16 February 1975).
7. J. R. Hale, *Machiavelli and Renaissance Italy* (London, 1961) p. 15.
8. *A Study of History*, abridged by D. C. Somervell (Oxford, 1946) p. 314.
9. See Felix Gilbert, 'The Venetian Constitution in Florentine Political Thought', in *Florentine Studies: Politics and Society in Renaissance Florence*, ed. Nicolai Rubinstein (London, 1968) esp. p. 466.
10. Daniel Waley, *The Italian City-Republics* (London, 1969) p. 32.
11. Denis Fustel de Coulanges, *The Ancient City* (1864; repr. New York, 1956) iii, 15, p. 205.
12. Victor Ehrenberg, *The Greek State*, 2nd edn (London, 1969) pp. 74–5.
13. See the discussion in Hannah Arendt, *On Revolution* (London, 1963) pp. 30, 289–90n. One of Machiavelli's formulations of the

thought is there located in the *Florentine Histories*, III, 7, which appears to be a slip. In III, 2, discussing the opponents of Pope Gregory XI, Machiavelli comments: 'So much did citizens at that time prefer the good of their country to their ghostly consolations.'

14. Michael Grant, *The Climax of Rome* (London, 1974).

15. Thucydides, *The Peloponnesian War*, III, 81 (Harmondsworth: Penguin, 1954) ch. 5, p. 208.

16. Ibid. II, 37, p. 117.

17. Ibid. I, 6, p. 51.

18. Plutarch, *Cato The Elder* (Harmondsworth: Penguin, 1965) p. 136.

19. Material on Athens, of course, dominates the thoughts of modern classicists. Sparta, however, was by no means forgotten. See Elizabeth Rawson, *The Spartan Tradition in European Thought* (Oxford, 1969).

20. Coulanges, *The Ancient City*, p. 221.

21. Waley, *The Italian City-Republics*, p. 100.

22. Coulanges, *The Ancient City*, III, 14, p. 201.

23. Herodotus, I, 170 (Harmondsworth: Penguin, 1954) pp. 81–2.

24. Thucydides, *The Peloponnesian War*, III, ch. 3.

25. Neal Wood, 'Machiavelli's Concept of Virtu', *Political Studies*, vol. XV, no. 2 (June 1967) 168.

26. Herodotus, I, 165.

27. Ehrenberg, *The Greek State*, p. 43.

28. *Leviathan*, ch. 21.

29. Cato, *Plutarch's Lives*, (Harmondsworth: Penguin, 1965) p. 128.

30. See Henri Pirenne: 'The mediaeval burger . . . was a different kind of person from all who lived outside the town walls': *Economic and Social History of Mediaeval Europe* (London, 1936) p. 56.

31. See, for example, Kant's *Perpetual Peace: a Philosophical Sketch*, whose first definitive article is that 'The Civil Constitution of Every State shall be Republican', wherein Kant explains that 'where the subject is not a citizen, and which is therefore not republican, it is the simplest thing in the world to go to war. For the head of state is not a fellow citizen, but the owner of the state, and a war will not force him to make the slightest sacrifices so far as his banquets, hunts, pleasure palaces and court festivals are concerned': *Kant's Political Writings*, ed. Hans Reiss (Cambridge, 1970) pp. 99–100.

32. Blaise de Monluc, *The Hapsburg–Valois Wars and the French Wars of Religion* ed. Ian Roy (London, 1971) p. 139.

33. Letter to Lady Theresa Lewis, 6 May 1857: *Memoirs, Letters and Remains of Alexis de Tocqueville*, vol. II (London, 1861) p. 376.

34. *An Argument Shewing that a Standing Army is inconsistent with Free Government, and absolutely destructive to the Constitution of the English Monarchy* (London, 1697) p. 3. Republished by *The Rota* (Exeter, 1971).

35. 'Machiavelli, Harrington and English Political Ideologies in the

18th Century', *Politics, Language and Time* (London, 1967).

36. As an example of this terminology, one might note J. R. Green's comment on John Hampden in 1627 as being 'as yet only a young Buckinghamshire squire' about to 'begin that career of patriotism which has made his name dear to Englishmen': *A Short History of the English People* (London, 1874) p. 500. Patriotism and monarchy are, in this powerful tradition, generally presented as opposites, though it is, of course, always monarchy presented as bordering on despotism.

37. *Absalom and Achitophel.*

38. *Boswell's Life of Johnson* (Oxford, 1953) p. 615; 7 Apr. 1775.

39. *The Rights of Man,* pt I (London: Everyman Edition, 1950) p. 24. Cf. pt II where Paine remarks that monarchy 'has a base original signification. It means arbitrary power in an individual person; in the exercise of which, *himself* and not the *res-publica*, is the object.' (p. 174)

40. *Notes on Nationalism* (1945) in *The Collected Essays, Journals and Letters* (London, 1968) vol. III, p. 362.

41. Ibid.

CHAPTER FOUR

1. Although the distinction between 'cultural' and 'political' nationalists is hazy, there are circumstances, notably those of Great Power intervention, which prevent nationalists from ever attaining political sovereignty. If this frustration is prolonged, as with the Kurds or Basques, a more limited regional–cultural autonomy becomes the habitual nationalist goal. Furthermore, there is a difference between those whose main aim is political sovereignty for its own sake, and those who see such sovereignty as a means of achieving certain cultural and social goals. The influence of Herder on the latter type of nationalist is marked.

2. In this chapter I am concerned solely with what Worsley has characterised as the 'elite' phase of nationalism (though it is hardly as 'moderate' and 'liberal' as he supposes). This is the decisive phase of nationalism from the standpoint of doctrinal formulation. Moreover, it is by no means certain that such an 'elite' or, better, 'middle strata' phase, always gives way to a 'mass' phase in which the proletariat or peasantry predominate; cf. P. Worsley, *The Third World* (London: Weidenfeld & Nicolson, 1964).

3. There is a large literature on 'enlightened despotism'. For Germany, see W. H. Bruford, *Germany in the Eighteenth Century* (Cambridge University Press, 1965), and more generally M. Beloff, *The Age of Absolutism 1660–1815* (London: Hutchinson, 1954); also H. Rosenberg, *Bureaucracy, Aristocracy and Autocracy, The Prussian Experience 1660–1815* (Harvard University Press, 1958).

4. See the essays by J. Strayer and C. J. Friedrich in *Nation-Building,*

ed. K. Deutsch and W. Foltz (New York: Atherton 1963), particularly on the role of *raison d'état*; also E. H. Kantorowicz, 'Pro Patria Mori in Medieval Political Thought', *American Historical Review*, 56 (1951) 472–92.

5. In France, in particular, the *parlements* from the 1760s onwards began to utilise the language of liberty and nationality in defence of their ancient privileges, borrowing both from English models and from the rhetoric of the *philosophes*. But such language had none of the regenerative and cultural meanings with which it was to be invested in the later 1780s by intellectuals of the Third Estate.

6. For the nationalist appropriation of the absolutist concept of territorial and legal sovereignty, see A. Cobban, 'The Enlightenment and the French Revolution', in his *Aspects of the French Revolution* (London: Paladin, 1971). As Cobban says, *lèse-majesté* becomes *lèse-nation*, and the *roi de France* became the *roi des Français* during the Revolution; but French nationalism acquired its concept of sovereignty from the absolutist monarchy, its practice as well as its theory.

7. The opinion of d'Alembert is cited by H. Honour, *Neo-Classicism* (Harmondsworth: Penguin, 1968) which provides a good introduction to the ideas, as well as the art, of this style.

8. Canova's chief monuments were Papal, and David's *Oath of the Horatii* and his *Brutus* (1789) were bought by d'Angiviller for the Crown. The reforms of de Tournehem and Marigny of the Academy and the system of royal patronage, 1745–73, were important in aiding the rise of neo-classicism in France.

9. 'We ought to preach it from the roof-tops that the ruler is instituted for the benefit of the people and not vice-versa; he is, as a ruler, the creation of the people, and not of the Almighty; hence he owes to his people *comptes rendus*, and that before the Day of Judgment': A. L. Schlözer, *Stats Anzeigen* (Gottingen, 1792) vol. xvii, p. 253; see F. M. Barnard, *Herder's Social and Political Thought, From Enlightenment to Nationalism* (Oxford: Clarendon Press, 1965) ch. 1.

10. For Diderot's artistic criticism and Winckelmann's cultural manifestos, see the extracts in L. Eitner (ed.), *Neo-Classicism and Romanticism, 1750–1850* (London: Prentice-Hall International Inc., 1971) vol. i, pp. 4–20, 54–67.

11. David's revolutionary works express aptly Diderot's dictum: 'Paint as they spoke in Sparta' (from *Pensées détachées sur la peinture, 1776–81*); see also W. Friedlander, *David to Delacroix* (New York: Schocken, 1968).

12. We should also not overlook the profound influence of the *Gefühlsphilosophie* of the third Earl of Shaftesbury's *Charackteristicks of Men, Manners, Opinions, Times* (London, 1711; 3rd edn 1723). This influence was particularly strong in Herder's Germany.

More generally, I do not wish to underrate the influence of England, both as a model of social and political organisation, and as a source of the liberal tradition. Yet as Cobban, *Aspects of the French Revolution*, points out, the liberal temper of English 'patriotism' is lacking in the impulse for collective reform and purification, which runs through neo-classicism.

13. On Fuseli and Flaxman, and their revival of Dante and Shake-speare, see the entries under their names in the section on 'Drawings and Prints' (and that on 'Paintings') in the Arts Council Catalogue of the Exhibition on *The Romantic Movement* (London: Arts Council, 1959).

14. For the role of ethnicity and ethnocentrism, see A. D. Smith, 'Ethnocentrism, Nationalism and Social Change', *International Journal of Comparative Sociology*, XIII (1972) 1–20. Examples of such 'ethnic messianisms' include ancient movements like the Maccabean and Zealot movements in Judea, and modern ones like Kimbanguism or Mahdism; see A. D. Smith, *Theories of Nationalism* (London: Duckworth, 1971).

15. On Justus Möser, see Barnard, *Herder's Social and Political Thought*, pp. 24–8, and H. Kohn, *The Idea of Nationalism* (New York: Macmillan, 1967) pp. 423–7. On the medievalising trend in painting in the 1770s and 1780s, see F. Antal, *Classicism and Romanticism, with Other Studies in Art History* (London: Routledge & Kegan Paul, 1966).

16. On German Romantic political thought and the German 'his-toricism' of A. W. Schlegel's 'secret longing for the chaos which is per-petually striving for new and marvellous births', see A. K. Thorlby, *The Romantic Movement* (London: Longmans, 1966) esp. 'Introduction' and sections on 'Historicism and Political Thought'; and H. S. Reiss (ed.), *The Political Thought of the German Romantics, 1793–1815* (Oxford: Black-well, 1955).

17. See M. Florisoone, 'The Romantic and Neo-Classical Conflict' in *The Romantic Movement* (London: Arts Council, 1959) pp. 21–6.

18. On the 'contagious fervour' of Winckelmann's eulogies of the spirit behind Greek sculpture, see L. D. Ettlinger, 'Winckelmann', in The Arts Council of Great Britain, *The Age of Neo-Classicism* (London and Harlow: Shenval Press, 1972) (Fourteenth Exhibition of the Council of Europe), p. xxxii.

19. The different versions of rejection of the political status quo, and of national self-assertion, given by thinkers in America, England, France, Germany, Switzerland and Italy, are analysed in S. Baron, *Modern Nationalism and Religion* (New York: Meridian Books, 1960), and A. Kemilainen, *Nationalism; Problems concerning the Word, Concept and Classification* (Yvaskyla: Kustantajat Publishers, 1964).

20. An example of freely accepted self-constraint was contained in the popular story of the Roman consul, Brutus, who ordered his sons to be executed for treason against the new republic. On the cult of Brutus in the French Revolution, see R. L. Herbert, *David, Voltaire,*

Brutus and the French Revolution: an essay in art and politics (London: Allen Lane, The Penguin Press, 1972).

21. See A. Jacobs, *A Short History of Western Music* (Harmondsworth: Penguin Books, 1972) ch. 12; and M. Laclotte, 'J.-L. David, Reform and Revolution', Arts Council, *The Age of Neo-Classicism*, pp. lxvii–lxxi.

22. On the parallels between Herder's concept of *Kraft* and the medieval notion of *vis*, and on Herder's biological analogies for cultural forms, see F. M. Barnard, *Herder's Social and Political Thought*, pp. 38–9.

23. On Lavater, see L. Eitner (ed.), *Neo-Classicism and Romanticism*, pp. 86–8. Lavater provides a good example of pre-Romantic and neo-classicist emphasis upon nature as an organic whole and of the inimitability of genius.

24. From Rousseau onwards, this educational evolutionism became an important facet of nationalism. For Rousseau's nationalist ideas, see A. Cobban, *Rousseau and the modern state*, 2nd edition (London: Allen & Unwin, 1964).

25. K. Minogue traces this moralistic and educational view of politics (and its dangers) to the French *philosophes*, in his *Nationalism* (London: Batsford, 1967).

26. For Burke's influence on neo-classical painters like Barry, see Arts Council, *The Age of Neo-Classicism*, pp. 9–11.

27. For Ledoux's ideas, see L. Eitner (ed.) *Neo-classicism and Romanticism*, pp. 126–9.

28. This was the burden of David's neo-classicist icons of Roman virtue, and of the Abbé Sieyès's famous pamphlet of 1789, *Qu'est-ce que le tiers état?* See R. Herbert, *David, Voltaire, Brutus . . .*; and A. Cobban, *Aspects of the French Revolution* (London: Paladin, 1971) pp. 23–8.

29. For an analysis of the restrictive social position of poets and artists at the German courts, and their 'escapist' classicism, see W. H. Bruford, *Germany in the Eighteenth Century, The Social Background of the Literary Revival* (Cambridge: Cambridge University Press, 1965) pp. 291–327.

30. H. Kohn, *The Idea of Nationalism, passim*, and his later restatement, *Nationalism, Its Meaning and History* (Princeton: Van Nostrand, 1955).

31. J. Locquin, *La Peinture d'Histoire en France de 1747 à 1785* (Paris: H. Laurens, 1912) emphasises the state's active role after 1747 in reviving the grandeur of the age of the Sun King, through commissions and national educational programmes based on a return to the classical authors.

32. Tocqueville's insight appears in chapter 3 of Part I of his *The Ancien Régime and the French Revolution,* translated by Stuart Gilbert and edited by Hugh Brogan (Manchester: Collins, Fontana, 1966) pp. 41–4. For some idea of neo-classicism's variety, see H. Honour, *Neo-Classicism*.

33. On Wilson, Barry, Hamilton, Flaxman and other British artists,

see Greater London Council, *British Artists in Rome, 1700–1800* (London, 1974) and D. Irwin, *English Neo-Classical Art* (London: Faber & Faber, 1966).

34. For 'historical mobility' and the more general meaning of the term 'historicism', to suggest 'the new retrospective and archaeological attitude towards the historical past that appeared in the mid eighteenth century . . .' and '. . . encompasses all historical revivals, Neoclassicism included . . .', see R. Rosenblum, *Transformations in Late Eighteenth Century Art,* paperback edition (Princeton: Princeton University Press, 1970) pp. 34 (note 106), 42–51, 78–85 (which indicates the close connections of historicism and nationalism).

CHAPTER FIVE

1. Acknowledgements and thanks are due to the University of Victoria Faculty Research and Travel Committee for funds, to Lynne Chisholm for research assistance and to R. I. Cheffins, E. Gruner, J. P. Menthor and A. D. Smith for comments on an earlier draft. None of the latter are responsible for statements made in the text.

2. See W. Sulzbach, *Imperialismus und Nationalbewusstsein* (Frankfurt-am-Main, 1959) p. 84; and A. D. Smith, *Theories of Nationalism* (London: Duckworth, 1971) pp. 181–2.

3. Sulzbach, *Imperialismus*, p. 81.

4 E. Lemberg, *Nationalismus, Bd II: Soziologie und politische Pädagogik* (München: Rowahlt, 1964) pp. 34, 60; and E. Hobsbawm, 'Some Reflections on Nationalism', in *Imagination and Precision in the Social Sciences*, ed. T. J. Nossiter *et al.* (London: Faber & Faber, 1972) p. 394.

5. Sulzbach, *Imperialismus*, p. 85; and Smith, *Theories of Nationalism*, pp. 182–4.

6. Ibid. p. 184.

7. Hobsbawm, 'Some Reflections on Nationalism', p. 394.

8. E. Gellner, *Thought and Change* (London: Weidenfeld & Nicolson, 1964) pp. 161–2.

9. Smith, *Theories of Nationalism*, p. 209.

10. H. Gerth and C. W. Mills (eds), *From Max Weber* (London: Routledge & Kegan Paul, 1964) pp. 175–6.

11. See Smith, *Theories of Nationalism*, 'Ethnocentrism, Nationalism and Social Change', in *International Journal of Comparative Sociology*, XIII, no. 1 (Mar 1972) 1–20, and ' "Ideas" and "Structure" in the Formation of Independence Ideals', *Philosophy of the Social Sciences*, 3 (1973) 19–39. Also see Gellner, *Thought and Change* and 'Scale and Nation', *Philosophy of the Social Sciences*, 3 (1973) pp. 1–17.

12. F. Znaniecki, *Modern Nationalities* (University of Illinois Press, 1952) pp. 53–5.

13. Hobsbawm, 'Some Reflections on Nationalism', pp. 400–1.

14. Royal Institute of International Affairs, *Nationalism* (New York: Kelley, 1963) p. 135.

15. Smith, 'Ethnocentrism, Nationalism and Social Change', p. 18.

16. See A. Hauser, *Schweizerische Wirtschafts– und Socialgeschichte* (Zürich: Eugen-Rentsch Verlag, 1961); and U. Im Hof, *Die Aufklärung in der Schweiz* (Bern: Francke, 1970).

17. See J. Furrer, 'Beleuchtender Bericht über den Entwurf der neuen eidgenössischen Bundesverfassung, 6. Aug. 1848', in *Bundesrat Dr. Jonas Furrer*, ed. A. Isler (Winterthur, 1907) appendix; W. E. Rappard, 'Pennsylvania and Switzerland: The American Origins of the Swiss Constitution', *Political Science and Sociology* (1941) pp. 49–121; W. Rupli, *Zollreform und Bundesreform in der Schweiz* (Zürich: Europa Verlag, 1949); F. Scheurer, 'Soziale Ideen in der Schweiz vor 1848', in *Schweizerische Blätter für Wirtschaft- und Sozialpolitik* (Bern, 1908); E. Franscini, *Neue Statistik der Schweiz*, Bd 2 (1848); E. Bonjour, *Die Gründung des schweizerischen Bundesstaates* (Basel: Benno Schwabe, 1948); and E. Gagliardi, *Alfred Escher* (Huber, Frauenfeld, 1919).

18. See S. B. Ryerson, *The Founding of Canada* (Toronto: Progress Books, 1963) pp. 321 ff.

19. See Ryerson, *Unequal Union: Confederation and the Roots of Conflict in Canada, 1815–1873* (New York: International Publishers, 1968) pp. 345–6; and P. B. Waite (ed.), *The Confederation Debates in the Province of Canada, 1865*, no. 2 (Ottawa, Carleton Library, 1963) pp. 67–8.

20. See D. Frei, *Das schweizerische Nationalbewusstsein: Seine Forderung nach dem Zusammenbruch der Alten Eidgenossenschaft 1798* (Zürich: Juris-Verlag, 1964).

21. H. Weilenmann, *Die vielsprachige Schweiz* (Basel: Verlag Rhein, 1925).

22. Ibid. p. 74; and Weilenmann, 'Les groupes linguistiques en Suisse', *Res Publica*, vol. IV (1962–3) 230.

23. See Weilenmann, *Die vielsprachige Schweiz*, p. 79, and 'Les groupes linguistiques en Suisse', 230; and also A. Hauser, *Das eidgenössische Nationalbewusstsein, sein Werden und Wandel* (Zürich/Leipzig, 1941) p. 50.

24. Weilenmann, *Die vielsprachige Schweiz*, p. 82.

25. Ibid. pp. 43–5.

26. K. B. Mayer, 'The Jura Problem: Ethnic Conflict in Switzerland', *Social Research*, vol. 35, no. 4 (1968) 704–41, this quote p. 711.

27. See H. Ammann, 'Die Grunflagen des Sprachfriedens in der Schweiz', in *Südtirol: Land europäischer Bewährung*, Kanonikus Michael Gamper zum 70 Geburtstag (Innsbruck: Wagner, 1955) p. 184.

28. See P. Zinsli, *Vom Werden und Wesen der mehrsprachigen Schweiz*, Schriften des deutsch-schweizerischen Sprachvereins, no. 1 (Bern: Verlag Feuz, 1964) p. 9.

29. K. Schwarber, 'National bewusstsein und Nationalstaatsge-

danken der Schweiz von 1700 bis 1789', Ph. D. dissertation (Basel, 1919) f. 66; and 'Zentralistische-politische Reformvorschläge in der Schweiz im 18. Jahrhundert', in *Festschrift Gustav Binz* (Basel: Benno Schwabe, 1935) p. 241.

30. Weilenmann, *Die vielsprachige Schweiz*, p. 30.

31. Ibid. p. 83.

32. See A. Masnata, *Nationalités et Fédéralisme* (Lausanne: Payot, 1933) p. 28.

33. The name given to the committee of representatives of each canton in the period before 1848.

34. See Schwarber, 'Nationalbewusstsein und Nationalstaatsge', folio 755; and W. Ninck, 'Vom Staatenbund zum Bundesstaat', Ph. D. dissertation (Zurich, 1922) f. 24.

35. Ninck, ibid. f. 24.

36. See J. D. Y. Peel, 'Cultural Factors in the Contemporary Theory of Development', *European Journal of Sociology*, vol. 14, no. 2 (1973) in which he refers to the growth of ideology in the eighteenth century – particularly its concern with intervening in the flow of social events in order to produce a better future.

37. See Zinsli, *Vom Werden und Wesen der mehrsprachigen Schweiz*, p. 10.

38. See H. Kohn, *Nationalism and Liberty: The Swiss Example* (London: Allen & Unwin, 1956) p. 37.

39. See G. Hunziker, *Die Schweiz und das Nationalitätsprinzip im 19. Jahrhundert*, Basler Beiträge zur Geschichtswissenschaft, Bd. 120. von Helbling u. Lichtenhahn (Stuttgart, 1970) pp. 21–2.

40. Frei, *Das schweizerische Nationalbewusstsein*, p. 12.

41. Ibid. p. 194.

42. See Weilenmann, *Die vielsprachige Schweiz*, p. 179.

43. See Hunziker, *Die Schweiz und das Nationalitätsprinzip*, p. 17.

44. Frei, *Das schweizerische Nationalbewusstsein*, p. 12.

45. Ibid. p. 28.

46. Ibid. pp. 3–6.

47. Ibid. pp. 145–8.

48. Weilenmann, *Die vielsprachige Schweiz*, p. 199.

49. W. E. Rappard, *Die Bundesverfassung der schweizerischen Eidgenossenschaft, 1848–1948* (Zürich: Polygraphischer Verlag, 1948) p. 67.

50. See E. Gruner, 'Die Schweizerische Eidgenossenschaft, 1789–1874', in *Handbuch der europäischen Geschichte* (Forthcoming).

51. *Protocole des délibérations de la commission chargée le 16 août 1847 par la haute diète fédérale de la révision du pacte fédéral du 7 août, 1815*, typed MS. deposited in Schweizerische Bundesarchiv, Berlin.

52. See K. Schmid, 'Versuch über die schweizerische Nationalität', in *Aufsätze und Reden* (Zurich and Stuttgart: Artemis, 1957); and Hunziker, *Die Schweiz und das Nationalitätsprinzip*.

53. See Schmid, ibid. p. 36; and Franscini, *Neue Statistik der Schweiz*,

pp. 567–71.

54. Franscini, ibid. pp. 504–6.

55. Ibid. p. 570.

56. H. Spreng, *Ulrich Ochsenbein, 1811–48*, Diss., Bern, 1918, pp. 129–32.

57. See E. Gruner, *Die Parteien in der Schweiz* (Bern: Francke, 1969) p. 76; and A. Götz, 'Dr. Ignaz Paul Vital Troxler als Politiker', in *Schweizer Studien zur Geschichtswissenschaft*, Heft. 2, Bd VII (März 1915).

58. See J. Fränkel, *Gottfried Kellers Politische Sendung* (Zurich: Oprecht, 1939) pp. 24–7.

59. See J. C. Bluntschli, *Stimme eines Schweizers für und über die Bundesreform* (Zurich, 1847).

60. Hunziker, *Die Schweiz und das Nationalitätsprinzip.*

61. See E. Gruner, *Das Bernische Patriziat und die Regeneration* (Bern: Verlag Herbert Lang, 1943) pp. 71–2; and his 'Die Schweizerische Eidgenossenschaft'.

62. See Gruner, *Die Parteien in der Schweiz*, p. 81; and Götz, 'Dr. Ignaz Paul Vital Troxler als Politiker', 430–1.

63. See D. Lasserre, *Étapes du fédéralisme: l'expérience suisse* (Lausanne: Éditions Rencontre, 1954) p. 219.

64. See Pedrazzini, 'Les principes du droit de langues en Suisse', p. 241.

65. See A. Humbel, 'Sprachpolitik', in *Sprache, Sprachgeschicte, Sprachpflege in der Deutschen Schweiz*, hrsgbn. v. der Geschäftsstelle des Deutschschweizerischen Sprachvereins (Zurich, 1964) p. 69.

66. H. Lüthy, 'Politische Probleme der Mehrsprachigkeit in der Schweiz', *Civitas*, 22 Jahrgang, no. 1–2 (Sep 1966) 39–47, this reference p. 45.

67. See K. Meyer, 'Die mehrsprachige Schweiz', *Neue Schweizer Rundschan*, neue folge, VII Jahrgang (1940) pp. 17 ff., this reference p. 34.

68. Schmid, 'Versuch über die schweizerische Nationalität', p. 13.

69. Ibid. p. 29.

70. An English rendering of this might be: 'Improvement of the nation can only begin within the family.'

71. See E. Gruner, 'Die Jurafrage als Problem der Minderheit in der Schweizerischen Demokratie', *Civitas*, 23 Jahrgang (Mar 1968) p. 524; and Mayer, 'The Jura Problem'.

72. Mayer, ibid. p. 734.

73. Ibid.

74. Zinsli, *Vom Werden und Wesen*, p. 34.

75. See R. Cook, *The Maple Leaf Forever* (Toronto: Macmillan, 1971) p. 70.

76. See M. Wade, *The French Canadians, 1760–1967*, 2 vols (Toronto: Macmillan, 1968), this reference to vol. I.

77. Ibid. p. 95.

78. Ibid. p. 111.

79. See H. R. Innis, *Bilingualism and Biculturalism: An Abridged Version of the Royal Commission Report* (Toronto: McClelland & Stewart, 1973) p. 12.

80. D. G. Creighton, cited in Ryerson, *Unequal Union*, p. 272.

81. Ibid. p. 369.

82. Ibid. p. 272.

83. Ibid. pp. 373, 376.

84. Ibid. p. 416.

85. See R. Jones, *Community in Crisis* (Ottawa, Carleton Library, 1972) p. 19.

86. G. Grant's *Lament for a Nation* (Toronto: McClelland & Stewart, 1965) is in some respects a recent version of it. See also C. Berger, *The Sense of Power* (University of Toronto Press, 1970).

87. See R. Cheffins, The Constitutional Process in Canada (Toronto: McGraw-Hill, 1969) pp. 128 ff.

88. See Wade, *The French Canadians*, vol. ii, pp. 901–12.

89. See D. Smith, *Bleeding Hearts – Bleeding Country* (Edmonton: Hurtig, 1971).

90. See Smith, '"Ideas" and "Structure" in the Formation of Independence Ideals'; and H. Guindon, 'Social Unrest, Social Class and Quebec's Bureaucratic Revolution', *Queens' Quarterly*, vol. 71 (Summer 1964) 150–62.

91. Cited in M. Chevalier and J. R. Taylor, *Dynamics of Adaptation in the Federal Public Service*, Studies of the Royal Commission on Bilingualism and Biculturalism, no. 9 (Ottawa: Information Canada, 1971) p. 2.

92. J. Porter, *The Vertical Mosaic* (University of Toronto Press, 1965) p. 60.

93. R. J. Ossenberg, 'Unity in Spite of Ourselves', *Queens' Quarterly*, vol. 81, no. 3 (Autumn 1974) 433, 435.

94. The first Indian Acts were passed after Confederation in 1867. They are pieces of legislation defining Indian people, their rights and privileges.

95. See D. Lockwood, 'For T. H. Marshall', *Sociology*, vol. 8, no. 3 (Sep 1974) 367 ff., this reference p. 367.

96. P. Carstens, 'Coercion and Change', in *Canadian Society: Pluralism, Change and Conflict*, ed. R. J. Ossenberg (Scarborough: Prentice-Hall, 1971) ch. 6.

97. R. L. Watts, *Multicultural Societies and Federalism*, Study no. 8 of the Royal Commission on Bilingualism and Biculturalism (Ottawa: Information Canada, 1970) pp. 27–8.

98. See D. I. Roussopoulos, *Canada and Radical Social Change* (Montreal: Black Rose Books, 1973); and A. Rotstein and G. Lax (eds), *Inde-*

pendence: The Canadian Challenge (Toronto: Committee for an Independent Canada, 1972).

99. B. Akzin, *State and Nation* (London: Hutchinson, 1964) pp. 103, 155.

100. Ibid. p. 155.

101. The distinction follows that of Smith, 'Ethnocentrism, Nationalism and Social Change', p. 13.

102. See Masnata, *Nationalités et Fédéralisme*, p. 206; K. B. Mayer, 'Cultural Pluralism and Linguistic Equilibrium in Switzerland', *American Sociological Review* (1952) 157–63; Mayer, 'The Jura Problem', and Gruner, 'Die Jurafrage als Problem der Minderheit', p. 525.

103. Some of these had been colonies of the old Confederacy.

104. F. R. Scott, 'Political Nationalism and Confederation', *Canadian Journal of Economics and Political Science*, vol. 8 (1942) 386–415, this reference p. 386.

CHAPTER SIX

1. See V. G. Kiernan, 'State and Nation in Western Europe', *Past and Present*, no. 31 (1965).

2. This is emphasised by F. Braudel in *Capitalism and Material Life 1400–1800*, English edn (London, 1973).

3. E. Renan, *Qu'est-ce qu'une nation?*, a lecture of 1882 (Paris: Calmann-Lévy, 1882) sec. III.

4. O. Jaszi, *The Dissolution of the Hapsburg Monarchy* (Chicago, 1929) p. 258.

5. *Barnaby Rudge* (1841) ch. 23.

6. H. Kohn, *The Idea of Nationalism* (New York, 1945) p. 528, remarks that the peasant in Hungary looked to enlightened Austrian rule for protection against his lord. E. Wangermann, *From Joseph II to the Jacobin Trials* (Oxford, 1959) pp. 34 ff., points out that patriotism was not monopolised by conservatives: others were hoping that a free Hungarian parliament would bring progress.

7. F. Fetjö, 'Hungary', in *The Opening of an Era, 1848*, ed. F. Fetjö (London, 1948) p. 316. Cf. p. 314: The minor nobility, half of it too poor to count, may have totalled 680,000 in a population of 12 million.

8. G. Brenan, *The Spanish Labyrinth* (Cambridge, 1950) p. 30. See also E. A. Peers, *Catalonia Infelix* (London, 1937) chs 7–9.

9. Karl Liebknecht, *Militarism and Anti-militarism*, English edn (Glasgow, 1917) p. 125.

10. This party was to stand for 'national independence as the indispensable ground-work of industrial emancipation': James Connolly, 'Patriotism and Labour' (1897), in *Socialism and Nationalism*, a selection from his writings, ed. D. Ryan (Dublin, 1948) p. 29.

11. As A. D. Smith points out, in *Theories of Nationalism* (London,

1971) p. 122.

12. D. Mitrany, 'Rumania', in *The Balkans*, ed. N. Forbes *et al.* (Oxford, 1915) p. 275.

13. 'Patriotism and Government', in Tolstoy's *Essays and Letters*, trans. A. Maude (London, 1903) p. 244.

14. See N. V. Riasanovsky, *Nicholas I and Official Nationality in Russia, 1825–1855* (University of California, 1959).

15. Introduction to *Des Prolétaires*, par l'auteur du 'Monde avant le Christ' (Paris, 1846).

16. See Kohn, *The Idea of Nationalism*, ch. 7, and for a summary of the German Romantic theory of nationalism Smith, *Theories of Nationalism*, pp. 16–17.

17. An English traveller writes of 'The pride with which a Prussian throws out his breast and erects his head, when he speaks of the "Liberation War"'; J. Russell, *A Tour in Germany* (Edinburgh, 1828) vol. ii, p. 55.

18. See J. G. Legge, *Rhyme and Revolution in Germany . . . 1813–1850* (London, 1918) pp. 159 ff.

19. See Liebknecht, *Militarism and Anti-militarism*, and V. G. Kiernan, 'Conscription and Society in Europe before the War of 1914–18', in *War and Society*, ed. M. R. D. Foot (London, 1973).

20. *Boswell on the Grand Tour: Italy, Corsica, and France 1765–1766*, ed. F. Brady (London, 1955) p. 174.

21. *Boswell: the Ominous Years 1774–1776*, ed. C. Ryskamp and F. A. Pottle (London, 1963) p. 329.

22. K. R. Greenfield, *Economics and Liberalism in the Risorgimento: A study of Nationalism in Lombardy 1814–1848* (Baltimore, 1934) pp. 149, 151.

23. Ibid. pp. 56, 58.

24. R. J. Rath, *The Fall of the Napoleonic Kingdom of Italy, 1814* (New York, 1941) p. 207.

25. Greenfield, *Economics and Liberalism in the Risorgimento*, p. 71.

26. Ibid., pp. 299–300.

27. Mazzini, *The Duties of Man*, English edn (London, 1907) pp. 1 ff., 246.

28. A. J. Whyte, *The Political Life and Letters of Cavour 1848–1861* (Oxford, 1930) p. 423.

29. Ibid. p. 319.

30. See *Selections from the Prison Notebooks of Antonio Gramsci*, ed. Q. Hoare and G. N. Smith (London, 1971) pp. 67, 101. Gramsci notes that the right-wing nationalist leader Crispi, a Sicilian, relied on the Sicilian landlords to support the central government after unification, because they needed its protection against their peasants. On Sicilian separatism as displayed in the revolutionary year of 1820, see R. M. Johnston, *The Napoleonic Empire in Southern Italy* (London, 1904) vol. ii,

pp. 122 ff. On the South in the Risorgimento see also M. A. Macciocchi, *Pour Gramsci* (Paris, 1974) ch. 4.

31. B. Croce, *A History of Italy 1871–1915*, trans. C. M. Adey (Oxford, 1929) p. 28.

32. R. F. Foerster, quoting P. Villari, in *The Italian Emigration of Our Times* (Harvard, 1924) p. 22.

33. See S. Kieniewicz, 'Polish Society and the Insurrection of 1863', *Past and Present*, no. 37 (1967). Cf. C. de Grunwald's comment on the 1830 rising, that there was 'something morbid in this political excitement of the Polish leaders: they lived in a world which no longer had any touch with reality.' *Tsar Nicholas I*, trans. B. Patmore (London, 1954) p. 117. R. F. Leslie emphasises how much dreams of past greatness, as distinct from concrete interests of the present, influenced younger patriots especially: *Polish Politics and the Revolution of November 1830* (London, 1956) pp. 95–6. See also his *Reform and Insurrection in Russian Poland, 1856–1865* (London, 1963).

34. Kieniewicz, 'Polish Society and the Insurrection of 1863' pp. 134, 139.

35. H. B. Davis, *Nationalism and Socialism. Marxist and Labour Theories of Nationalism to 1917* (New York, 1967) pp. 134 ff.

36. Hroch, quoted by E. J. Hobsbawm, 'Some Reflections on Nationalism', pp. 385–406 in *Imagination and Precision in the Social Sciences*, ed. T. J. Nossiter *et al.* (London, 1972); 'But this must be seen as the spirit of an old self-sufficient community, resenting interference. The Argentine hinterland, as opposed to Buenos Aires, was content with Spanish colonial rule, resentful of British intrusion, free trade, and competition'; see H. S. Ferns, *Britain and Argentina in the Nineteenth Century* (Oxford, 1960) chs 2, 3.

37. 'Marxism and the National Question' (1913), in Joseph Stalin, *Marxism and the National and Colonial Question* (London, 1936) p. 17. He argued that Marx had been right to desire an independent Poland, but Polish Marxists were now right to reject it because economic and cultural changes had drawn Poland and Russia much closer (p. 21).

38. *Cambridge History of Poland 1697–1935*, ed. W. F. Reddaway *et al.* (1941) p. 496.

39. V. Serge, *Year One of the Russian Revolution* (1930) trans. P. Sedgwick (London, 1972) pp. 186–91.

40. H. Marczali, *Hungary in the Eighteenth Century* (Cambridge, 1910) p. 222. Cf. Jaszi, *The Dissolution of the Habsburg Monarchy*, p. 301: In the 1840s the lower nobility, with an ideology compounded of old feudal and French Revolutionary elements, 'became the real *tiers état* of Hungary'.

41. A. Massingberd, *Letter on Kossuth and the Hungarian Question* (London, 1851) p. 12; cf. Jaszi, ibid. p. 225.

42. Massingberd, ibid. p. 20.

43. Fetjö, 'Hungary', pp. 340–1.

44. K. Tschuppik, *The Reign of the Emperor Francis Joseph 1848–1916*, trans. C. J. S. Sprigge (London, 1930) p. 161.

45. Down to 1914 only 6·5 per cent of the Hungarian population had votes, and voting was not secret: cf. Jaszi, *The Dissolution of the Habsburg Monarchy*, p. 227.

46. Davis, *Nationalism and Socialism*, pp. 143 ff. On the Habsburg Slavs see also A. J. May, *The Hapsburg Monarchy 1867–1914* (Harvard University Press, 1951) pp. 375 ff., and J. Plamenatz, 'Two Types of Nationalism', in *Nationalism. The nature and evolution of an idea*, E. Kamenka (Canberra, 1973) pp. 30 ff.

47. Tschuppik, *The Reign of the Emperor Francis Joseph*, p. 312.

48. See R. A. Kann, *The Multinational Empire* (New York, 1950) p. 261.

49. L. S. Stavrianos, *The Balkans since 1453* (New York, 1958) pp. 245 ff. Cf. H. M. Chadwick, *The Nationalities of Europe and the Growth of National Ideologies* (Cambridge, 1945) p. 12.

50. Stavrianos, ibid. pp. 274–5.

51. R. Clogg, 'Aspects of the Movement for Greek Independence', in *The Struggle for Greek Independence*, ed. R. Clogg (London, 1973) p. 14.

52. C. M. Woodhouse, *The Greek War of Independence* (London, 1952) p. 59.

53. Ibid. pp. 35–6.

54. M. Roller, 'The Rumanians in 1848', in Fetjö, 'Hungary', pp. 303 ff.

55. Stavrianos, *The Balkans since 1453*, p. 252.

56. H. G. A. V. Schenk, *The Aftermath of the Napoleonic Wars* (London, 1947) pp. 136 ff.

57. M. S. Anderson, *The Ascendancy of Europe: Aspects of European History 1815–1914* (London, 1972) pp. 188 ff. This is a work that may be referred to for many illuminating comments on nationalism and nationalist movements.

58. W. M. Ball, *Nationalism and Communism in East Asia* (Melbourne, 1952) p. 198. Cf. W. Z. Laqueur, *Communism and Nationalism in the Middle East* (London, 1956) pt 8: 'Communism and the National Minorities'.

59. *A Speech delivered by Ghazi Mustapha Kemal . . . October 1927*, English edn (Leipzig, 1929) p. 309. The speech is a lengthy narrative of the national revolution.

60. See V. Purcell, *The Boxer Uprising* (Cambridge, 1963) ch. 11; and Wu Yung, *The Flight of an Empress*, trans. I. Pruitt (Yale, 1936) pp. 24 ff. There is a judicious estimate of the 'concept of China in the hearts and minds' of the people, after millennia of national unity, in J. Strachey, *The End of Empire* (London, 1961) p. 128.

61. E. J. Hobsbawm, op. cit.

62. See Wu Yu-chang, *The Revolution of 1911* (Peking, 1962) ch. 11.

63. C. A. Johnson, *Peasant Nationalism and Communist Power: The Emergence of Revolutionary China 1937–1945* (Stanford, 1962) p. 87. Cf. Cabral's discussion of what he calls, for want as he says of a better word, the *déclassés* who 'proved to be extremely important in the national liberation struggle' in Portuguese Guinea: Amilcar Cabral, *Revolution in Guinea* (London, 1969) p. 48.

64. See S. Y. Teng, *The Taiping Rebellion and the Western Powers* (Oxford, 1971) pp. 54–5, etc.; and J. Chesneaux, Preface to J. Reclus, *La Révolte des Tai-Ping* (Paris, 1972) p. 12; and on the Boxers, see Purcell, *The Boxer Uprising*, pp. 55, 210–11, and J. Chesneaux, *Secret Societies in China*, trans. G. Nettle (London, 1971) pp. 70–1.

65. Engels to Paul Lafargue, 3 Nov 1892, in *Frederick Engels, Paul and Laura Lafargue. Correspondence*, vol. 3 (Moscow, n.d.) p. 208.

66. This is the main thesis of Johnson, *Peasant Nationalism and Communist Power*. Of the Japanese peasantry, B. Moore remarks that it seems not to have been much infected by ultra-nationalism, though this was utilised by the upper classes to keep it docile: *Social Origins of Dictatorship and Democracy* (1966) (London edn 1967) pp. 307–8.

67. J. L. Buck, *Chinese Farm Economy* (Chicago, 1930) p. 145.

68. See Hira Lal Singh, *Problems and Policies of the British in India 1885–1898* (Bombay, 1963) chs 1, 3. A threshold stage was marked by semi-political bodies representing upper-class vested interests, like the British Indian Association, founded in 1851; see A. Seal, *The Emergence of Indian Nationalism* (Cambridge, 1968) pp. 202–3.

69. On British tariff policy and the Indian bourgeoisie, see Bipan Chandra, *The Rise and Growth of Economic Nationalism in India* (Delhi, 1966) ch. 6; and V. I. Pavlov, *The Indian Capitalist Class* (Delhi, 1964) ch. 11.

70. See Moore, *Social Origins of Dictatorship and Democracy*, p. 316: The British presence, and its reliance on landed interests, 'prevented the formation of the characteristic reactionary coalition of Landed élites with a weak bourgeoisie'.

71. Much light is thrown on social structure and national movement in Bengal by Premen Addy and Ibne Azad, 'Politics and Society in Bengal', in *Explosion in a Subcontinent*, ed. R. Blackburn (London, 1975).

72. Competing national and class appeals to the peasantry are well illustrated in Majid Hayat Siddiqui, 'Peasant Movements in the United Provinces: 1918–1922', unpublished Ph. D. thesis (Jawaharlal Nehru University, Delhi, 1975).

73. See *Speeches and Writings of Mr. Jinnah*, ed. Jamil-ud-Din Ahmad (Lahore, 1942) vol. 1 (1935–44) pp. 164, etc.

74. G. W. Choudhury, *The Last Days of United Pakistan* (London, 1974) pp. 55, 133.

75. See 'Theses on the Eastern Question' of the Fourth Congress, Nov 1922, in J. Degras, *The Communist International 1919–1943: Docu-*

ments, vol. 1 (London, 1956) pp. 382 ff.; as well as other documents in this collection. P. C. Joshi, a former general secretary of the Communist Party of India, reviews the issues between Lenin and M. N. Roy, from a point of view favourable to the former, in 'Lenin and National Revolution' (Working paper IV. 1 of the Lenin Centenary Seminar held by the Indian Council of World Affairs, Feb 1970). After the Second World War, Owen Lattimore wrote that nationalism, discarded in Western Europe, was being left to the emergent peoples, and added somewhat over-hopefully, 'It is a heritage that has fallen to whole peoples, rather than to classes': *The Situation in Asia* (Boston, 1949) p. 51. Kamenka points to the Mexican revolution as the first to combine national with social ideals: 'Political Nationalism – the Evolution of the Idea', in *Nationalism,* p. 18.

76. See, for example, *Collected Works,* English edn (Moscow, 1966) vol. 31, pp. 122–8.

77. J. A. Silén, *We, the Puerto Rican People,* trans. C. Belfrage (New York, 1971) p. 113.

78. See J. S. Saul, 'The State in Post-Colonial Societies: Tanzania', in *The Socialist Register,* ed. R. Miliband and J. Saville (London, 1974), pp. 350–2, 355–6. P. Worsley, *The Third World* (London, 1964) pp. 192 ff., seems too optimistic on this question.

79. See V. A. Olorunsola (ed.), *The Politics of Cultural Sub-Nationalism in Africa* (New York, 1972) pp. 220–1, 223, 263, etc.

80. Stalin, *Marxism and the National and Colonial Question,* p. 13.

81. See, for example, Dona Torr (ed.), *Marxism, Nationality and War* (London, 1940) pt 1.

82. V. I. Lenin, *Collected Works* (Moscow, 1964) vol. 20, p. 396; written in 1914.

Index

177

Food +
Farming

FARMYARD FLYERS

EGMONT

We bring stories to life

First published in Great Britain in 2007 by Egmont UK Limited, 239 Kensington High Street, London W8 6SA

Text and illustrations copyright © Mike Bostock 2007

Mike Bostock has asserted his moral rights

A CIP catalogue record for this title is available from The British Library

ISBN 978 1 4052 2152 8 (Hardback)

ISBN 978 1 4052 2153 5 (Paperback)

1 2 3 4 5 6 7 8 9 10

Printed in Italy

On Flippety Farm,

Farmer Jolly's jobs were in a muddle.
One by one the animals began to notice.

Pig looked up from his
aeroplane story.
**"Where's
my straw?"**
he said, peering at his
lemonade.

"HEY!" honked the geese.
"Who shut the gate?"

Over in the meadow,
no one fetched Sheep.
"This just won't do!"
she sighed.

Cow shook her head.
"This isn't
my dinner!"
she huffed.
"Nope, Siree!"

But Farmer Jolly didn't notice.
He was too tired.

That night, Pig couldn't sleep.
He read his book.
He counted stars.
Then he heard **a noise**
from inside the
BIG
red
barn.

"There it goes again," he said.
He'd heard the noise before.

Pig peeped through a gap in the boards.
Farmer Jolly was busy fixing something.
"So, that's why he's tired," said Pig.

Early next morning, Pig gathered the other animals.
"Farmer Jolly needs help," he said.

"And I've got a plan."

Under the shady sycamore tree Pig drew in the mud with a pointy stick.
When everyone knew what to do, Cow scuffed the drawing out with her feet.
"Keep it secret," whispered Sheep.
"Yup, Siree!" nodded Cow.

As the sun came up,
Pig rolled
into action.

From the payphone by the bridge on Crimson Creek
he dialled Farmer Jolly's number.

"HELLO?"

said Pig, disguising his voice.

"Urgent . . .

Goose loose . . .
far side of
Flippety Farm . . ."

"Goose loose?"

yawned sleepy Farmer Jolly.

"I'll be right there."

He put down his tools
and jumped **straight** onto his tractor.

"**IT WORKED!**" giggled the animals.

As soon as Farmer Jolly was out of sight they
scooted up the hill . . .

. . . to see what he'd been fixing in the

BIG
red
barn.

They

poked

their heads

round the

BIG

barn door.

"It's an **aeroplane!**"
said Pig.

"**Let's get busy**," said Pig. "**If we fix it, the jobs won't be in a muddle any more.**"
"**Good plan,**" said Sheep.
"**Yup, Siree,**" nodded Cow.

Pig read the instructions,

and he SAWED,

while the geese GLUED,

and Cow PATCHED

and Sheep PAINTED . . .

. . . until Farmer Jolly's
aeroplane
was fixed
and ready
to fly.

Pig was excited.
"Coming for a spin?" he called.

They all piled in and Pig
revved the engine.

"Quack!" squawked the ducks as the plane **splashed** into the pond.

When Farmer Jolly came back from his **wild goose chase,**
he couldn't believe his eyes.

"sorry," said a very soggy Pig.

"**I'd better have a look,**" sighed Farmer Jolly.

He got back on his tractor and pulled the aeroplane out of the pond.

He patted the **wings**,

and tapped the **wheels**,

and looked into the **cockpit**.
"**You should have asked before you took it**," he said, "**but you've done a very good job.**

Thank you. And now I really MUST go to sleep."

Pig had a think about what Farmer Jolly had said,
then he came up with **one last plan**.

He fetched

Sheep

from the
meadow . . .

. . . and opened
the gate
for the
geese.

He gave
Cow
the right
dinner.

And found a straw
for his lemonade
all by **himself**.

When he woke, none of Farmer Jolly's jobs
were in a muddle. He was delighted.

"what a wonderful surprise!" he said.
**"I didn't think we would be
ready in time."**

**"Ready in time
for what?"**

asked Pig.

"Aha!"
said Farmer Jolly.
"Now I have a
surprise for you.
Jump in!"

And as a special treat,
Farmer Jolly flew all the
animals to the air show
on Morgan's Field.

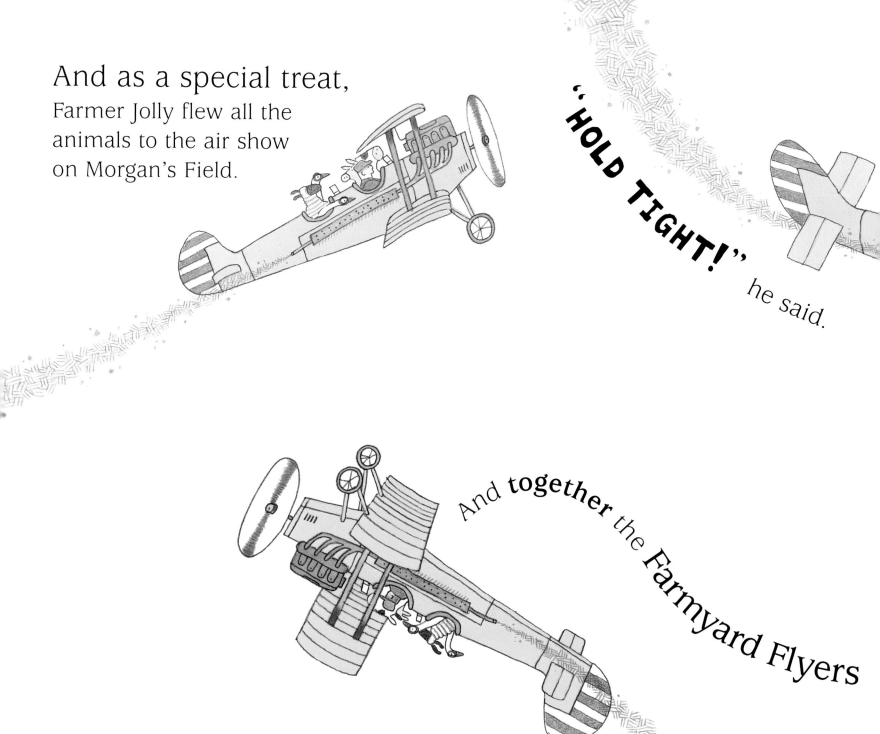

"**HOLD TIGHT!**" he said.

And **together** the Farmyard Flyers

looped-the-loop high above the **cheering** crowd.

"**wheee!**" said Pig.

Everyone agreed it was the best
flying display they had ever seen.
The judges clapped and gave
a standing ovation.

"Farmer Jolly wins
First Prize," they said.

"whooohooo!"

said the animals.

AIR SHOW

As they flew home to Flippety Farm, Farmer Jolly let Pig take the controls.
"Hold her steady now," he said.

It took a while for Pig to answer.
"I can do it!" he said quietly. **"I can really fly!"**